LOCOMOTION PAPERS

By Great Western to Crewe

The Story of the Wellington to Nantwich and Crewe Line

by

Bob Yate

THE OAKWOOD PRESS

British Library Cataloguing in Publication Data
A Record for this book is available from the British Library
ISBN 0 85361 639 6

Typeset by Oakwood Graphics.
Repro by Ford Graphics, Ringwood, Hants.
Printed by Cambrian Printers, Aberystwyth, Ceredigion.

BR Standard class '2' 2-6-0 No. 78036 speeds towards, the by now closed, Wollerton Halt with the RCTS 'St George' railtour on 23rd April, 1966. *Michael Mensing*

Front cover: You can almost hear the exhaust, as Collett 'Hall' class 4-6-0 No. 5955 *Garth Hall* gets under way from Market Drayton with a southbound class 'C' fully fitted freight around 1963. *R. Mulford*

Rear cover, top: Churchward Mogul No. 6368 arrives at Wellington with a freight from the Crewe line on 4th July, 1959. *Michael Mensing*
Rear cover, bottom: Railway Clearing House map showing the route from Wellington to Crewe and connecting railways.

Published by The Oakwood Press (Usk), P.O. Box 13, Usk, Mon., NP15 1YS.
E-mail: sales@oakwoodpress.co.uk
Website: www.oakwoodpress.co.uk

Contents

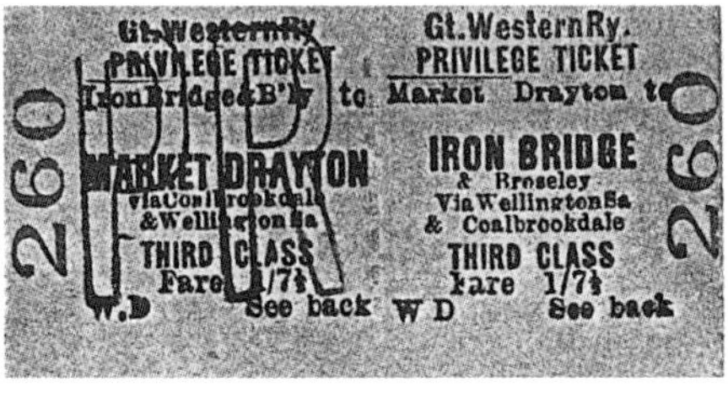
Gt.WesternRy.
PRIVILEGE TICKET
Market Drayton to
IRON BRIDGE
& Broseley
Via Wellington Sa
& Coalbrookdale
THIRD CLASS
See back
260

Introduction

The centrepiece of this railway history is the town of Market Drayton. This ancient town is set amidst a fertile farming area of very gently rolling Shropshire countryside, quite close to the western edge of Staffordshire. The town was mentioned in the Domesday Book of 1086 by King William I as 'Draitune', but did not achieve its 'Market' sobriquet until it was granted a charter for a market by King Henry III in 1245, and even so, was still often referred to as Drayton-in-Hales.

The ensuing centuries saw the town prosper as a marketplace for the agricultural products of the area, and it became well known for its dairy products, especially cheese, and its later speciality of gingerbread. Another claim to fame was that Robert Clive (Clive of India) was born nearby at Moreton Saye, and attended the town's grammar school. Canals did not reach the town until the full opening of the Birmingham & Liverpool Junction Canal (later the main line of the Shropshire Union Canal) in 1835. At last the produce of the area could reach the West Midlands and the North West of England with a reasonable chance that much of it would be acceptably fresh.

Just as the town was beginning to feel the benefits of canal transport, so railways began to appear connecting neighbouring towns. Once again the town felt that the latest transport medium was beyond its reach, and dissatisfaction grew during the 1850s that outside investors were ignoring it. Nonetheless, the town demonstrated its independence by attempting to modernise its own facilities, and, for example, sewers were built during 1848 and 1849, being further added to during the 1850s. Unfortunately, these were poorly designed and lined with bricks laid without cement, which later contributed to a most unsanitary state of affairs. But at least they had tried.

Eventually, the 'railway mania' spawned a number of schemes that promised to include the town and thus provide transport links to the outside world. However, these were mostly independent and as all failed to materialise, some disillusionment in the town was inevitable. Events once again seemed to be passing by the town. Consequently, the local townspeople made several petitions to the London & North Western Railway (LNWR) to be considered in their schemes, without any success. However, the Great Western Railway (GWR) (with its eye on a target further north) was more responsive, although at the earliest stage it wished to remain firmly in the background.

The placement of the town on a through route to enable traffic to proceed with ease in all directions of the compass, rather than being at the end of yet another minor branch line, took about six years from the first steps. This rather dilatory progress caused a degree of impatience locally, but once achieved was welcomed wholeheartedly, and eventually led to the addition of a further route, by the North Staffordshire Railway (NSR) to Stoke in 1870. The town had at last achieved what it had desired - good communications with an element of competition. The benefits of the railways to the business communities of Market Drayton, and the other smaller towns and numerous remote agricultural enterprises along the routes, were enjoyed for nearly a hundred years. The Wellington to Nantwich line was never a major passenger route, and did not generate large amounts of freight, nor had it ever been anticipated as such. But it was a major strategic route for freight traffic, as evidenced particularly

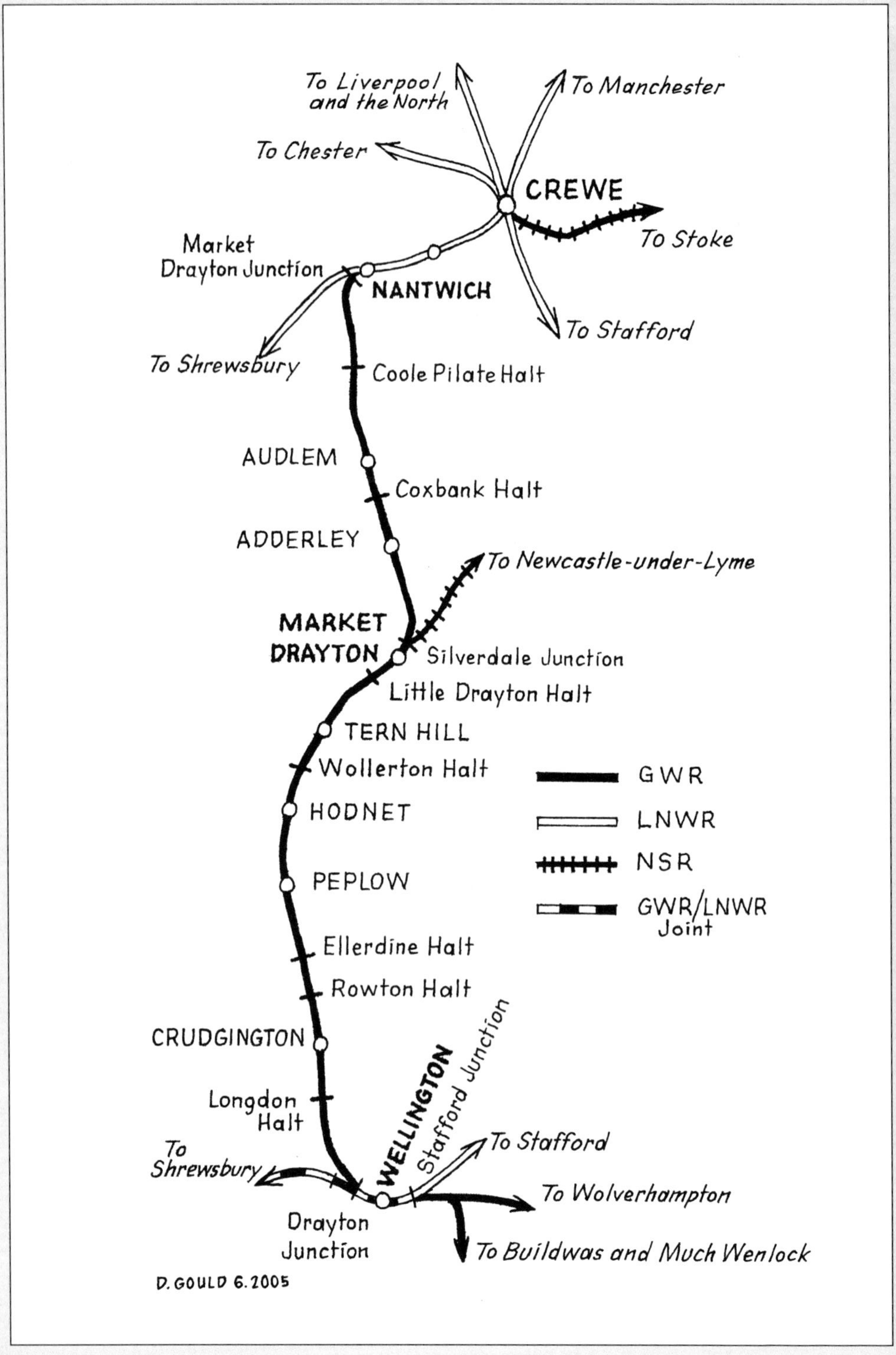

To Liverpool and the North
To Manchester
To Chester
CREWE
To Stoke
Market Drayton Junction
NANTWICH
To Stafford
To Shrewsbury
Coole Pilate Halt
AUDLEM
Coxbank Halt
ADDERLEY
To Newcastle-under-Lyme
MARKET DRAYTON
Silverdale Junction
Little Drayton Halt
TERN HILL
Wollerton Halt
GWR
HODNET
LNWR
NSR
PEPLOW
GWR/LNWR Joint
Ellerdine Halt
Rowton Halt
CRUDGINGTON
WELLINGTON
Stafford Junction
Longdon Halt
To Shrewsbury
To Stafford
To Wolverhampton
Drayton Junction
To Buildwas and Much Wenlock
D. GOULD 6.2005

throughout the two world wars, and even in the days of major route closures was called upon to act as a primary diversionary route during the electrification of the West Coast Main Line in the early 1960s.

During British Railways (BR) days, the route was principally under the control of the London Midland Region, but it never lost its Great Western flavour and traditions, as we shall see.

Abbreviations

The following abbreviations are used throughout the text:

BR	British Railways (later British Rail)
GWR	Great Western Railway
LMS	London Midland & Scottish Railway
LNER	London & North Eastern Railway
LNWR	London & North Western Railway
MSJ&AR	Manchester South Junction & Altrincham Railway
NMDR	Nantwich & Market Drayton Railway
NSR	North Staffordshire Railway
OEWR	Oswestry, Ellesmere & Whitchurch Railway
OWWR	Oxford, Worcester & Wolverhampton Railway
PSNWR	Potteries, Shrewsbury & North Wales Railway
S&BR	Shrewsbury & Birmingham Railway
S&NWR	Shrewsbury & North Wales Railway
S&PJR	Shrewsbury & Potteries Junction Railway
SR	Southern Railway
WDR	Wellington & Drayton Railway
WMCQR	Wrexham, Mold & Connah's Quay Railway

Chapter One

Early Proposed Schemes

The first proposed railway for Market Drayton was the conversion of the Shropshire Union Canal, running from Autherley Junction (on the northern outskirts of Wolverhampton) to Calveley (west of Chester and adjacent to the LNWR Crewe to Chester line). The proposed line of 45 miles and 7 chains entailed the construction of only four miles of entirely new railway, the remainder being conversion of the existing canal. The plans were deposited at Shrewsbury County Court by the Shropshire Union Railways and Canal Company on 30th November, 1845, and also showed junctions with the proposed Crewe to Newtown railway at Nantwich, and with the proposed Stafford to Shrewsbury line at Gnosall. However, the canal and railway interests of the Shropshire Union company were leased by the LNWR under an enabling Act passed in June 1847 (10 & 11, Vict. Chapter 121). Subsequently, the LNWR did not proceed with this conversion part of the scheme, preferring to protect its own lines from the West Midlands to Crewe and Chester, and retain the existing canal.

Plans were deposited in Shrewsbury on the same date in 1845 by the nominally independent Shropshire Mineral Railway, for a railway of 43 miles and 5 furlongs from Craven Arms to Norton Bridge (near Stone), surveyed by Sam Clegg. This line would not actually have reached Market Drayton, but its route would have taken it nearby through Munslow, Much Wenlock, Buildwas, Madeley (Salop), Dawley, Wombridge, Lilleshall, Newport, Norbury and Chebsey. Nothing more was heard of this over ambitious scheme.

Almost coincidentally, was a scheme for which the plans were deposited on 1st December, 1845 by the Oxford, Worcester & Wolverhampton Railway (OWWR) for a grandly titled Oxford & Worcester Extension and Chester Junction Railway. This was to run from the OWWR south of Kidderminster via Sutton Maddock, Stirchley, Wombridge, and Hodnet to Chester. No engineer was given, but the scheme was overtaken by events when the OWWR merged with the Worcester & Hereford Railway from 1st January, 1860 to form the West Midland Railway, which was itself leased to the GWR from 1st July, 1861. Obviously such a line would have duplicated existing GWR routes from the West Midlands to Chester, and so it was dropped.

In chronological order, the next scheme was that of the Nantwich & Market Drayton Railway (NMDR), which as we shall see in more detail in the next chapter, was successful. The plans were deposited in Shrewsbury on 28th November, 1860.

A year later, on 30th November, 1861 plans were deposited for the Market Drayton & Newport Junction Railway. After the NMDR scheme had got underway, local people were frustrated that the GWR seemed uninterested in exploring a southern route from Market Drayton. This local scheme was once again led by Mr Henry Reginald Corbet of Adderley Hall, and was surveyed by the same engineer, John Gardner. It would have linked the NMDR to the LNWR Stafford to Shrewsbury line at Newport by a railway of 12 miles, 7 furlongs and 4 chains. However, as this line did not link into the GWR system, it failed to win its backing. Moreover, as the NMDR had approved of the Wellington, Drayton &

Newcastle Railway scheme (*see below*) at a Board meeting of 11th June, 1862 this latter scheme was preferred, and the Newport extension plan was dropped.

On the same date, plans for a further line, the Drayton Junction Railway were deposited. This independent concern was promoting a 10½ mile line from the LNWR main line at Mill Meece through Market Drayton to a south-facing junction with the LNWR Crewe to Shrewsbury line 3½ miles north of Wem. Not surprisingly, the LNWR objected and the line never achieved its enabling Act. However, the small but ambitious Wrexham, Mold & Connah's Quay Railway (WMCQR) revived the scheme the following year, and on 29th November, 1862 deposited plans for a similar scheme. This time the eastern end of the line ran parallel with the LNWR from near Mill Meece to Stafford, where it formed a junction. At the other end, the railway would have formed a junction with, then crossed, the LNWR Crewe-Shrewsbury line at Whitchurch to join a separately promoted WMCQR line. This too ran into fierce opposition from the LNWR. Undaunted, a further scheme was deposited a year later on 30th November, 1863 this time including a triangular junction at Prees, south of Whitchurch, from where a branch of the authorised Oswestry, Ellesmere & Whitchurch Railway (OEWR) would connect. The line continued south-east to make an end-on connection with the now opened NMDR at Market Drayton, then proceeded further east towards Eccleshall, and ran parallel southwards with the LNWR line, this time from Great Bridgeford, before joining the LNWR line from Shrewsbury just outside Stafford. A spur was also planned to join the NSR at Norton Bridge. Strong objections by the LNWR prevented the authorisation of this line.

However, the WMCQR was evidently persistent in its objectives, for the following year it presented further amendments to its plans, on 29th November, 1864. This time the line near Whitchurch was rerouted to form a junction with the OEWR near Bettisfield (5 miles south-west of Whitchurch). Once again it failed in Parliament, but the following year presented further plans with its Drayton Railway Extensions, deposited on 30th November, 1865. This incorporated a revised junction near Stafford to take a further line towards Cannock Chase (and thus tap the newly emerging coalfield there). The LNWR must have breathed a sigh of relief when this plan was thrown out of Parliament, and proved to be the last from this particular direction. B. Percy was given as the Engineer for all of these plans, although the final plans also included a Mr Stileman, and John Robinson McClean (who had earlier championed the South Staffordshire Railway). Although this line was never built, the Railway Inn near Eccleshall is believed to have been so named in anticipation of this scheme.

Returning to 1861, on 30th November of that year plans for another line were deposited at Shrewsbury. This time it was the Wellington, Drayton & Newcastle Railway, whose line was to run from the GWR at Admaston (just west of Wellington) via Market Drayton to Silverdale (one mile north of Keele) with connecting spurs to join the LNWR main line in each direction. These plans were amended soon after, on 22nd March, 1862, showing the north of the line to terminate at Wolstanton. The Engineer was given as John Ashdown. The scheme was backed by the NMDR, as well as the GWR and the West Midlands Railway, but the first section from Wellington to Market Drayton was rejected in the House of Commons, and the section from Market Drayton to Newcastle was rejected in the House of Lords. The scheme was not renewed and was allowed to fade after the emergence of the Wellington & Drayton Railway (WDR) later that year.

Continuing in date order, the next proposal in the area was the WDR which, as we shall see in Chapter Four, was the line built. The plans were deposited at Shrewsbury on 29th November, 1862.

Finally we come to the saga of the Potteries Junction Railway, later to become the Shrewsbury & Potteries Junction Railway (S&PJR). This was promoted by the same individuals who had started the abortive Drayton Junction Railway a year earlier, and was an attempt to eliminate the stranglehold of the NSR in the Potteries, as much as to provide a through route to Wales. So it gained the backing of many of the businesses in the Potteries as well as that of the LNWR, which at that time was involved in several disputes with the NSR, although this support was short lived. The first plans were deposited on 29th November, 1862 and the Engineers given as Sir Charles Fox and John Ashdown. The line was to run from Newcastle-under-Lyme through Market Drayton to Whitchurch to join the LNWR Crewe to Shrewsbury line, and on to Pulford (5 miles south of Chester) to join the GWR Chester to Shrewsbury line. At Madeley (Staffs) there would be a connecting spur to the LNWR main line.

The plans were modified in the following year, when the sections from Market Drayton to Whitchurch and on to Pulford were dropped, doubtless because they duplicated those of the aspiring WMCQR (*see above*). Further connections were included in the Potteries and with the newly opened NMDR at Market Drayton. Some revisions were necessary as, on the original plans, the line would have crossed the NMDR on the level and at an angle, right through the middle of its booking office in the station at Market Drayton! The approved WDR was recognised by running parallel to Hodnet, from where the line ran across country to join the LNWR line at Battlefield, just outside Shrewsbury. By this time, the plans had been opposed by the LNWR, GWR, West Midland Railway, NSR, WMCQR, NMDR, WDR, various landowners and owners of mines, quarries, mills and farms along many sections of the route. There were also allegations that the Parliamentary Deposit (required to be paid when presenting a scheme for approval) had been paid out of a loan, rather than from subscribed monies, as required by law. As a result the proposal was thrown out by Parliament in 1863.

Further alterations were included in the plans deposited on 30th November, 1864, whereby the parallel route out of Market Drayton was extended to Peplow, then at Battlefield the line ran parallel with the LNWR line rather than making a junction, as previously. After 1½ miles of parallel running the line was to turn south and make an east-facing junction with the joint LNWR/GWR Wellington line outside Shrewsbury. At this point, a further line would proceed westwards to make an end on junction with the Shrewsbury & North Wales Railway (S&NWR) at Red Hill. This scheme finally received Parliamentary approval. However, the only part of this line ever built was the latter section from its junction with the Wellington line in Shrewsbury to the junction with the S&NWR at Red Hill, which opened in 1866. These two companies merged on 16th July, 1866 to form the Potteries, Shrewsbury & North Wales Railway (PSNWR), even before the official opening of their line on 13th August, 1866. No other part of the proposed lines was ever built, mainly because the PSNWR had severe financial problems which caused it to cease traffic on 22nd December, 1866 - the same year that it had opened! After further stops and starts, the company was finally wound up in 1881.

Chapter Two

The Nantwich & Market Drayton Railway

Formation

As we have seen, the local people of Market Drayton wanted a railway connection to their town and district, and so lacking the support of the main line companies, and in the spirit of many other such localities, sponsored their own railway. The first meeting of the provisional company took place on 23rd August, 1860 although the precise venue has gone unrecorded. At this meeting it was unanimously resolved that the name of the company was to be 'The Market Drayton and Madeley Railway', although events would prove this to be short lived. Henry Reginald Corbet of Adderley Hall was elected as Chairman of the Provisional Committee. Others present were Will Tayleur, Thomas Twemlow, Egerton W. Harding, Richard Corbet and Charles Townshend. It was resolved to appoint John Gardner (of 18 Adam Street, Adelphi, London) as Engineer of the line, and, on 15th September of that year, the Provisional Committee instructed him to survey the line from Market Drayton to Nantwich. At a meeting a few days later, on 19th September, it was resolved that the line should not cost more than £60,000 and that was the amount set for the capital of the company. Plans for the line to run from a junction with the LNWR at Nantwich for 10 miles, 6 furlongs and 2½ chains to Market Drayton, were deposited at Shrewsbury County Court on 28th November, 1860 (at one o'clock). The length is equivalent to 10 miles and 50½ chains, which compares to the measured 10 miles and 67 chains as finally built.

On 9th January, 1861 the Provisional Committee met at the offices of the local solicitors Warren & Onions of Market Drayton, but dealt with only some local correspondence, although at the next meeting at this venue, on 12th February, the Committee requested that Mr Gardner should peg out the route of the line for inspection by the contractor.

The next meeting of note was that on 3rd April, 1861 at the offices of Mr Charles Townshend of Market Drayton at which time the name of the railway has been changed to the Nantwich and Market Drayton Railway, although the actual date at which it was changed may have been earlier. The railway company was formally incorporated on 7th June, 1861 after the passing in Parliament of the required enabling Act (Vict. 24 & 25, Chapter 44) in 1861.

On 21st June, 1861 the meeting was held at the residence of Richard Corbet at 40 Portman Square, London. This meeting seems to have been the first official meeting of the company, as H. Reginald Corbet was formally elected as Chairman of the Nantwich & Market Drayton Railway Company, and John Gardner as Engineer. At the risk of being pedantic, I should point out here that although various other publications, including the Board minutes, spell his name as 'Gardiner', correspondence has been examined as signed by him as 'Gardner'. *Appendix Two* lists the Directors as appointed at the first Board meeting.

The present day Corbet Arms Inn in Market Drayton, where the first meetings concerning the formation of the Nantwich & Market Drayton Railway were held. *Author*

Plaque on the wall of the Corbet Arms Inn recording the first meetings of the promoters of the Nantwich & Market Drayton Railway. Not many railways have been commemorated in such a public manner. *Author*

All subsequent Board meetings were held at the Corbet Arms Hotel, Market Drayton. The next meeting, held on 3rd July, 1861, proposed that when complete, the line should be worked by the LNWR such that a dividend of 4½ per cent would be paid to the shareholders out of the gross receipts. In the original Prospectus of 1860 (*see Appendix One*), the Directors had mentioned that they expected the line to be worked by the LNWR 'upon fair and proper terms'. There is no record of the response from the LNWR, but this proposal was evidently unacceptable, as at a Board meeting over a year later, on 19th October, 1862, it was agreed that the line would be worked on the same terms by the GWR. In a seemingly related move, it is worthy of note that the Duke of Sutherland (an LNWR Director) was elected as a Director on 17th December, 1861, but retired from the Board on 22nd October the following year. In any event, the initial working agreement was made with the fledgling WDR, which under Section 55 of its Act of Incorporation in 1862 was to work the NMDR. The terms of this agreement were evidently less than satisfactory to the latter, and this view was expressed at several Board Meetings between August and October 1863. Subsequently the NMDR negotiated directly with the GWR over its working agreement to the satisfaction of all concerned, although quite what the difference could have been is difficult to imagine.

By 31st December, 1861 matters seemed to be moving ahead quite quickly, as the called-up share capital was reported to have been £11,608. This meeting also viewed with favour the proposals of the Wellington & Cheshire Junction Railway, and it was resolved that Heads of Agreement with this concern should be drafted by 9th April next. The subsequent events relating to this company are traced in Chapter Four. Meanwhile, other local schemes had come to the notice of the Board, and the Newport extension was deemed practical to the extent that on 16th January, 1862 a loan was obtained for the Parliamentary deposit of £9,600 to pave the way for the enabling Act to proceed. Strictly speaking, this practice was not legal, as the deposit was required to be paid from subscribed monies. The plans for this railway, provisionally titled the Market Drayton & Newport Junction Railway, had earlier been deposited at the County Court, Shrewsbury on 30th November, 1861. However, a further scheme, the Wellington, Drayton & Newcastle Railway, then took the favour of the Board, whose formal approval was recorded on 11th June, 1862. Because these two schemes overlapped to a degree, the Newport extension plan was dropped at a meeting on 30th August, 1862. This same meeting noted that the Wellington, Drayton & Newcastle Railway would be backed by both the GWR and the West Midland Railway (even though this railway had been acquired by the GWR on 1st August of the preceding year), and that the Board considered it would be beneficial to have this line worked by either company. In the event, the GWR subsequently dropped its support for this railway and the scheme was allowed to fade.

Construction

Two bids for the construction of the line were received by the Board, but the initial amounts are not recorded in the Board Minutes, whose only comment is that on 31st December, 1861 'the tender by Mr Brassey is lower than (that submitted) by Mr Furness, who made another, but he is still higher'. We do know, however, that the contract issued to Thomas Brassey on 10th March, 1862 was for an estimate of £52,500.

Construction of the line appears to have gone without any particular problems, which is not surprising considering that the line was generally across fairly flat countryside, particularly the northern half towards Nantwich. There were no tunnels, nor any lengthy embankments or cuttings even on the southern half which is slightly more undulating. A skew bridge was required to carry the line over the Shropshire Union Canal just south of the later Coole Pilate Halt, and another over the Audlem to Market Drayton road near to Coxbank. The line was single throughout.

The contractor was actually Thomas Brassey in partnership with William Field, and their agents were Messrs Mackay and Gallaher. The Board agreed to pay Brassey and Field £21,000 on acceptance of the contract on or before 30th June, 1862 then a further £18,000 between 1st July, 1862 and 30th June, 1863. The balance was to be paid during the following six months in ⅔ cash and ⅓ shares in the company. No mention is made in the company records of the final amount paid to the contractors for the initial construction of the line, although the Engineer, John Gardner, was paid a total of £6,992 3*s*. 9*d*. for his professional services, which in addition to engineering the line included work in connection with the Parliamentary agreements. However, the final cost including the purchase of land meant that the company's share capital had to be doubled from its initial amount to £120,000. The Resident Engineer was a Mr Lister.

Inspection and approval

Prior to the official inspection of the line, the NMDR was required to submit to the Railway Department of the Board of Trade two undertakings pertaining to the manner of operation of the line. These were both dated 12th October, 1863 and signed by the Chairman, H. Reginald Corbet and the Secretary, G.H. Wickham. The first was as follows:

> This is to certify that this railway, being a single line, shall be worked by the assistance of the Electric Telegraph, separate wires and instruments at each station and the junction being provided for working the up and down traffic in addition to an instrument for sending messages, so that only one engine in steam, or two or more coupled together and forming part of one train, shall be between two adjacent stations, or a station and the junction, at one and the same time.

This confirms the original arrangement that has become known as 'one engine in steam working', but in this case applied to sections rather than the whole branch.

The second undertaking read:

> We hereby undertake that a turntable shall be fixed at Nantwich station within three months from this date unless arrangements shall have been made for working into Crewe station. In the meantime tank engines only shall be used upon this line.

No turntable was ever installed at Nantwich. However, workings were not permitted into Crewe, as the NMDR did not have any running powers into Crewe at this time and the LNWR was not inclined to permit regular daily workings beyond Nantwich. Thus the evidence is clear that the line can only have been worked by tank engines until the second line was installed.

The line was inspected by Captain (later Colonel) J.H. Rich on 16th October, 1863. His report to the Board of Trade was dated the following day, and remarked that the single line was 10 miles and 67 chains in length, with sidings at Audlem, Adderley, Market Drayton and Nantwich Junction. Further, the land, overbridges and one underbridge (at Adderley) had been provided for subsequent doubling of the line. The double-headed rail was of 75 lb. per yard, with chairs of 26 lb. secured by wooden keys and spiked to sleepers which were on average three feet apart, resting on ballast one foot thick. There were six brick overbridges and one with cast-iron girders. Three underbridges had wrought-iron girders, one had cast-iron girders, one had wooden beams and one with a brick arch. The bridge over the River Weaver was a brick-arched viaduct, and the bridge over the Shropshire Union Canal at Coole Pilate had wrought-iron girders. It was further remarked that a turntable was provided at Market Drayton, although as we have seen above this was to be of limited value until the complete line from Wellington was opened. The report concluded that the line was complete and ready for opening, which was confirmed by the Board of Trade on 17th October, 1863.

The line opened with considerable festivity on 19th October, and the following chapter is devoted to a full description of this occasion.

Doubling the line

During 1863, it became apparent to the Board in their discussions with the newly promoted Wellington & Drayton Railway, that this railway, strongly supported by the GWR, would form part of the GWR's aspirations for a through route to Manchester. In this case, it was considered that the Board of Trade would press for their line to be of double track formation to take the anticipated volume of a fairly major route. During 1865, tenders were sought for the doubling, apparently only from Brassey and Field, which is understandable as their work was already known to be highly satisfactory, and they were thoroughly familiar with the line and countryside. By this time relationships with the GWR had become much firmer, as the GWR had been operating their railway for nearly two years, and the prospect of an amalgamation had been suggested. At a Board Meeting on 17th August, 1865 the contract for the doubling of the line was submitted to the GWR for approval. At the same time, a draft manuscript for the proposed merger was also submitted to the GWR.

Finally, the contract for the doubling was awarded to Brassey and Field on 5th May, 1866 for £42,144 15*s*. 3*d*. This amount included maintenance of the existing line from the expiry of the prior maintenance agreement, 19th October, 1864 until the completion of doubling (£1,125) and maintenance of the completed line for one year (a further £1,350). John Mackay and a Mr Reid were noted as agents. The conditions of the contract required that 'the contractor will be required to conform to orders and regulations of the General Manager of the Great Western Railway for the working of traffic during the construction of the works, and to pay for all of the expenses of all temporary signalmen, signals and watchmen during the construction'. This emphasised that the GWR was already in charge and was actually working the line. It is also of interest that the detailed schedules attached to the contract included the alteration or replacement of bridges and other structures on the route to provide for a double track formation, thereby indicating that, despite previous assurances, much of the earlier permanent way was constructed for single track only.

Work commenced almost immediately, and was completed just over a year later in July 1867. This rate of progress was quite acceptable, as the original formation had been largely created to permit double track. The final contractor's cost of the doubling of the line came to £48,497 3*s*. 2¾*d*. which had included much reworking of station buildings and some bridges, as well as a three year maintenance contract from completion.

The NMDR issued a formal First Notice of intention to open the line within three months on 15th May, 1867 and then a Second Notice (to open within 10 days) on 9th July, 1867. Finally, the double track line was inspected by Colonel Yolland of the Board of Trade who reported on 23rd July, 1867 that the rails were satisfactory at 75 lb. per yard in lengths varying between 21 and 27 feet, fixed by compressed elm keys, in chairs secured by fang bolts to sleepers of 9 feet by 10 inches by 5 inches. The ballast of sand and fine gravel was one foot deep, and surfaced by furnace cinders. However, the following deficiencies were to be corrected:

> Rail chairs of 25½ to 26¼ lb. were inadequate and should be of 28 to 30 lb., so as to avoid fractures.
>
> The goods lines at Market Drayton and Audlem were not protected by blind sidings and interlocked signals.
>
> Rails on longitudinal timbers on some underbridges were not adequately supported and required cross transoms, and tie rods for better support.
>
> The locking mechanism at Nantwich Junction required amendment so that points are locked when the signal is at danger, and the distant signal worked from the junction is required at the station.

These matters were cleared to the inspector's satisfaction, with the exception of the rail chairs, for which a similar criticism was made in his report concerning the WDR inspected at the same time. Similar to the WDR, this matter delayed the opening of the second line. This matter is expanded upon further in Chapter Four. Consequently, the Second Notice was withdrawn on 23rd August. The existing chairs were eventually replaced, and a fresh Second Notice issued on 20th September. After the inspection of the line by Colonel J.H. Rich on 8th

October, the Board of Trade gave formal consent to its opening on 11th October, 1867.

No date for the full opening of the double track line has been positively confirmed, but it is thought to have been coincidental with the opening of the WDR on 16th October, 1867. Similarly, it is assumed that whilst there may have been some disruption to the services on the NMDR during the course of this work, some form of interim working was adopted during the conversion. Certainly, there is no evidence that services were suspended during this period.

Although Brassey and Field are not known to have used locomotives during the construction of the line, nor on the WDR construction, it is known that one was used on the doubling of the NMDR. This was a Manning, Wardle 'Old I' class 0-6-0ST with 11 in. x 17 in. inside cylinders, built in 1866 (Works No. 192) and named *Christopher*. After completion of this work, it was sold in 1872 to Brassey & Field's agent, John Mackay, who having worked on the line, was now setting up on his own account. He renamed it *Christiana*, and probably first used it on the doubling of the LNWR Central Wales line in that year. Certainly, it was used in the construction of the Treforest to Hafod section of the Barry Railway in 1885-1889. Its subsequent fate has gone unrecorded.

Brassey and Field's account for the conversion was finally accepted and paid on 5th August, 1868.

Subsequent events

Despite the earlier suggestions of a merger with the GWR, the time was evidently inappropriate for either or both parties, as the Board minutes from January 1871 record that that there was 'no immediate prospect of amalgamation'. This did not, of course, change the routine operation of the railway, as the GWR now operated the entire line from Wellington to Nantwich, with running powers on to Crewe and Manchester.

However, eventually the GWR was authorised on 21st July, 1873 'to make financial arrangements for the amalgamation'. Evidently the GWR was in no hurry, but an amalgamation did occur, as from 20th December, 1896 by which all books and documents were handed over in accordance with clause 9 of the agreement dated 30th December, 1896. The NMDR company was fully absorbed with effect from 1st July, 1897 under an authorising Act dated 6th August, 1897. The GWR had guaranteed 5 per cent on £18 of each of the £20 shares of the NMDR, effectively a cash surrender value of £18 18*s.* 0*d.*

OPENING OF THE NANTWICH AND MARKET DRAYTON RAILWAY.

PROGRAMME OF PROCEEDINGS,

ON MONDAY, 19TH OCTOBER INSTANT:—

A PROCESSION will be formed in the High Street, Market Drayton, at 10-30 a.m., consisting of

The 2nd Shropshire Rifle Volunteers, headed by their Band.

The Chairman and Directors of the Railway.

The Engineer, Contractors, and other Railway Officials.

The Committee of Management for the day's proceedings.

The Shareholders of the Company.

The Inhabitants of the Town and Neighbourhood.

The Procession will proceed to the Railway Station, when the Line will be formally Opened.

The Train conveying the Directors, Shareholders, and their Friends, will start at 11 a.m. for Nantwich, stopping at Adderley and Audlem Stations, and will return to the Drayton Station at 12-30, where the Procession will be re-formed, and will be joined by the recipients of Tickets for the Dinner in the Waterloo Tent, and by the Children of the various Schools.

Dinner for 700 Men, in the Waterloo Tent, Stafford Street, at 1-30 p.m.

Tea for the Children at the different Schools at 3 p.m.

A PUBLIC DINNER,

At the Corbet Arms Hotel, at 4 p.m., H. REGINALD CORBET, Esq. in the Chair. Dinner Tickets, including Champagne and other Wines, 5s. 6d. each.

A Grand Display of FIREWORKS

Will take place in the High Street, at 7 p.m.

Dancing will commence in the National School Rooms at 8 precisely. Admission 1s. each.

ON TUESDAY, 20TH OCTOBER INSTANT:—

Tea for 700 Women, in the Waterloo Tent, Stafford Street, at 3 p.m.

Dinner for the Rifle Volunteers, at the Corbet Arms, at 5-30 p.m.

Market Drayton, 14th October, 1863.

John Lockett, Printer Hith Streer, Market Drayton.

Handbill with details of opening ceremony of the Nantwich & Market Drayton Railway.

Chapter Three

Opening of the First Railway

To promote the opening of the railway, a programme of events was organised and advertised throughout the district. For such a small railway the amount of celebrations seems somewhat overdone, but this was the first railway to the town of Market Drayton, and the enthusiasm of the people as to the potential benefits it would bring is understandable. A copy of the original leaflet distributed in the locality is shown opposite and this was reproduced in advertisement format in the *Newport and Market Drayton Advertiser* issue of 17th October, 1863.

The contemporary press description (from the *Newport & Market Drayton Advertiser* of 24th October, 1863) of the events of the day is rather lengthy, and so extracts only are reproduced here, complete with all original spellings and punctuation. The account is perhaps rather repetitious, and somewhat verbose, and presents precious little of detail to the student of railway history. Nonetheless, this account has an undoubted period charm about it, and provides an interesting insight into the attitudes and humour of the time.

MARKET DRAYTON

OPENING OF THE NANTWICH AND MARKET DRAYTON RAILWAY

The position in these days of a town without a railway may be fitly compared to a man with his hands tied. He is not able to help himself, nor to do much for others; and, therefore, it is no wonder that the struggle made by the inhabitants of Market Drayton for the liberty enjoyed by other towns should have been, from time to time, earnest and sincere; for we cannot consider any event so important to the common interests of the neighbourhood as that which would give them convenient access to the rest of the world, and would connect them with the general network of the railway system which lies on all sides within a few miles around them. Various attempts have been made by them to relieve themselves of their isolated position, but in them all they had been thwarted. Two years ago, however, the present line (which was entirely a local project) was proposed, and it succeeded, and it is eighteen months since the first sod was cut. From that time the proceedings have been prosecuted with great energy and and success, and the fruit of their labours was rewarded on Monday last by a demonstration, such as was never witnessed in Drayton before. The shops were closed, and the town wore the general appearance of a holiday. Not less than 5,000 spectators crowded the High-street, - almost every door and post in the centre of the town was crowded. The line is about 10¾ miles in length, and the cost about £4,000 per mile. It affords a ready access to Liverpool, Manchester, and the north, and even the journey to London and other places south can now be accomplished in much less time than by the ordinary route of driving to Newport. The line to Wellington will be commenced at once, which will place Drayton in direct communication with all parts of the Kingdom. The new line is in the hands of the Great Western, but whether on lease or absolute possession we are not aware. As the details of the proceedings will appear in the subjoined report, we will make no further comment, but proceed at once to a description of their character and extent.

On approaching the town the steeple presented itself in prominent relief, bearing at its summit a flag of the Union Jack and Danish Cross; also from the National schools was another flag of the Danish Cross. These two objects form the main features of this picturesque scene from the Newport road, and, standing side by side, fitly represent Christianity and education as the bulwarks and strongholds of our land. On turning the corner towards the

This photograph is believed to be of the opening ceremony of the Nantwich and Market Drayton Railway at Market Drayton station on 17th October, 1863. Of particular interest is the original station building, and the water tower placed in front of the still newly constructed wooden single-road goods shed. A locomotive appears to be to the left of this building but is too indistinct to be identified. The signal is one of the early pattern with opposing arms at the top, and the lamp some four feet below the arms. Many of the group standing on the permanent way are dressed in railway uniform, although there is at least one Army officer in full uniform. A 'bobby' is standing in the bottom centre of the picture, with his hands on his hips and his back to the camera. The down platform is discernible bottom left of the view. *D. Houlston Collection*

post-office, a vast archway of evergreens, by the George inn, overspread the street, and Union Jack and Danish Cross were suspended in like manner. At the George were flags of 'Prosperity to the Market Drayton and Nantwich railway.' Similar demonstrations were also shown at the Red Lion. Mr Rodgers, watchmaker, had a good flag, also, Mr Bradbury, draper; Mr Snow had the balcony of his house ornamented with laurels and flowers, with appropriate flags. From the Corbet Arms were suspended across the High-street, large and handsome bunting flags of Danish Crosses, in various devices, and Union Jacks, and from a front window hung a Royal Standard, which bore evidence of time-honoured loyalty and length of service. In fact, the High Town was a perfect garden of evergreens and flowers, and the flags and streamers which hung from almost every house had an effect, perhaps, never witnessed in Market Drayton during the history of many generations. Over the entrance to Stafford-street was another archway, with mottoes, & numerous decorations were observable in other instances. Among the chief in that street were the works of Messrs Gower, implement manufacturers. The entire range of these works were bedecked with mottoes of various form and signification, such as 'Success to the Nantwich and Market Drayton Railway,' 'Long looked for come at last,' &c. There was also a large tablet, extending along the whole compass of the building, with the words 'May trade, agriculture, and commerce flourish.' Mr W.D. Green's house was nicely ornamented with festoons and mottoes; this was about the only decoration of that description noticed in the town, and it formed a pleasing contrast with the great sameness of the generality of the ornamentations. The Horse Market was well represented with objects of gaiety, as also Shropshire-street. As the train was preparing for departure, a photographic artist of high local standing, occupied an elevated stage adjoining the line, and took photographs of the opening scene.

At half-past ten, the Market Drayton rifle corps were marched into the High town, under the command of Major Hill, and headed by their excellent band. These then formed the head of the procession - followed by the chairman and directors of the railway - the engineer, contractor, and other railway officials - the shareholders of the company - and a long train of the inhabitants of the town and neighbourhood, among whom were observed a fair proportion of the agriculturists of the district. There were also present the rifle corps band from Nantwich, and the drum-and-fife band from Hodnet. The procession thus arranged proceeded to the railway station, where there congregated about 1,000 persons; and the crowd gradually increased until it reached the creditable number of 3,000 persons. After the necessary preliminaries were gone through, those persons having free passes took their seats, and the important event of a first ordinary railway train from Market Drayton was declared to be accomplished. Over the gateway to the station was a massive triumphal arch, with central garland and flags. We must however, express our regret that when the train started there was not the slightest demonstration on the part of the people. Probably the event is one which for general purposes cannot be surpassed for importance and usefulness, and there is no public object which for many years has been a matter of greater complaint than the want of a railway; and therefore, we did expect to hear what is the usual form of showing Shropshire appreciation - 'a jolly good hurrah.' Onward with its crowded vehicles the iron horse proceeded, calling at Adderley, where there were also triumphal archways and flags across the line, and throngs of rural spectators. Thence they proceeded to Audlem, where like demonstrations were made; & from thence to Nantwich. After waiting a few minutes the train was brought back to Market Drayton, where an immense concourse of persons had assembled. A succession of fog signals announced its return.

The procession then re-formed, containing most of the gentlemen and others who took active steps in the proceedings of the day. It was also joined by the men who were to have dinner, who were estimated at 700 or 800. These were followed by the scholars of the various schools, computed at upwards of 1,000 children - respectable and intelligent-looking children. The long string of juveniles was materially enlivened by a gay and countless variety of streamers, mottoes, and flags. We must here remark that the whole procession was of the most orderly character, and did much credit to those whose superintendence it was intrusted.

At half-past one 700 men were feasted with a most substantial and capital dinner, in spacious tents erected in a field adjoining Stafford-street; and we are bound to remark that, for such monstrous joints, we have seldom seen a dinner served up in a more edible form. At three o'clock about 1,000 children were regaled with tea, cake, and bread-and-butter. At a little after four o'clock about 150 gentlemen sat down in the Assembly Room at the Corbet Arms Hotel to a dinner, which was well suited to the importance of the day, and which was served up as well as could be expected under the excitement, confusion, and crush of such a great occasion. The wines, also, (particularly the champagne) gave great satisfaction, and were rolled about the tables as freely as water. It is many years since Drayton witnessed a dinner upon such a liberal scale before. The room was handsomely decorated with flags of many descriptions, rich in quality, colour, and device.

One important incident in this memorable occasion was that the train was driven there and back by Mrs Reginald Corbet, the lady of the worthy chairman of the directors. It will be a pleasing item in the future history of the town to know that the starting, stopping, whistling, and all other operations of the first railway train that ever started from Market Drayton, were conducted by the fair fingers of a lady.

The entire proceedings were marked with great order, and not a single offence gave trouble to the police.

TUESDAY

The festivities were continued this day, when nearly 1,000 women partook of an excellent tea, provided in the tents that had been used for the dinner to the men. After tea dancing was commenced, and kept up with unflagging spirit until about ten o'clock at night.

A similar report, and of similar length, was also contained in the *Wellington Journal* of 24th October, 1863.

Chapter Four

The Wellington & Drayton Railway

Formation

We have seen how the GWR had backed the NMDR from a distance, but when nearing completion it became apparent to the GWR that this line could form part of its aspirations to reach Manchester. It is true that by 1860 the GWR had gained access to Manchester via the Birkenhead Railway, which was jointly vested in the LNWR and the GWR in that year. But this access was somewhat limited at the LNWR goods and passenger premises. So it backed a rather less than independent line, the Wellington & Drayton Railway, which was incorporated on 7th August, 1862 with an authorised capital of £200,000 shares of £10 each. Plans were deposited at Shrewsbury County Court on 29th November, 1862 which, apart from the section from Wellington to Drayton, included extensions from the WDR at Market Drayton to the Cheshire Midland Railway south of Knutsford, with connections to the LNWR south of Minshull Vernon station, and a line from Middlewich to Northwich. Also included was a connection from the Manchester South Junction and Altrincham Railway (MSJ&AR) to a double junction with the Bolton Railway at Salford. The Engineers were given as John Fowler of Birmingham, Edward Wilson and George Kent Radford. These extension plans were part of the scheme of an earlier enterprise known as the Wellington and Cheshire Junction Railway. It was clear that the GWR intended to make its presence felt in Manchester! The plans also included a line to reach the Potteries at Newcastle, running eastwards from Market Drayton. However, any thoughts in that direction were soon dispelled by the combined opposition of the LNWR and NSR. It is often believed that the lack of this proposed line was the primary reason for the GWR to restrict its activities in this area to the Wellington to Nantwich section.

However, the backing for the MSJ&AR eventually came from the Great Northern Railway and the Manchester Sheffield & Lincolnshire Railway (later to become the Great Central Railway). Furthermore, the GWR and West Midland Railway Amalgamation Act of 1863 granted running powers (Section 2, Article 5) to the GWR and West Midland Railway from Nantwich to Crewe over the LNWR, and on to Manchester, London Road. So the GWR had no further need of the independent lines through Cheshire. Further plans were therefore deposited at Shrewsbury, this time dropping the northern extensions, and altering the connection at the southern end from near Admaston to Wellington, as built. The Consulting Engineer was given as John Fowler, and the Engineer-in Chief as Edward Wilson. A Mr Pryce was later appointed as the Resident Engineer. The company solicitors were Baxter, Rose, Norton & Co. of 6 Victoria Street, Westminster and George Gordon Warren of Market Drayton.

The first Directors' Meeting was held on Thursday 4th November, 1862 at the Imperial Hotel, Great Malvern at which William Fenton was elected as Chairman, and the other Directors elected were Messrs Porter, Jervis and

Warren, with Gordon Graham serving as Secretary. Subsequently, all Directors' Meetings were held at Paddington station. On 17th February, 1864 Sir Watkin Wynn and Mr A.C. Sherriff were also appointed as Directors. Later in that same year, an Act of 14th July, 1864 authorised the transfer of the WDR company to the GWR upon completion.

It was also during 1864 that the local people of Hodnet became aware that the station to serve their community was to be sited at Wollerton, over a mile from the principal village of Hodnet, and therefore considered to be inconvenient. The siting of this station was evidently to suit the inhabitants of Wollerton Hall rather than the local population. A 'memorial' of 101 signatures of local people was sent to the Chairman, expressing their dissatisfaction, and asking for the station to be sited at Hodnet Heath where the railway was due to pass within a ¼ mile of the village. They cited their reasons as being:

> It (Hodnet Heath) is the most central place for the whole neighbourhood.
>
> Two-thirds of the population of the neighbouring villages lie south-east of the line, and if the station is at Wollerton, will have a further mile to reach it.
>
> That the comfort and accommodation of a community should not be sacrificed for the gratification and interest of one or two individuals.

The petition was signed by a Mr Percy of Hodnet Hall. The petition evidently worked, as the site of the station was changed to Hodnet Heath, and the residents of Wollerton Hall had to wait until 1931 for facilities in the shape of a halt to be provided there.

A Working Agreement for a term of 50 years between the GWR and the WDR was approved on 30th January, 1864 in which the line was required to be of double track. The GWR agreed to work the line entirely at its own expense for which it would receive 50 per cent of the gross receipts, and guarantee a dividend of 4½ per cent to the WDR shareholders.

A Board Meeting of the WDR on 18th May, 1865 agreed that the WDR and the NMDR should be under one management, so further extending the GWR influence. It is also therefore significant that at a later Board Meeting of the WDR, on 6th July, 1865, the decision was taken to have the NMDR line doubled.

Evidence of the escalating costs of construction of the line is that the GWR Act of 1869 provided for the Authorised Share Capital of the WDR Company to be increased to £300,000 (of which £217,770 had been issued by this time) and additional Loan Stock of £66,600. The Directors continued to be provided by the GWR, and a list of those elected at 31st December, 1873 is given in *Appendix Two*.

Construction

Progress on the line during 1865 seems at first to have proceeded well, as Edward Wilson reported to the Board on 15th March, 1865 that the line would be ready to open by May 1866. But the reappearance of the Whitchurch to Stafford line proposed by the WMCQR in 1864 included the intention to run parallel with the WDR from Hodnet into Market Drayton. Although this line was later dropped, a similar formation was proposed by the Potteries Junction Railway for its section from Market Drayton to Shrewsbury, and was later extended to run from Peplow. This proposal caused the contractors to cease work on this section for a year from September 1865, until the exact alignment of the line could be determined. In the event, the Potteries Junction line was never built, nor were there ever any earthworks constructed in this area. Other delays were caused by three revisions to the siting of the junction with the GWR joint line at Wellington.

Apart from these considerations there were no major engineering works to be overcome, as no tunnels were constructed, and only bridges over the River Tern at Crudgington, and two more between Wollerton and Tern Hill could be considered as being of some importance.

John Fowler received an initial fee of £500 in 1862, followed by further payments in 1862 of £3,850 4*s.* 5*d.* and £1,665 in 1863. These fees reflected not only his work on the engineering of the line, but also Parliamentary expenses and 'promotion' work in respect of the northern extensions (that were never built) from Nantwich to Knutsford, Northwich to Middlewich and two short lines in Manchester.

The contract issued to Thomas Brassey and William Field was dated 1st June, 1864 and required that the railway be completed within 21 months from the date of contract (i.e. by 1st March, 1866) unless time was extended, which it clearly was. The contract also provided for the contractors to be paid in shares of the company, which were not to be sold for two years after the opening of the line. An earlier letter, dated 1st October, 1863, fixed the maximum amount to be paid in shares at £170,000.

The original estimate by Brassey and Field for the construction of the line had been £150,000. However, there were inevitably many 'extras' added during the course of construction, not least of which were the station buildings (not originally included in the contract, but also eventually built by Brassey and Field), plus the various deviations as mentioned above. Details of the original estimate, plus a comparison with his final account for the line, totalling £196,344 13*s.* 7*d.*, are given in *Appendix Three*, of which works totalling £168,000 had been certified up to 18th April, 1868. It is worthy of note that the signals were supplied by Saxby & Farmer in August and October 1866, its invoices totalling £700, and that the telegraph equipment was supplied by the Electric Telegraph Company in June 1866 for the indicated £431 19*s.* 0*d.* Brassey and Field had erected much of the telegraph by April 1867 but the supplier completed the installation. This confirms that the line was fully signalled and provided with full telegraphic equipment right from the opening. Land and other compensation totalled a further £69,402 15*s.* 8*d.* The only payments traced to Edward Wilson are £1,000 in June 1868, £2,000 in June 1869 and £1,000 in December 1872. However, there must surely have been further, more regular payments.

One fatal accident is known to have occurred in connection with the building of the line, and was reported as follows in the *Wellington Journal* of 20th May, 1865:

COLD HATTON - FATAL ACCIDENT - On Yesterday evening week [12th May, 1865 - *author*] an accident, causing immediate death, occurred to a young man named Baxter, in the employment of Messrs Brassey and Field, as a carter. Deceased was returning with his team from Wellington, and when a short distance past the Stars Inn, was knocked down by his horse, and the cart, which was heavily loaded with sleepers, passed over him, crushing him to death. An inquest was held on the following day at the Stars Inn, before J. Bidlake, Esq., deputy coroner, when a verdict of 'Accidental death' was returned. Deceased was only 18 years of age, and was a young man of steady habits, and, as it was stated at the inquest, was quite sober when he met his untimely death.

Thus the accident did not actually occur on the construction of the line. The unfortunate youth was buried at All Hallows Church, Rowton.

The Secretary of the WDR, Gordon Graham, advised the Board of Trade of the intention to open the line within three months by issuance of a formal First Notice on 30th April, 1867. This was followed by a Second Notice on 7th June, 1867 of intention to open within 10 days. However, Graham withdrew this notice on 18th June as the line was not ready. A fresh Second Notice was issued on 6th July, in order for the inspection to be arranged.

Colonel Yolland made his inspection of the completed line on behalf of the Board of Trade and submitted his report on 22nd July, 1867. He reported that the width between the running rails was 6 feet, and that the formation was a maximum of 30 feet below the land level in cuttings, and 32 feet on embankments. The sharpest curve was 40 chains radius (apart from two short lengths), and the steepest gradient was 1 in 104. The rails were, as prescribed, of 72 lb. per yard in 24 foot lengths, laid on part cinder and part gravel ballast, and the rail chairs were 25 lb. each, fixed by oak keys and by 7 inch wrought-iron spikes to the sleepers. The half-round sleepers were 9 feet by 10 inches, by 5 inches, placed 2 feet 8⅝ inches apart on ballast of cinder and gravel about one foot deep. There were 19 overbridges, 11 underbridges and 5 viaducts, with the widest span being of 38 ft 9 in. on the skew. Stations had been provided at Crudgington and Hodnet, with additional goods sidings made or intended at Tern Hill, Wollerton and Peplow. Turntables had been installed or were available at Wellington and Market Drayton. His report specified the following amendments required:

The chairs, varying between 24¼ to 26 lb. are inadequate for this type of main line intended to reach Nantwich, Crewe and Manchester. Chairs should be 28 to 30 lbs each so as to eliminate fractures.

At Crudgington, Peplow and Hodnet, the goods lines should be interlocked with signals and blind sidings. If intended sidings are installed at Tern Hill and Wollerton, these should be similar.

Platforms opposite the station buildings at Crudgington and Hodnet should have shelter for the passengers.

Some signals require resiting, as follows: the branch distant cannot be seen from the Wellington signal box, the down distant at Wollerton siding cannot be seen from the siding, the up distant is not well seen from the line approaching the siding at Wollerton, and the up distant at Peplow is not well seen by the driver on the up main line.

The line requires to be shifted midway on the girders of wrought iron bridges at 3 miles 18 chains, and at 11 miles 32 chains.

The matter of the apparently inadequate weight of the rail chairs was commented on by Colonel Yolland on his inspection of the completed double track NMDR at the same time, and was taken up by the WDR Secretary, Gordon Graham. He very quickly lodged an appeal, on 25th July, 1867 to the Lords committee of the Privy Council for Trade, citing this requirement as not having been originally specified by the Board of Trade. The Engineer of the line, John Gardner, wrote a lengthy appeal, also dated 25th July, claiming the adequacy of the chairs, and their compliance with Board of Trade guidelines. He further cited other railways (e.g. the Llangollen & Corwen, Severn Valley, Stafford & Uttoxeter and Stourbridge Railways) as having lighter chairs than their own. Further discussion took place, such that the WDR was obliged to withdraw its Second Notice on 20th August, although this was replaced by a fresh notice the following day.

A last minute delay was reported by Edward Wilson to the Board on 18th September, 1867 in which he recorded that he was having difficulty in getting the remaining chairs from the foundries, and so the line would not be ready for opening on 1st October. Presumably the weight of the GWR was brought to bear on the foundries concerned, and the remaining chairs delivered shortly afterwards.

This prompted a new inspection, which this time was performed on 8th October by Colonel Rich (as Colonel Yolland was on leave). He reported to the Board of Trade the following day that all requirements from the first inspection had been attended to, with the exception of the shelters for Crudgington and Hodnet, but as these were not safety issues, they did not prevent the opening of the line. With the outstanding matters now resolved, the Board of Trade finally agreed on 11th October, 1867 that the railway could open.

The *Newport and Market Drayton Advertiser* reported on 12th October, 1867 on Colonel Rich's further tour of inspection, as follows:

> WELLINGTON - Completion of the Wellington and Market Drayton Railway
> The line of railway has, we believe, received the sanction of the Government Inspector, who went over the works on Tuesday last [8th October, 1867 - *author*]. We are informed that the public may now rely on the opening of the line taking place on or about the 1st. proximo.

Opening of the line

Evidently the GWR was anxious to open the line as soon as possible, for hardly had the ink dried on the above newspaper report, then the line opened, actually on 16th October, 1867. And it opened without any of the elaborate ceremonies that had taken place when the NMDR line opened. Indeed, there seems to have been little time to advertise in advance the opening of the line. Once again, the *Newport and Market Drayton Advertiser* reported on the occasion, this time in their issue dated 19th October, 1867:

MARKET DRAYTON - Opening of the Wellington and Market Drayton Railway
This short line was opened on Wednesday [16th October, 1867 - *author*], after many delays which have tried the patience of the neighbourhood. There was little display or public rejoicing on the occasion. But the ultimate usefulness and prosperity of the enterprise must not on that account be slightly spoken of. The line will be important to the Great Western Company, as giving them direct communication through Nantwich and Crewe with the Potteries, Manchester, and the North. It will give the people of the district increased facilities for distant journeys North and South, and those aids to communication with neighbouring districts, by which their resources will be developed, and turned to the best advantage.

This short report was certainly not in error, for the line now afforded the people opportunities to travel north, south, east and west, whereas previously they had only been able to travel west to Shrewsbury with some convenience.The lack of formal celebrations on the opening of the complete line by either the WMD Company or the GWR is somewhat disappointing, but the contractors were not to be denied this fairly simple pleasure, and so they held their own celebratory dinner on an unspecified date, as reported in the *Wellington Journal* of 26th October, 1867:

WELLINGTON AND MARKET DRAYTON RAILWAY
In connection with the opening of this line Messrs. Brassey and Field last week provided an excellent spread at the Wrekin Hotel, for their employees and a few others connected with the Railway. Of these about 40 sat down after the last train from Drayton, Mr John Mackay occupied the chair. The health of the worthy contractors was given and most vigorously cheered, their representative, the chairman, also coming in for most cordial applause. Some good songs were sung, and an extremely pleasant evening was passed.

Subsequent events

With the opening of the through double track line, trains from Wellington to Nantwich travelled in the down direction, and those from Nantwich to Wellington in the up direction.

Public goods sidings had already been provided at Peplow, even though there was no station there, but at a Board Meeting on 17th February, 1868 it was agreed to install a private siding for Sir V. Corbet at his cost. Sir V. Corbet had taken residence at the nearby Peplow Hall.

Earlier, on 18th April, 1867 a draft agreement had been signed for amalgamation with the GWR and this was formalized on 16th December, 1868. Next, an Act of 12th July, 1869 authorized the amalgamation, although it was not until 30th August, 1877 that this agreement was sealed at a Board Meeting on that date. This was to be the last Directors' Meeting of the nominally independent company.

Thus the entire line was formally vested in the GWR until Nationalisation on 1st January, 1948. However, it should be remembered that Nationalisation of all the railways in the country had been first mooted by the Liberal government in 1913, who appointed a Royal Commission to investigate the possibility and practicality of such a move to public ownership. Only the onset of World War I prevented any further progress, although for the duration of the war all of the railways were taken under the control of the government-appointed Railway Executive. With the cessation of hostilities, the first Minister of Transport, Sir Eric Geddes (a former General Manager of the North Eastern Railway), proposed the resumption of Nationalisation and began to prepare plans with this objective in mind. Once again these plans were curtailed, this time in 1920 when the Government withdrew support for his plans. But the scene for eventual Government control had been set, and in August 1921 the Railways Act received the Royal Assent and established the formation of the 'big four' companies. Unlike the London Midland & Scottish Railway (LMS), London North Eastern Railway (LNER) and Southern Railway (SR) who each grouped several main line companies, the GWR absorbed mainly minor companies and was the only one to retain its former title. These minor companies were absorbed at set dates over a period of time, viz 1st January, 1922, 1st July, 1922, 1st January, 1923, 1st July, 1923 and 1st January, 1924. Regrettably, it became necessary for the control over the country's railways to be once again vested in the Railway Executive Committee from 1st September, 1939 for the duration of World War II. The final scenario at the conclusion of the war left little alternative but to nationalise the entire run down railway system.

Chapter Five

Later Proposed Schemes

We have seen the number of failed schemes that predated the building of the NMDR and the WDR, but quite a few more were proposed in subsequent years, and these are detailed below. It should be borne in mind that the number of schemes around this time was enormous. Not for nothing is this period known as the 'Second Railway Mania'. For example, in 1865/66 there were 804 Bills lodged for the construction of railways. Money was cheap at this time, but then the unthinkable happened, with the collapse of a major bank, that of Overend & Gurney. This severely curtailed the optimism of the time, and probably for good reason.

Many of the newly promoted lines were often an attempt to get the main line companies to buy them out at a profit before work could even begin, hoping that the big companies would want to stifle competition in this manner. Certainly, many of the big companies had resorted to this tactic in the past, but the economic times had changed, and the managements had become a lot more discerning. Other promoters hoped to sell out as soon as the lines were built, if only they could get the finance, but there were still a few who genuinely believed in the quality of their lines. Generally by 1880 it has to be said if any new lines were really required, then the big companies were in the best position to decide to do so.

Birkenhead, North Wales & Stafford Railway, 1872

Plans were deposited at Shrewsbury County Court on 30th November, 1872 for this complex series of railways. The first line left the WMCQR at Wrexham, then made a connection with the GWR Shrewsbury-Chester line north of Ruabon, continuing eastwards from Cefn to the LNWR at Whitchurch, then across to the WDR at Market Drayton, then over the NSR at Market Drayton for a short distance before heading south-eastwards to join the Stafford & Uttoxeter Railway at Stafford. The surveyor was given as Charles R. Cheffins and the Engineers as W.H. Barlow and T.E. Minshall. In April 1873 several 'influential townsmen' of Market Drayton were said to have supported this proposal. Although this line had indeed been properly surveyed, it faced the combined opposition of the GWR, LNWR and NSR and never received its enabling Act.

Whitchurch, Nantwich & Cheshire Lines Junction Railway, 1883

This proposal was for two lines. The first left the Cambrian Railways south of Whitchurch, with a further junction from the LNWR Whitchurch-Tattenhall line north of Whitchurch and was to run north to join the Winsford branch of the West Cheshire Railway. The second was from the NMDR south of Nantwich to join the first line near Brindley Bank (4 miles north of Nantwich). The Engineer was given as Edgar O. Ferguson. Nothing more was heard of this line.

North Staffordshire Railway Line from Shrewsbury to Market Drayton, 1885

In this year, the NSR Engineer, William Henry Stubbs, was instructed to make a study into the feasibility of reopening the PSNWR line from Llanymynech to Shrewsbury, and of continuing this line onwards to Market Drayton to join their line to Stoke. Of the extension, he concluded that it would cost around £100,000 to construct a single line railway, with intermediate stations at Shawbury and Drakeley Heath. He further concluded that this line seemed to have a better traffic potential than their own existing line! Nonetheless, no plans were registered, and nothing more was heard of this scheme.

Shropshire Railways, Shrewsbury to Market Drayton, 1887

Prior to acquiring the erstwhile PSNWR, this company deposited plans at Shrewsbury on 30th November, 1887 which entailed the doubling of the erstwhile PSNWR line from Abbey Foregate to the Shrewsbury-Wellington joint line, then over a new line to a junction with the NSR near Market Drayton. The Engineers were John Russell and Edgar O. Ferguson. No Parliamentary powers were ever obtained, but this company continued in its efforts to promote the old PSNWR line, as below.

Shropshire Railways, Shrewsbury to Hodnet, 1888

With the revival of the PSNWR completed in 1888, the Shropshire Railways revised their earlier proposals with a line from Shrewsbury to Hodnet, thence via running powers over the GWR to Market Drayton and the NSR to Stoke. The GWR would not agree to the running powers required, and despite filing the plans and being granted extra time until 1891 to construct the line, the company was never sufficiently funded to enable this to proceed. Such work as had been started ceased in 1891.

Sheffield, Shrewsbury & South Wales Direct Railway

This unlikely line was only ever provisionally registered. It was intended to run from Sheffield via Bakewell, Leek and then use part of the Colwich to Macclesfield line of the NSR to reach Newcastle (Staffs). From here it would use NSR tracks to Market Drayton, and GWR tracks to Hodnet. A new line would take it to Shrewsbury, where it would connect with the Hereford line and so on to South Wales. Its London-based promoters boasted that it would form 'one of the most important railways in the kingdom, connecting as it does, all the principal Manufacturing Towns in the country with Shrewsbury and North & South Wales. The Surveyor has made a most favourable Report, and on no portion of the projected Line does any Engineering difficulty present itself'. There was little to commend this proposal, and it soon disappeared.

Shropshire (Light) Railways, 1918

The plans for this scheme were deposited at Shrewsbury on 30th November, 1918 by Colonel H.F. Stephens, who had been operating the Shropshire & Montgomeryshire Railway since 1909. It was a revival of the 1887 scheme from Shrewsbury to Market Drayton, but it would appear that a lack of finance for the construction of this railway prevented it ever proceeding.

Walcot Marshalling Yards, BR, 1959

The plans were deposited at Shrewsbury on 13th November, 1959 for a new line to run from a north-facing junction on the Wellington-Market Drayton line to meet a west-facing junction on the Wellington-Shrewsbury line near Admaston. This line effectively formed the boundary of a proposed new marshalling yard at Walcot. This was intended to enhance the Wellington-Nantwich line by routeing additional freight traffic between South Wales and the North West around the chord at Shrewsbury station, instead of through the station and thus to this yard and onwards to Crewe. There was to be a group of 48 sidings, with a hump at one end and departure sidings at the other. It could be accessed from either direction. There were to be facilities for the repair of wagons, servicing of diesel locomotives and transhipment of loads (where necessary) including road access. The proposals were made public in 1961, but before any more work could proceed, BR had decided to abandon the traditional traffic of single wagon loads, and to concentrate on the movement of bulk loads. To this end, it decided to develop its Bescot site, and the Walcot plans were shelved.

NANTWICH & MARKET DRAYTON

	Week Days A		Week Days B		Sun.
UP TRAINS.	1 2 3	1 2	1 2 3	1 2	
Mkt. Drayton..*Dep.*	8 30	11 55	2 45	7 45	..
Adderley	8 47	12 12	3 2	8 2	..
Audlem............	8 55	12 20	3 10	8 10	..
Nantwich..........	9 5	12 30	3 20	8 20	..
Shrewsbury ..*Arr.*	10 15	1 30	4 50	9 40	..
DOWN TRAINS.	1 2 3	1 2	1 2 3	1 2	
Shrewsbury ...*Dep.*	8 25	11 50	2 30	8 0	..
Nantwich..........	9 30	1 0	4 0	9 5	..
Audlem............	9 40	1 10	4 10	9 15	..
Adderley	9 48	1 18	4 18	9 23	..
Mkt. Drayton. *Arr.*	10 5	1 25	4 25	9 40	..

A—Third Class from Market Drayton Branch to Shrewsbury, stations on the Shrewsbury and Hereford line, and to Great Western stations.

B—Third Class from Market Drayton Branch to Crewe, L'pool, Manchester, &c.

Public timetable from the *Newport and Market Drayton Gazette*, 24th October, 1863.

Chapter Six

Working the Line

The First Railway

The initial services provided four weekday trains in each direction on the NMDR, and no services on Sunday. All trains called at Adderley and Audlem, the only two intermediate stations open at that time. The timetable from 24th October, 1863 (*shown opposite*), reveals that all of them took 35 minutes to traverse the line. The departures were from Market Drayton at 8.30, 11.55 am, 2.45 and 7.45 pm, with return workings at 9.30 am, 1.00, 4.00 and 9.05 pm. All provided first and second class accommodation, with the first and third trains in each direction also giving third class travel. This presumably entailed the provision of extra carriages or an alternative set of carriages for these services, possibly in connection with goods services, as mentioned below.

As would be expected at this time, most of the travellers from Market Drayton would be inclined to visit the county town, Shrewsbury. Therefore, the trains were carefully timed to facilitate travel onwards or returning from Shrewsbury and local advertising promoted this facility. Connecting times for the trains onwards to Shrewsbury at this time required waits at Nantwich of 11 minutes, 8 minutes, 28 minutes and 8 minutes respectively, and of 5, 15, 32 and 7 minutes in the opposite direction. Crewe was quite well served, with connection waiting times of 20, 15, 8 and 38 minutes in the down direction, and 14, 22, 12 and 37 minutes in the up direction.

By 1865 the services remained broadly the same, except that there was now an additional late night service on Wednesdays only, leaving Market Drayton at 10.20 pm and returning from Nantwich at 11.00 pm. Also, the last return trip of all other days was some two hours earlier, leaving Market Drayton at 5.50 pm instead of 7.45pm and returning from Nantwich at 7.00 pm instead of 9.05 pm. The Working Timetable (*Appendix Four*) from this time also gives the first information on goods services. As will be seen, the first and third train was listed as conveying goods traffic, and therefore operated as a mixed train. In all probability this method of working was adopted from the opening of the line.

We have seen that the GWR worked the line from its opening, so that the times given above easily facilitated the working of the single line by 'one engine in steam'. In addition, as the first train of the day started from Market Drayton, and the last one terminated there, it is presumed that the locomotive and stock were stabled there. The locomotive shed at Market Drayton is believed to have been opened with the line in 1863, and was a single-road shed of wooden construction, measuring approximately 50 feet by 18 feet, sufficient to house one tender locomotive or two tank engines. Indeed, the undertakings given to the Board of Trade prior to opening required the use of tank engines. So it may well have been that a second engine would be allocated to the line, especially as it was remote from the remainder of the GWR system, in order to provide an

WELLINGTON AND MARKET DRAYTON.

Week Days Only.	1 2 3	1 2	1 2 3	1 2 3				
Wellington ....dep.	7 45	11 5	2 10	5 15	..	..	..	..
Crudgington	8 10	1120	2 21	..	..	..	..	..
Hodnet	8 15	1135	..	5 37	..	..	..	..
Market Drayton	8 30	1150	2 45	5 50	..	..	..	..
Adderley	8 40	12 0	2 55	6 0	..	..	..	..
Audlem	8 45	12 5	3 0	6 5	..	..	..	..
Nantwich ....dep.	9 0	1220	3 15	6 20	..	..	..	..
Crewe ....arr	9 15	1233	3 36	6 38	..	..	..	..
Do ....dep.	9 25	1243	3 50	7 0	..	..	..	..
Stockport ......dep.	9 40	1 10	4 0	7 20	..	..	..	..
Manchester ....arr.	1055	2 0	5 10	8 20	..	..	..	..

Week Days Only.	1 2 3	1 2	1 2 3	1 2 3				
Manchester ....dep.	7 45	1045	1 30	5 15	..	..	..	..
Stockport ......dep.	8 50	1210	3 0	6 18	..	..	..	..
Crewe ....arr.	9 0	1230	3 40	6 40	..	..	..	..
Do ....dep.	9 10	1240	3 52	6 51	..	..	..	..
Nantwich ......dep.	9 30	1250	4 5	7 0	..	..	..	..
Audlem	9 45	1 5	4 20	7 15	..	..	..	..
Adderley	9 50	1 10	4 25	7 20	..	..	..	..
Market Drayton......	10 0	1 20	4 35	7 30	..	..	..	..
Hodnet	1015	1 32	..	7 45	..	..	..	..
Crudgington........	1030	..	..	8 0	..	..	..	..
Wellington ....arr.	1045	1 55	5 5	8 15	..	..	..	..

Public timetable from the *Wellington Journal*, 26th October, 1867.

WELLINGTON AND MARKET DRAYTON.

	Week Days.						*Sundays.*	
Down Trains.	1 2 3	1 2	1 2	1 2	1 2 3	1 2	1 2 3	1 2 3
Wellington ....dep.	7 50	1110	1152	2 25	5 20	8 20	9 0	7 55
Crudgington	8 6	1126	..	..	5 36	.	9 15	8 10
Hodnet	8 21	1141	..	..	5 51	8 43	9 31	8 26
Market Drayton	8 33	1153	1225	2 57	6 3	8 55	9 43	8 38
Adderley	8 41	12 1	..	..	6 11	..	9 51	8 46
Audlem	8 46	12 6	..	..	6 16	..	9 56	8 51
Nantwich ....dep.	9 0	1220	..	..	6 30	9 15	1010	9 5
Crewe ....arr	9 10	1230	1255	3 25	6 40	9 25	1020	9 15
Do ....dep.	9 40	..	1 10	3 30	6 55	9 40	..	..
Stockport ......dep.	1040	..	1 50	4 13	7 33	1043	..	..
Manchester .....arr.	1055	..	2 0	4 25	7 45	11 5	..	..

Up Trains.	1 2 3	1 2	1 2	1 2	1 2	1 2 3	1 2 3	1 2 3
Manchester ....dep.	..	8 45	12 0	1 30	4 15	5 55	..	4 15
Stockport ......dep.	..	8 57	1210	1 54	4 25	6 5	..	4 25
Crewe ....arr.	..	9 50	1253	3 0	5 8	6 45	..	5 8
Do ....dep.	7 50	10 0	1 5	3 10	5 15	6 50	7 10	6 10
Nantwich ......dep.	8 0	1010	..	3 20	..	7 0	7 20	6 20
Audlem	8 14	..	.	3 34	..	7 14	7 34	6 34
Adderley	8 19	..	..	3 39	..	7 19	7 39	6 39
Market Drayton......	8 27	1028	1 30	3 47	5 40	7 27	7 47	6 47
Hodnet	8 39	1037	..	3 59	..	7 39	7 59	6 59
Crudgington........	8 55	..	..	4 15	..	7 54	8 15	7 15
Wellington ....arr.	9 10	1057	2 0	4 30	6 10	8 8	8 30	7 30

Public timetable from the *Wellington Journal*, 9th November, 1867.

emergency source of motive power. Certainly, the branch engine would have had to travel to Shrewsbury (presumably as light engine) for its periodic boiler washouts, and any other servicing and repairs. A 35 ft turntable was installed just behind the shed, and to the east of it. As the shed passed into the hands of the NSR from 1870, its subsequent history will be detailed later.

Motive power for the line would undoubtedly have been provided from Shrewsbury's allocation of GWR standard gauge locomotives. These included those taken over as part of the absorption of the Shrewsbury & Chester Railway on 1st September, 1854 which comprised three 0-4-0 tank locomotives by Bury, and Sharp Brothers. On the same date, the Shrewsbury & Birmingham Railway had been absorbed by the GWR, and a further 0-4-0 tank locomotive by Sharp, Stewart came into the GWR stock. In addition, the West Midland Railway had been absorbed by the GWR as from 1st August, 1863 and so any of its 16 tank engines of 0-4-2, 2-2-2, 2-4-0, and 0-6-0 wheel arrangements by E.B. Wilson, Robert Stephenson, Jones and Son, Beyer, Peacock, and Dodds could have been used here. Virtually all of these types would have been suitable for the less than demanding work required of them.

These early days before the doubling of the line and opening of the WDR seem to have proceeded quietly, although not even this sleepy railway backwater was without its moments of drama, as the following report from the *Newport & Market Drayton Advertiser* of 5th October, 1867 (shortly before the opening of the WDR) recalls:

> MARKET DRAYTON - Burglary at the Railway Station
>
> Some months ago we had occasion to notice that the safe and its contents were carried off at Market Drayton railway station. Between Saturday night and Monday last the station was again entered, apparently by means of skeleton keys, and a considerable sum of money carried away by the thieves. We regret to hear that Mr Collett, our station master, as the responsible agent of the company, is likely to be the loser of the amount. We wish the daring delinquents may be brought to account.

Passenger Traffic from 1867

The opening services on the complete line from Wellington to Nantwich operated at the same frequency as those over the NMDR had done for the prior two years, i.e. four on weekdays only, as shown in the October timetable *opposite*. First, second and third class fares were now available on three of the trains, the exception being the second train of the day. It should be noted that second class fares did not disappear from the GWR until 1910, at which time the basic fare was 1¼*d*. per mile as against 1*d*. per mile for third class. Somewhat surprising are the omissions of stops at Crudgington on the last down and third up services, and at Hodnet on the third down and third up services. This timetable shows through services to Crewe and Manchester, and with its running powers granted over the LNWR to Crewe by the GWR and West Midland Railway Amalgamation Act of 1863. However, although carriages may have worked right through, there is no evidence that the GWR ever provided the motive power north of Crewe, either at this time or at any later date.

Market Drayton and Manchester Branch.

	Week Days a.m.			Week Days p.m.				Sun. p.m.
Wellingt'n	7 40	9 45	12 0	2 40	...	5 55	8 38	7 40
Crudg'nt'n	7 50	...	1210	2 50	...	6 5	...	7 52
Peplow ...	8 0	...	w&s	3 0	...	6 15	...	8 4
Hodnet ...	8 7	10 3	1225	3 7	...	6 22	8 56	8 11
M. Draytn	8 19	1014	1236	3 18	5 35	6 34	9 7	8 23
Adderley..	8 27	...	1244	3 26	5 43	6 42	...	8 31
Audlem ...	8 32	1023	1249	3 32	5 48	6 47	...	8 36
Nantwich.	8 45	1032	1 0	3 45	6 0	7 0	9 25	8 50
Crewe......	3 55	1042	1 10	3 55	6 10	7 10	9 35	9 0
M' chester	10 0	1150	2 15	5 30	7 30	8 20	11 5	10 0

	Week Days a.m.			Week Days p.m.			Sun. a.m.
M' chester	...	8 30	1145	3 15	4 15	5 20	
Crewe......	7 30	9 40	1 10	4 35	5 12	6 50	7 10
Nantwich.	7 40	9 50	1 20	4 45	...	7 0	7 20
Audlem ...	7 53	10 3	1 33	4 55	...	7 13	7 34
Adderley..	7 58	10 8	...	5 5	...	7 18	7 39
M' Draytn	8 6	1016	1 43	5 15	5 28	7 26	7 47
Hodnet ...	8 17	1026	1 53	...	5 48	7 37	7 59
Peplow....	8 25	Thu	...	...	...	7 45	8 6
Crudg'nt'n	8 34	1039	Th.	...	6 0	7 54	8 15
Wellingt'n	8 45	1050	2 14	...	6 10	8 5	8 30

Public timetable from the *Wellington Journal*, March 1883.

It had long been the GWR's desire to serve Manchester with passenger services from the South, and it actually managed to achieve this in 1864 by two standard gauge trains per day from Wolverhampton (where, of course, broad gauge passengers would have had to change). These ran from Low Level station via Cannock Road Junction to the Grand Junction line at Bushbury, where the carriages were attached to LNWR trains through to Manchester. This service continued until 1st November, 1867 after which the trains ran from Low Level to Wellington and on to Nantwich and Crewe. Although this route was much longer, the principal reason for change was that the GWR previously only gained revenue on the mileage from Low Level to Bushbury (perhaps 3 miles), whereas on the revised routeing they were given credit for the mileage through to Crewe (60 miles).

Thus one month later, in November 1867, the second illustrated timetable shows a 50 per cent, increase in services. The weekday trains have increased to six in each direction, of which four can be described as stopping trains (albeit that one in each direction does not call at Crudgington, Adderley and Audlem), and there are the two 'expresses' mentioned above, stopping only at Market Drayton, and not even at Nantwich. Furthermore, there are now two services in each direction on Sundays, stopping at all stations. The last of these Sunday up trains advertises a service through from Manchester, although there was an hour long wait in Crewe. Surprisingly, third class accommodation was then only available on two of the weekday trains each way, plus all of the Sunday services. The Working Timetable from 1870 (*see Appendix Five*) confirms a similar level of services.

Moving forward to 1883 (*see opposite*), one of the weekday 'expresses' has been cut, but an additional stopping service has been added, and a further limited stopping train added, running from Market Drayton to Crewe and return. The Sunday service was reduced to just one train each way, departing from Crewe at 7.10 am and Wellington at 7.40 pm. In the 1890 Working Timetable this level of passenger traffic continued, except that the last remaining 'express' was no longer running.

By 1898 (*see Appendix Six*) the Sunday service had remained the same, but the weekday services were now all stopping trains, totalling eight down and seven up. Of the down trains, three were through trains to Manchester, one ran from Wellington to Market Drayton only and one ran from Market Drayton ostensibly to Manchester. The 11.40 am from Wellington was actually the 9.55 am from Worcester to Manchester through service, and the 2.55 pm departure included a through carriage detached from the 9.43 am Paddington to Birkenhead train. Similarly, the 5.45 pm departure included a carriage slipped from the 2.10 pm Paddington to Birkenhead. The use of slipped coaches on the GWR reached a pinnacle in 1908, when each day there were 79 so detached, at no less than 43 different locations around the GWR system. The main problem with slipping carriages, is that they are unbalanced, in that they cannot be 'slip-attached' to trains going in the reverse direction, and this was the cause of their gradual decline. Of the up trains, two were through trains from Manchester, one from Crewe, and one ran from Crewe to Market Drayton. The 9.40 am departure from Crewe had originated in Manchester at 8.35 am, and was attached in Wellington to the 8.15 am from Birkenhead to Wolverhampton,

Armstrong '481' class 2-4-0 No. 19 was built at Swindon in 1869, and subsequently rebuilt at Wolverhampton in 1886 and 1896. It worked on the Wellington to Crewe line for 30 years before being withdrawn in 1906. Here it is seen with its crew and some other GWR staff, in typically immaculate condition at Market Drayton, probably around 1900. *Shropshire Archives*

An unidentified Dean 'Barnum' or '3206' class 2-4-0 approaches Tern Hill station around 1920 with a two-coach stopping train from Crewe to Wellington. *Shropshire Archives*

where it was then attached to the 9.30 am Birkenhead to Paddington corridor train. The 1.07 pm departure from Crewe was the 11.50 am from Manchester which was a through train to Wolverhampton, where it was split. Through carriages for Worcester (Foregate Street), (arrival 5.05 pm) were attached there to the 3.45 pm to Hereford, and through carriages to Paddington were attached to the 12.00 noon from Birkenhead. The remainder of the trains shown as serving Manchester were those utilising connections at Crewe rather than actual through services. Not generally advertised was the NSR train that ran through from Market Drayton to Hodnet on alternate Tuesdays from 3rd May of that year. This was to enable visitors from the Potteries to the fortnightly Hodnet Sale Day to spend more time at that activity, rather than rely on the unfortunate connections that otherwise existed at Market Drayton.

Sunday services comprised one train stopping at all stations (except Tern Hill which although shown in the timetable had not yet opened at this time) in each direction, leaving Crewe at 8.00 am and Wellington at 7.40 pm.

After World War I services continued much as before, with the 1922 timetable comprising six weekday down and five up stopping trains between Wellington and Crewe (of which only one ran through to Manchester, and one started from Worcester, departing at 9.35 am). Additionally, a through carriage between Bournemouth and Manchester in both directions was operated, not stopping at Nantwich. In the down direction, this service arrived in Wellington at 2.50 pm as the 9.40 am from Bournemouth to Birkenhead. The last four carriages were detached to form this through service to Manchester going forward at 3.17 pm, which a GWR locomotive worked as far as Crewe. In the opposite direction, the 10.10 am from Manchester paused only at Market Drayton and arrived in Wellington at 11.43 am, where it was added to the 9.35 am from Birkenhead to Bournemouth. One of the through carriages in each direction served Portsmouth. Sunday services were limited to one stopping train in each direction.

There was little change by 1933, with five up stopping trains from Crewe to Wellington, of which four ran from Manchester. There were six down stopping trains from Wellington to Crewe of which three ran through to Manchester, and one was through from Worcester (now departing at 9.42 am) to Crewe. The Manchester to Bournemouth express still stopped at Market Drayton, but not at Nantwich. Sunday trains comprised two stopping trains through to Crewe (one on to Manchester), plus one round trip from Wellington to Market Drayton and return.

One interesting working took place during World War II, and for some time afterwards, in which a special train ran from RAF Sealand (near Chester) to Tern Hill on Saturdays for the benefit of transferring recruits to continue their more advanced training there. This was usually formed of non-corridor stock and hauled on alternate occasions by LMS and GWR engines. The LMS power usually consisted of an ex-LNWR 'Precursor' 4-4-0, and the GWR of a 'Bulldog' class 4-4-0.

Wartime services can be appreciated from the Working Timetable issued with effect from 4th May, 1942, which comprised four up weekday stopping trains departing Wellington at 7.45 am, 12.00 noon, 5.55 and 9.25 pm over the whole

Dean double-framed '3201' class 2-4-0 No. 3507 pulling into Crewe with a train from Wellington on 2nd June, 1923. This locomotive had a very complex history, having been built in 1885 as a broad gauge 2-4-0T, converted to a broad gauge 2-4-0 in 1890, then into its final standard gauge form in July 1892. It was withdrawn from service in October 1929.

Kidderminster Railway Museum: A.W. Croughton Collection

Dean '3232' class single-framed 2-4-0 No. 3234 at Crewe, with the driver having just presumably finished oiling round his engine prior to departure for Wellington on 15th August, 1925. Note that the locomotive carries the early GWR separate brass numerals on the rear driving wheel splasher. The first vehicle of the train is a low-roofed six-wheel siphon van.

Kidderminster Railway Museum: A.W. Croughton Collection

Dean double-framed '3206' 2-4-0 No. 3223 enters Crewe station from the south with a stopping train from Wellington, probably in the late 1920s. This engine, which was built in 1889, was a member of the class better known as 'Barnums'. The first carriage is a comparatively modern Collett non-corridor brake third, whilst the second is a Churchward clerestory corridor composite and probably downgraded from main line service. Note the LMS 'Jinty' 0-6-0T on the adjacent track, and the magnificent LNWR gantry. *A.V.W. Mace/Milepost 92½*

A delightful study of Dean double-framed '3201' or 'Stella' class 2-4-0 No. 3201, built in 1884, standing in the bay platform at Crewe with a train for Wellington. The date is probably some time in the late 1920s. Note that the carriage set has been labelled as being 'Wellington and Crewe No. 2', indicating its dedicated usage. *A.V.W. Mace/Milepost 92½*

Dean double-framed '3201'class or 'Stella' 2-4-0 No. 3518 leaves Crewe station around 1930 with a southbound Wellington train. The leading carriage is a GWR clerestory-roofed vehicle.
Kidderminster Railway Museum: C.A.J. Nevett Collection

Dean '3571' class 0-4-2T No. 3574 leaves Crewe with a Wellington train around 1928. This engine, built in 1895, was the last of the class to be left in service. The formation also includes a clerestory-roofed carriage as the first vehicle. On the right, Fowler LMS Compound 4-4-0 No. 1120 is waiting its next turn of duty. *Kidderminster Railway Museum: C.A.J. Nevett Collection*

Dean double-framed '3206' class or 'Barnum' 2-4-0 No. 3210 at Crewe South shed in August 1935. This locomotive was built at Swindon to Lot 75 in May 1889 and withdrawn in March 1937.
Kidderminster Railway Museum: C.A.J. Nevett Collection

Collett '5101' class 2-6-2T No. 5165 pauses at Nantwich with a two-coach train for Wellington on 28th May, 1939. Note the station nameboard proudly proclaiming 'Nantwich Junction, change for Great Western trains to Market Drayton, Wellington, Wolverhampton, Birmingham, Oxford and London'.
J.M. Bentley

The 5.10 pm from Crewe to Wellington was also a through train to Worcester at the time of this photograph, on 31st May, 1950. It is headed by Wellington shed's Collett '5101' class 2-6-2T No. 4154, and has just left the Crewe to Shrewsbury line at Market Drayton Junction, Nantwich and is about to pass beneath the Nantwich to Whitchurch road (A531), with Bridge Farm in the background.
E.A.J. Saunders

Collett '5101' class 2-6-2T No. 5178 stands in the shed yard at Wellington in the early 1950s.
Stephenson Locomotive Society

line, plus one for Market Drayton only at 1.00 pm. On Sundays there were departures at 9.15 am and 10.45 pm. The down weekday trains left Crewe at 6.15 am, 1.02 and 5.10 pm for Wellington and at 10.00 am (Wednesdays only) and 8.10 pm for Market Drayton. Sunday services were at 6.40 am and 10.35 pm from Crewe to Wellington. The last services in each direction were not booked to call at the halts.

In 1947 the frequency was five stopping trains each way between Wellington and Crewe, and two return workings between Wellington and Market Drayton, and two in each direction over the entire line on Sundays. Through carriages from further afield had been dropped during the war years. Passenger services were occasionally required to interrupt their journeys to collect or deposit special vehicles from the intermediate stations. These were normally horse boxes, or other special perishable traffic. However, on one occasion recalled by Don Houlston, a former Wellington footplateman, he was required to attach a 'Siphon G' bogie van to his Crewe train at Tern Hill. Only later did he discover that it contained the coffins of two young airmen, killed in a flying accident, and being returned to their homes. The van was detached at Crewe to continue its sad journey further north. This type of traffic was carried regularly on the railways, but of course was usually kept away from public view.

During the 1950s the line was often used by excursion trains travelling from the North West to destinations further south. For example, on 9th January,1955 Holyhead BR Standard 'Britannia' class 4-6-0 No. 70045 (then unnamed) worked such an excursion via the line from Manchester (London Road) to Birmingham (Snow Hill). These particular Sunday excursions became quite frequent, and during the Winter of 1956/57 a regular pattern of such trains emerged, running from Manchester, and from Liverpool (Lime Street) and Blackpool, mostly calling at intermediate stations *en route*. For example, on 17th February, 1957 Stanier 'Black Five' 4-6-0 No. 45401 (Edge Hill) and No. 44947 (Blackpool North) were seen on such trains from Liverpool and Blackpool respectively. In fact, the Liverpool train was composed of a full Liverpool-Newcastle-upon-Tyne set, complete with 12-wheeled buffet car and roof boards still proclaiming its Newcastle destination.

The 1953 timetable (*see Appendix Seven*) reveals a slight increase in passenger services to seven up, and seven down weekday services. However, these require a little further explanation, as all but one of the up trains were through from Crewe to Wellington. The exception was the 8.00 am departure from Market Drayton to Wellington, which was listed as a 'passenger and milk train', thereby evidently collecting milk churns at stations along the route. In addition, there was an unadvertised train from Crewe (departure 1.35 am) to Donnington (arrive 2.57 am), presumably for the benefit of munitions workers at the Ordnance Factory, Donnington. A further oddity was that the 5.10 pm departure from Crewe called at Willaston, presumably for the benefit of workers returning home, but this was the only train ever known to have called there on its way to or from the Wellington line. The down workings also included one Wellington (departure 1.00 pm) to Market Drayton train, and the through working from Worcester survived, but now departed there at 9.32 am. The two up and two down services on Sundays ran between Crewe and Wellington.

An unidentified English Electric type '4' (later class '40') 1Co-Co1 diesel locomotive heads through Market Drayton with the southbound 'Pines Express' and watched by a ganger standing in the 'four-foot' of the down line. A '57XX' class pannier tank is shunting the down yard in the distance. *M. Temple*

An unidentified English Electric type '4' diesel passes beneath the Adderley Road bridge and enters Market Drayton station with the down 'Pines Express' from Bournemouth to Manchester in 1963. *Shropshire Archives*

Moving right up to the final years of 1962/63, there was indeed little further change as the service remained at six up and down weekday stopping trains, plus two between Wellington and Market Drayton (of which one ran onwards to/from Crewe on Wednesdays and Saturdays only). However, four down weekday parcels workings were introduced (from Penzance, Paddington, Southampton Docks and Evesham), but only one up parcels working (to Bristol). The Sunday service comprised two return trips between Crewe and Wellington which stopped only at Nantwich, Market Drayton and Tern Hill. The early hours of Sundays also saw one down parcels train from Penzance, and one up mail train to Plymouth.

One further through service was finally introduced as from 10th September, 1962. This was the rerouteing of 'The Pines Express' due to electrification work on the West Coast Main Line south of Crewe. The original route had been from Manchester (London Road - subsequently, Piccadilly) to Crewe, Stafford, Bushbury Junction, then along the original Grand Junction line via Bescot to Birmingham (New Street), where it arrived on the former Midland Railway side, and after an engine change took the former Midland Railway route to Bristol and Bath, then over the Somerset & Dorset Joint Railway to Bournemouth. This new route diverged at Crewe, where it took the line to Nantwich, then via Market Drayton, Wellington and Wolverhampton (Low Level) to Birmingham (Snow Hill). It then headed south via Banbury, Oxford and Reading through Basingstoke and arrived at Bournemouth. Thus our line was now on the route of a 'titled train', which passed through Market Drayton at 11.10 am in the up direction, and 3.55 pm in the down direction. During this period, the normal motive power over the line for this working was an English Electric type '4' (later class '40') diesel-electric locomotive. However, this state of affairs only continued until the cessation of passenger traffic on the line, i.e. 9th September, 1963, after which time the line was downgraded for freight traffic only. Subsequently, 'The Pines Express' carried straight on at Nantwich to Shrewsbury, then along the Joint Line through Wellington to Wolverhampton, until further rerouteing after the completion of the electrification work in 1967 took it through Macclesfield, Stoke and Stafford to Wolverhampton (High Level), then via Coventry and Leamington and so back on to the former GWR route to Reading and thus to Bournemouth.

Although the booked motive power for 'The Pines Express' was an English Electric type '4' diesel, there were a number of occasions on which steam was substituted. For example, during May and June 1963 'Royal Scot' class 4-6-0 No. 46110 *Grenadier Guardsman* of Edge Hill shed was noted at least once a week on this duty. More remarkable was the final day of this working over the line (15th June, 1963) when the normal type '4' diesel had been appropriated to work a preceding train, the 9.28 am relief from Bournemouth that had been extended to Manchester. Wolverhampton's Stafford Road shed was left with no option but to grab BR Standard class '4' 4-6-0 No. 75004 of Machynlleth shed from its turn on the 7.35 am Pwllheli-Paddington relief for use on the northbound 'Pines'. Perhaps someone had not appreciated the difference between a steam class '4' and a diesel class '4', because the unfortunate No. 75004 made five stops for steam before reaching Wellington. It subsequently

Collett '5101' class 2-6-2T No. 4158 pulls into Market Drayton from Crewe with a passenger train for Wellington. Note that the engine is displaying the GWR headlamp code for a local passenger working, and not the correct BR code. *M. Temple*

Collett '57XX' class 0-6-0PT No. 9774 diverges from the Shrewsbury line at Drayton Junction, Wellington with a one-coach local service to Market Drayton around 1960. *R. Mulford*

needed 145 minutes to reach Crewe from Wolverhampton instead of the booked 65 minutes!

As a result of the rerouteing of the 'Pines', the booked motive power between Oxford and Crewe was scheduled for a 'Warship' class diesel-hydraulic, but ironically on the first day the southbound train was headed by 'Castle' class 4-6-0 No. 5026 *Criccieth Castle,* one of Stafford Road's dwindling fleet.

In summary, it can be said that there was no particular pattern of growth among the passenger traffic to lead to a corresponding increase in the level of services from around 1870 until termination of passenger facilities in 1963, with the possible exception of a slight increase around the end of the 19th century. However, that increase was not sustained, and it must be remarked that there was no great increase in the population of the area during the 100 years that the line provided a passenger service. The lack of working timetables for the war years (First and Second) does not give any clues as to how passenger levels were affected during those times, but such circumstances are unlikely to have had any lasting effect anyway. However, it should be stressed that services arriving and departing from Wellington were generally timed to make good connections, especially for travellers heading southwards or returning therefrom. The one notable exception was in the 1947 timetable, where the last Sunday train (departure 8.35 pm from Crewe) managed to arrive in Wellington at 9.27 pm, 12 minutes after the last train had left for Wolverhampton and any other southerly destinations! However, by this time the great travelling public had got used to the unreliability of the timetables, and/or the unpunctuality of the rail services during the war. In fact, it is recalled that the 6.20 pm from Market Drayton on a Saturday was notoriously late, sometimes over an hour. Even when it did arrive, it was likely to be without heat or lights or both. Perversely, this train arrived on time on one occasion, thus causing untold confusion along the line. Several intending passengers at Market Drayton were dismayed to find that they had missed the 'on time' train, and were compelled to take instead the 7.05 pm LMS train to Stoke and change there for Crewe!

Carriages used on the stopping services would initially have been of the four-wheeled variety, then during the 19th century improving to the use of six-wheeled stock. All of these were of course non-corridor stock and, like the locomotives, were seeing out their days in some form of revenue earning service. Eventually, Dean clerestory-roofed carriages reached the line, and became a familiar sight up to the outbreak of World War II. After this time, much of the stock was from the Churchward and Collett era, although it is recalled that in the early 1950s some new Hawksworth carriages appeared. Almost always the formation was two or three carriages, usually non-corridor, and obviously including a brake third (later second) in the formation.

Motive power for the line from its opening was provided by the locomotives allocated to the GWR shed at Wellington. After 1867, Market Drayton became simply a stabling point for locomotives on the branch, although its usefulness to the GWR was limited, as we shall see. Early passenger turns were undoubtedly in the hands of the former West Midland Railway, Shrewsbury & Chester Railway, or Shrewsbury & Birmingham Railway locomotives, but with the opening of the locomotive shed at Wellington in 1868, its allocation of

BR Standard class '3' 2-6-2T No. 82009 runs into Market Drayton station with a down Crewe train, as Riddles 'WD' class 2-8-0 No. 90485 stands by the water column on the up line. The crew member of this locomotive is rearranging the lamp on his locomotive, so it could be about to depart southwards as a light engine, or it has arrived from the north as such, and is about to proceed to the yard, 4th November, 1957. *R.K. Blencowe*

An unidentified Ivatt class '2' 2-6-2T stands with a single BR-built non-corridor coach on a siding adjacent to the northern face of the island platform at Wellington in September 1963. This train formation was usually used for services solely between Wellington and Market Drayton. The 1950s replacement coaling plant of steel with corrugated asbestos cladding is behind the train. *R. Mulford*

locomotives thereafter worked the line. These included some of the Wolverhampton-built 2-4-0T and 0-6-0ST to the designs of Joseph Armstrong, and then latterly there was established a lengthy relationship with various ageing designs of 2-4-0 tender engines. Indeed, the line became well known for the various designs to seen working out their remaining years on the less than arduous passenger workings. For example, three of the '481' class, Nos. 12, 19 and 20 (all built in 1869) were sent to the GWR Northern Division, and saw regular use on the line before being withdrawn between 1899 and 1906. At the start of the 20th century, several of the double-framed '149' class were working the line, notably Nos. 150, 151, 154, 155 and 156, and continued until being withdrawn between 1916 and 1920. Although shedded at Wolverhampton, one of the last two Dean single-framed '3226' class engines, No. 3231, is known to have worked the line after World War I. Similarly, the last of the Armstrong '806' class, No. 810 was shedded at Wellington until withdrawn in 1926. Other designs ekeing out their remaining years included Nos. 3234 and 3240 of the '3232' class, which were at Wellington in 1921. More well known, perhaps, were the remaining small-wheeled, double-framed 2-4-0s of the '3201' class, otherwise known as 'Stellas'. Nos. 3204 and 3507 worked the line during the 1922 to 1925 period, whilst No. 3505 worked until withdrawal in 1929, and Nos. 3201, 3205 and 3518 were withdrawn from Wellington shed between 1931 and 1933. Some of these locomotives had very convoluted histories having been originally built as broad gauge 2-4-0T, then some were converted to standard gauge 2-4-0 tender engines, whilst others ran as broad gauge 2-4-0s for a while, before conversion to standard gauge. Others were built as standard gauge 2-4-0T before conversion to tender engines. The final class of 2-4-0 to see service on the line was the Dean '3206' class otherwise known as 'Barnums'. Nos. 3220 and 3221 were shedded at Wellington during 1921, and Nos. 3210, 3221, 3222, and 3223 also featured on the line, right up until 1937.

During the 1920s and 1930s many of the passenger duties were increasingly being taken over by the larger Dean 4-4-0 tender engine classes, not because of any great increase in the weight of trains on the line, but simply that these were being cascaded down from their earlier express duties to light work in their final years. For example, the 1921 allocation at Crewe (Gresty Lane) included '3252' or 'Duke' class No. 3267 *Cornishman* and '3300' or 'Bulldog' class Nos. 3314 *Mersey*, 3362 *Albert Brassey*, and 3400 *Winnipeg*. Subsequently, further engines of these types appeared at Wellington shed, notably 'Duke' class Nos. 3266 *Amyas*, 'Bulldogs' Nos. 3309 *Maristow*, 3405 *Empire of India*, 3414 *Sir Edward Elgar*, 3417 *Lord Mildmay of Flete*, and 3445 *Flamingo* and the rebuilt 'Dukedog' No. 3208 *Earl Bathurst*.

Although these engines lasted until the outbreak of World War II (and No. 3417 actually until 1948), they were eventually, and perhaps understandably, replaced by some of the later Swindon standard designs. In particular, Wellington had a number of the very successful Collett '5101' class 2-6-2T engines from around 1936 onwards for use on the Much Wenlock and Wolverhampton services as well as to Crewe. None of these seemed to spend a lengthy time at Wellington, for by this time it had become normal GWR (and later BR) practice that when a locomotive went into the shops, it was replaced

An Ivatt class '2' 2-6-2T enters Market Drayton with an evening Wellington to Crewe service in 1960. *R. Mulford*

Collett '57XX' class 0-6-0PT No. 9639 pulls away from Audlem station with a two-coach 'B-set' forming a southbound service to Wellington, around 1962. At this time the goods yard was still in use, evidenced by the open wagon in the mileage siding. *J. Maden Collection*

by one of the same class newly outshopped, so that locomotives spent time at a number of widely dispersed sheds during their lives. Similarly, those members of Collett's extremely numerous '57XX' class of 0-6-0PT at Wellington varied considerably, and members of this class were often seen on the local turns to Crewe, although in earlier times the Dean and Wolverhampton built 0-6-0PT classes did not seem to feature on passenger turns, presumably due to the lack of a vacuum brake. Gresty Lane shed also managed to include Collett 2-6-2T and 0-6-0PT classes in its allocation from the late 1930s until the 1950s.

Wellington usually had one or more of the Churchward, and later Collett 2-6-0 tender locomotives of the '43XX' class, principally for express freight turns, but these too often turned up on passenger workings. Of course, in times of a shortage of motive power, virtually anything that could be borrowed did also appear on these workings, and the Collett 'Halls' were far from unknown.

Don Houlston recalls how on one occasion in the early 1950s, his Collett 'Large Prairie' was failed at Crewe with inoperable injectors, and the only locomotive available there was a former Midland Railway '2P' 4-4-0, which had to be worked tender first to Wellington. It was apparently not in the first flush of youth, and its 7 ft driving wheels did not make life easy with the frequent stops and starts along the route. By complete contrast, on another occasion when a spare locomotive was hastily arranged at Crewe, he was given a Stanier class '4' 2-6-4T, straight out of Crewe works. This was in superb order, ran quietly and effortlessly, and used hardly any coal and water.

Into the BR days, the motive power situation remained unchanged at first. However, changes began with the transfer of the line from Nantwich to Crudgington to the London Midland Region in 1950, although this was in effect for administration purposes only. But it was not long, actually on 19th April, 1953 that Gresty Lane shed became part of the Crewe Motive Power District, and from this date it was intended that all locomotives and crews were to be provided for the local workings over the line. Gresty Lane shed became a sub-shed to Crewe North, and its allocation increasingly reflected the LMR influence. Most noticeable was the allocation of Ivatt class '2' 2-6-2T locomotives, which became the staple (but not exclusive) motive power for the next 10 years until passenger services ceased. Despite the new boundaries being established, Wellington locomotives and crews continued to turn up on a wide variety of duties, and latterly, their BR Standard class '3' 2-6-2T locomotives of the 82000 series frequently provided power for the passenger services.

Diesel multiple units were never used on the local services, and even though it seems probable that there must have been tests of this type of power in the 1950s and early 1960s, no such tests have been found to have been recorded. However, it is known that one of the GWR's diesel railcars built by AEC was tested on the Wellington to Much Wenlock route in March 1936. Don Houlston can recall seeing one coming off the Nantwich line at Wellington around this time, which would suggest that it was probably tried on this route too, although no reports of such testing have been traced. This railcar was found wanting on the steep gradients of the Much Wenlock line, but this can hardly have been the cause for the failure to introduce railcars on to our route. More likely, it was a problem of achieving a satisfactory utilisation of such units during a typical

Collett '57XX' class 0-6-0PT No. 3607 arrives in Market Drayton with the terminating service from Wellington. Although this photograph is believed to date from 1962, the locomotive still bears its original 'lion and wheel' BR emblem. *R. Mulford*

Collett '57XX' Class 0-6-0PT No. 4605 drifts into Crudgington station around 1963 with a single-coach service for Market Drayton. This was probably the 12.50 pm departure from Wellington. *A.J.B. Dodd*

day. Whereas the steam locomotives on passenger duties would undertake sundry goods and shunting work during the quieter moments of the day at Wellington and Market Drayton, the same could not be undertaken by the diesel railcars.

The cessation of regular passenger services on 7th September, 1963 did not, however, mean an end to passenger workings over the line. For even on the following two Saturdays the line carried excursions from the Midlands to the Blackpool Illuminations. Shortly afterwards, on Sunday 29th September Willesden's 'Coronation' class Pacific No. 46245 *City of London* was used to power an enthusiasts' special from Birmingham (Snow Hill) to Crewe works via Market Drayton, returning via Shrewsbury. A little over a month later, on 17th November the same engine was used on another enthusiasts' special, this time from Euston to Crewe, returning over our line and via Birmingham (Snow Hill) to Paddington.

A month later the line was graced by the presence of 'Castle' class 4-6-0 No. 7012 *Barry Castle* working the 12.30 pm Wellington to Crewe parcels post special.

On 15th February, 1964 Stanier class '5' No. 45205 of Rose Grove, passed along the line with a football supporters' special from Acccrington to Oxford. More excitement occurred in April 1964 when excursions from Manchester to Stratford-upon-Avon passed through on the 14th headed by 'Britannia' class Pacifics Nos. 70030 *William Wordsworth* and 70052 *Firth of Tay*. The first excursion was piloted by 'Hall' class 4-6-0 No. 6926 *Hackness Hall* from Gresty Lane to Birmingham (Snow Hill).

An RCTS 'North Staffordshire Railtour' visited the line on 30th May, 1964 headed by Stanier 'Black Five' 4-6-0 No. 45020, and on 11th September, 1965 another member of this class, No. 44818 passed through with the joint Stephenson Locomotive Society / Manchester Locomotive Society 'Shropshire Rail Tour'. It had taken over this train at Manchester (Piccadilly) and it headed it as far as Wellington, where it was relieved by Ivatt class '2' 2-6-0 No. 46512 which took it through to Shrewsbury for a visit to the Minsterley branch. Upon return to Shrewsbury, the 'Black Five' took over for the return run, this time via Whitchurch.

More exotic motive power appeared on the line on 24th June, 1966 when rebuilt Bulleid 'Merchant Navy' class 4-6-2 No. 35026 *Lamport & Holt Line* passed through at the head of the Warwickshire Railway Society's three-day 'Aberdonian' railtour, on the first leg of its journey from Waterloo via Crewe to Scotland.

Freight Traffic

Freight was the lifeblood of this line, not particularly that much was generated along the way, but that it formed a strategic route from the Midlands and the South to the industrial North-West and the ports of Manchester and Liverpool. The first mixed trains of the NMDR have already been described, and so we shall move straight into the traffic operating along the full line, from 1867 onwards.

PLEASE RETAIN THIS PROGRAMME FOR REFERENCE

N25R/D

PROGRAMME OF

REGULAR DAY TRIPS

TO

SEASIDE RESORTS and PLACES OF INTEREST

from

CREWE AND STAFFORD

and

ADDERLEY
AUDLEM
BEESTON CASTLE & TARPORLEY
CRUDGINGTON
ELLERDINE HALT
GOOSTREY
HODNET
HOLMES CHAPEL
MARKET DRAYTON
NANTWICH
PEPLOW
PREES
SANDBACH
TATTENHALL ROAD
TERN HILL
WEM
WHITCHURCH
WRENBURY
YORTON

17th JUNE to 8th SEPTEMBER 1963

(unless otherwise stated)

OR UNTIL FURTHER NOTICE

DURING THE AUGUST BANK HOLIDAY PERIOD THE TRAIN SERVICES SHOWN HEREIN MAY BE SUBJECT TO ALTERATION AND CANCELLATION AND PASSENGERS ARE REQUESTED TO VERIFY SAME PRIOR TO TRAVEL.

The Combined Rail and Steamer Trip, shown on page 9, is subject to weather and other circumstances permitting.

Children under 3 years of age, free; 3 years and under 14, half-fare (fractions of 1d. to be charged as 1d.).

Issued by C. R. STUART, District Manager, Stoke-on-Trent. Telephone: Stoke-on-Trent 44121, Ext. 26 (Hours of opening: Monday to Friday, 9.0 am to 5 p.m. Saturday 9.0 am to 12 noon)

"Take a Trip and Go by Train"

May 1963

BR 35008/6

LONDON MIDLAND

Arthur Gaunt & Sons (Printers) Ltd., Heanor, Derbyshire

Programme of regular day trips, 1963.

Stanier class '4' 2-6-4T No. 42482 stands in Market Drayton station with an SLS special on 31st May, 1958 and about to traverse the former North Staffordshire Railway line to Stoke.
A.J.B. Dodd

Stanier 'Black Five' 4-6-0 No. 44818 pauses in Market Drayton on 11th September, 1965 with the joint Stephenson Locomotive Society/Manchester Locomotive Society 'Shropshire Rail Tour' which it worked from Manchester to Wellington, and back from Shrewsbury to Manchester via Whitchurch. *RCTS*

A local private owner 10 ton coal wagon, photographed in the goods yard at Market Drayton. From the date on the solebar (6/04), and from the relatively new appearance of the wagon, this must have been taken shortly after June 1904. *Shropshire Archives*

Horse shunting in the goods yard at Market Drayton, around 1900, with a North Staffordshire Railway cattle wagon in the background. *Shropshire Archives*

The 1870 Working Timetable (*see Appendix Five*) shows eight up weekday goods trains plus one to run as required. Of these, only one was classed as a 'Local Goods' calling at all stations including Peplow Siding (the station not yet being open). All started from Crewe, although there were various connections from Manchester and Leeds, and travelled to Wolverhampton, Victoria Basin (one), Oxley (four), Worcester (one), with two terminating in Wellington. One ran on Sundays, from Crewe to Oxley. There were eight down goods trains on weekdays, including two classed as 'Local Goods' although one of these made only one stop *en route* (at Market Drayton, and this 'conditional') - so its classification seems a little strange. The others originated at Paddington Goods (one), Bordesley Junction, Birmingham (one), Worcester (one), Wolverhampton Victoria Basin (one) and the remaining four from Oxley (including the 'Local Goods'). There were none on Sundays.

By 1890 there were 15 up goods trains of various categories, including express goods, return broccoli (considered as an express goods service), Goods Empties, and Local Goods. Wolverhampton Victoria Basin now received five trains, Worcester had five, Bordesley Junction one, Shrewsbury/Baschurch two, Wellington one and Southampton one. There were five on Sundays, to Victoria Basin (two), Worcester (two) and Bordesley Junction (one).The down trains comprised one from Paddington Goods, one from Bordesley Junction, five from Worcester, seven from Victoria Basin, one from Wellington, and one from Baschurch, totalling sixteen. On Sundays there were six: one each from Paddington Goods, Bordesley Junction and Worcester and three from Victoria Basin.

This traffic had further expanded by 1898 (*see Appendix Six*) with a total of 19. Paddington now received one, Shrewsbury two, Worcester five, Victoria Basin seven, Oxley three and Wellington one. On Sundays there were four: three for Victoria Basin and one for Worcester. The down trains comprised 21 trains; one from Paddington Goods, one from Bordesley Junction, one from Shrewsbury, eight from Worcester, seven from Victoria Basin, one from Oxley, one from Wellington and one from Market Drayton. Of the seven trains on Sundays, one was from Paddington, one from Worcester, three from Victoria Basin, one from Oxley and one from Wellington.

The number of services had stayed virtually the same by 1933, although the pattern of origins and destinations had changed somewhat. Of the 17 up weekday trains, only one went through to Worcester, with 10 terminating in Oxley, and two each at Shrewsbury, Stourbridge Junction and Wellington. Sundays produced two for Oxley, one for Wellington and one for Worcester - a total of four. The down trains totalled 21; one from Shrewsbury, six from Worcester (including Littleton & Badsey), 12 from Oxley, one from Wellington and one from Cradley. The five Sundays trains originated from Oxley (three), Cradley (one) and Worcester (one).

During the 1930s, the Great Western Railway adopted the unofficial names given to many express goods workings by its own railwaymen, although the names were never carried by the trains. The following workings passed along the line:

A rare photograph of a former GCR-designed 'ROD' class 2-8-0, obtained by the GWR after World War I. This engine, No. 3020, is working an up freight between Rope Lane bridge, Crewe and Willaston on 25th January, 1948. *D. Rowland*

Collett '2884' class 2-8-0 No. 2898 backing past Gresty Lane No. 2 box into Gresty Green sidings prior to working an up goods train on 10th July, 1948. *D. Rowland*

Collett 'Hall' class 4-6-0 No. 4931 *Hanbury Hall* emerges from beneath Rope Lane bridge, Crewe on 10th September, 1948 with a southbound freight. *D. Rowland*

Churchward '28XX' class 2-8-0 No. 2861 just west of Crewe, between Rope Lane bridge and Willaston with the 1.35 pm up freight for Bristol, 21st September, 1948. *D. Rowland*

9.35 pm	Basingstoke to Crewe 'The BBC' (Basingstoke, Birmingham, Crewe)
8.42 pm	Manchester to Wolverhampton 'The Early Riser'
11.40 am	Southall to Crewe 'The Grocer'
7.35 pm	Westbury to Manchester 'The Lancashire Lad'
4.00 am	Wolverhampton to Crewe 'The Northern Exchange'
8.35 pm	Worcester to Crewe 'The Sparagras'

In 1936, the GWR advertised that general merchandise loaded before specified times at stations along the line would be delivered by the following morning to Birkenhead, Birmingham, Bristol, Cardiff, Chester, Hereford, Manchester, Paddington, Wellington, Welshpool and Wolverhampton. Those for Craven Arms and Ironbridge would be delivered by the following noon, and for Bridgnorth, Leominster and Ludlow by the next afternoon. These latter reflect the smaller number of goods workings to these destinations.

In 1953 (*see Appendix Seven*), the freights passing along the line varied slightly from one day to another; on Mondays there were 17 up and 14 down, Tuesday to Fridays there were 19 up and 20 down, Saturdays there were 14 up and 15 down, and on Sundays 9 up and 9 down. As usual most of these most terminated or started at Crewe Gresty Lane for resorting, although there were two through workings to Haverton Hill, near Middlesbrough and Leeds (Neville Hill). There was one through working from Manchester, London Road. Southwards, most again started or terminated at Oxley, but there were two workings in each direction to Worcester and others in the Midlands at Stourbridge Junction, Kingswinford Junction, Hockley and Oldbury. Further afield workings were made to and from Basingstoke, Tavistock Junction and Didcot. The Shrewsbury to Market Drayton early morning freight continued, and there was the usual local pick-up freight in each direction on weekdays. Of the nine up Sunday workings eight were from Crewe to Oxley and the remaining one from Crewe to Hockley. In the other direction, although all terminated at Crewe, only four were from Oxley, the remainder originating from Worcester, Stourbridge Junction; Kingswinford Junction, Basingstoke, and Tavistock Junction.

Albert Simester started work at Tern Hill as a junior porter in 1941, earning the princely sum of 17*s*. 6*d*. per week, later he graduated to porter and although latterly based at Market Drayton, he eventually spent time as a relief porter at all of the stations on the line until 1958 (except for military service), when he became a passenger guard on the line. One of his memories is that 18 small calves could be and were shipped in a horse box, being more economical to the farmers, at the rate of six calves equals one horse. The calves were individually put into bags with just their heads sticking out, so that they would not hurt themselves.

By the Summer of 1961 there had been a slight change in the emphasis of freight workings over the line. On Mondays there were 15 up and 13 down workings, Tuesdays to Fridays there were 18 up and 18 down, Saturdays 12 up and 16 down, but only four up and five down on Sundays. Doubtless this enabled economies to be made in the staffing of signal boxes on Sundays. There were three up and down workings from the North Staffordshire branch Mondays to Fridays, and two each way on Saturdays. 'Q paths' for special workings have been excluded, although one interesting path was that for a Sunday 1.00 am Holyhead to Broad Street, which probably presaged the diverted freights from the West Coast Main Line during electrification work in following years. A similar indication was that of the booked class 'C' Sunday 5.53 pm Camden to Crewe. Otherwise the workings started or terminated mostly at Oxley, Worcester and Stourbridge Junction, but also further to the south at Reading, Southampton, Marazion (Penzance) and Tavistock Junction. The West Country workings indicate the usual Summer pattern of perishable fruit and vegetable traffic from that area. To the north the through workings served Crewe, Glasgow, Edge Hill (Liverpool) and Manchester.

During the electrification work on the West Coast Main Line from 1960 until completion in 1965, many freight workings were diverted over this line, particularly on Sundays. However, as these were diversions they did not appear in the working timetables for the line.

By 1966 the frequency of freight traffic was basically similar to that for the prior 20 years, except that no such traffic was booked along the line during Sundays. However, because of the electrification work on the West Coast Main Line at this time, it is likely that the line was opened for diverted traffic to pass along. Normal freight workings were around 17 down and 20 to 22 up workings on weekdays , and 14 down and 18 up on Saturdays. But the changing patterns of industry were reflected in many different destinations, such as Southampton, Eastleigh, Basingstoke, Stoke Gifford (Bristol), Avonmouth, Middlesbrough, Tees Yard, Edge Hill, as well as the traditional workings between Crewe and Oxley, Stourbridge Junction, and Round Oak, although Bordesley Junction now only received one train, and dispatched none. There was still one local pick-up freight each way, calling at Crudgington, Peplow and Adderley as required. The up working left Crewe at 7.15 am arriving at Wellington at 10.28 am, and the return working left at 11.40 am arriving back at Crewe at 1.44 pm. Another interesting working was a long distance light engine movement from Old Oak Common at 7.15 pm for Barrow, which passed through Market Drayton just after midnight on weekdays and Saturdays. This was curiously balanced by a light engine movement in the opposite direction which left Barrow at 9.20 am, passing through Market Drayton at 3.02 pm and Wellington at 3.35 pm on its way to Old Oak Common.

During 1962 the electrification work at Crewe was causing considerable congestion, so one palliative adopted was to use Market Drayton as the centre for the reorganisation of two parcels services, instead of at Crewe. The first to arrive was 3M09, the 8.21 pm class 'C' parcels (Sundays and Mondays excepted) from Paddington at 5.08 am, which was routed into the northern side of the down platform (known as the 'Stoke Bay'). At 8.36 am 3M01, the 8.20 pm from Southampton parcels arrived and was positioned in the adjacent down platform. The contents of the vans were re-sorted, and any unwanted vans were removed to the down sidings. The remaining vans were marshalled into a combined service, which went forward at 1.26 pm as the 3K26 parcels to Wavertree parcels depot, Liverpool. The empty vans were cleared from the sidings twice a week, on Tuesdays and Thursdays only. This was a through empty vans train to Willesden Junction, which departed at 7.30 pm, and was often loaded to as many as 20 bogie vehicles, so that it required a minimum of class '7' power. This resulted in the train being frequently powered by a Stanier

An unidentified Collett 'Grange' class 4-6-0 threads its northbound freight into Market Drayton around 1960. *Courtesy Shropshire Star*

'Modified Hall' class 4-6-0 No. 6980 *Llanrumney Hall* charges through Adderley station with a southbound goods train around 1962. The once well-tended platform gardens have become rather overgrown by this date. *J. Maden Collection*

Collett '57XX' class 0-6-0PT No. 9639 arrives in Hodnet with the daily down local goods service on 1st May, 1962. The single-road goods shed can be seen in the background. *M. Priestley*

Collett '57XX' class 0-6-0PT No. 9639 shunts a few wagons into the goods yard in front of Hodnet signal box, after arrival with the daily down local goods service on 1st May, 1962. *M.Priestley*

Collett '57XX' class 0-6-0PT No. 3744 in the down side goods yard at Market Drayton with the daily pick-up goods from Wellington around 1963. *M. Temple*

Ivatt class '4' 2-6-0 No. 43024 in the down side goods yard at Market Drayton, around 1963, with an LMS type brake van. It is believed to have arrived from the Stoke direction. *M. Temple*

'Princess Coronation' Pacific, a 'Britannia' Pacific or even a BR Standard class '9F' 2-10-0. In prior years, when the parcels traffic had been dealt with at Crewe, this train left there at 6.50 am (Saturdays only) to Willesden. However, from July 1963, this working was changed to depart at 4.30 pm on Mondays, Wednesdays and Fridays from Market Drayton.

Following the cessation of passenger traffic on the line in September 1963 there were insufficient staff at Market Drayton to deal with the parcels sorting, so this operation was switched to Whitchurch for a few months, then transferred to Wellington. In 1965/66 the northbound combined parcels (3K26) left Wellington at 1.10 pm to Crewe (arrive 2.10 pm). For the return of the empty vans, a light engine left Crewe North at 6.53 am to Wellington, arrive 8.00 am, then worked the empty vans train to Willesden at 9.12 am.

The types of traffic varied considerably over the years, but was for the main part comprised of vacuum-fitted trains of general merchandise and steel products. During the Summer and Autumn months there was much in the way of fruit and vegetable traffic from Worcester (actually originating in the Vale of Evesham, and the orchards of rural Worcestershire and Herefordshire). Summer broccoli specials from the West of England, and the returning empties were also generally classed as 'express goods'. There was little of the heavy, slow moving coal or other mineral traffic passing along the line. During the 1960s BR became more committed to the principle of bulk traffic, which led to the introduction of trains consisting solely of one company's traffic. Such trains over the line during 1966/67 included automotive products in services from Morris Cowley to Liverpool (Edge Hill) and to Johnston High, near Glasgow as mentioned above. Two other 'company trains' at this late stage ran from Heysham Moss to Basingstoke or Bristol, as required.

It will have been noticed that many of the Wolverhampton goods trains originated or terminated at the Victoria Basin depot (opened in 1859), and that traffic from here gradually fell away in favour of Oxley Sidings. This reflects the inability of the Victoria Basin goods yard (near to the centre of the town, and a goods terminus) to deal with through goods traffic. Although the facilities here were improved several times over the years, it was not until 1931 that the depot was completely modernised with the latest materials-handling equipment. At this time, it was also renamed as Herbert Street Goods Depot, by which name it had actually become known for many years anyway. In the meantime, Oxley Sidings, which had originated as a small collection of up and down sidings after the opening of the Shrewsbury & Birmingham Railway in 1849, was finally extended in 1897 to incorporate a further dozen up and down sorting sidings. The up yard was divided into the new and old yards, and the down yard into the Crewe and Birkenhead yards. This reflected the northwards direction of the traffic flow, and the increased importance of traffic to be sent along our railway.

At the other end of the line, in Crewe, a similar reorganization was required to the handling of freight traffic at Gresty Lane, as the patterns and volumes of such traffic changed over the years. This traffic included much also coming from Whitchurch (and thus over the Cambrian Railways), but principally that from Shrewsbury and beyond (including Bristol and South Wales). The original few sidings here had long been inadequate to handle this traffic, which by the

Ivatt class '2' 2-6-2T No. 41232 departs Market Drayton with the 1.02 pm Crewe-Wellington service on Easter Monday, 15th April, 1963. *Michael Mensing*

Collett '2884' class 2-8-0 No. 3825 powers an up class 'H' freight through Crudgington station around 1963. *A.J.B. Dodd*

Stanier Pacific No. 46235 *City of Birmingham* taking water in Market Drayton at the up platform, having just arrived light engine from Crewe, and about to work forward the 7.30 pm empty vans train to Willesden Junction. The date is sometime in the 1963/64 period. *M. Temple*

BR Standard Pacific No. 70004 *William Shakespeare* standing in Market Drayton station with the 7.30 pm empty vans train for Willesden Junction, sometime in 1963/64. Crewe North had a sizeable allocation of these engines at the time. *M. Temple*

'Modified Hall' class 4-6-0 No. 7906 *Fron Hall* has just arrived in Market Drayton with the 8.20 pm (Mondays excepted) parcels working from Southampton Docks. The vans of an earlier working, the 8.21 pm (Mondays and Saturdays excepted) parcels from Paddington can be seen across the platform in the 'Stoke Bay'. *M. Temple*

'Castle' class 4-6-0 No. 4090 *Dorchester Castle* taking water at the up platform in Market Drayton around 1963. It had just worked in from the Wellington direction with a train of some 40 wagons, which eventually left behind an LMR locomotive for the Stoke direction. A considerable demotion for this once proud express locomotive. *M. Temple*

end of the 19th century was regularly routed into the Basford Hall Sidings south of Crewe, and alongside the Stafford line. This gradually created a severe bottleneck around Crewe South, as traffic from the Shrewsbury direction was moved in two different directions regardless of where it was destined. Eventually, a scheme was started in 1927, for the creation of 19 new down sidings with a total capacity of 1,227 wagons and two new arrival lines. This work was completed in 12 months, and the new sidings were controlled by a newly installed signal box, Gresty Lane No. 2. At the same time, the Basford Hall up sidings and the approach lines were remodelled and extended. This considerably eased the passage of freight traffic from the Shrewsbury line, permitting an independent passage through Crewe, and for traffic requiring sorting, frequent trip workings were made between Gresty Lane and the Basford Hall Sidings instead of routeing complete trains there. A further benefit was that locomotives could turn on the triangle created between the independent lines, Basford Hall and the Shrewsbury line, instead of having to visit either the North or South shed to access the turntables there. A further three new sorting sidings were installed at Gresty Lane during 1940.

Similar to the passenger services, the early goods trains were worked by locomotives inherited from the Shrewsbury & Chester and Shrewsbury & Birmingham railways. These were very shortly supplemented by locomotives built at Wolverhampton by the GWR for its Northern Division standard gauge lines. These were mainly 0-6-0ST designs by Joseph Armstrong, most of which were subsequently rebuilt as 0-6-0PT engines. These were eventually replaced by Dean engines of similar configuration, such as his '645', '655', '1501', '1791', '1854', '2021' and '2721' classes. The outside-framed '388' class 0-6-0 'Standard Goods' tender engines (built from 1866 to 1876) also became a familiar sight, but were eventually eclipsed by the long lasting '2301' or 'Dean Goods' 0-6-0 engines built at Swindon from 1883 onwards. These were accompanied by the double-framed Dean '2600' class of 2-6-0, better known as 'Aberdares', some of which, against all expectations, survived to see use right through World War II. In the meantime, Churchward's celebrated '28XX' class of 2-8-0 was introduced in 1902 and his '43XX' class of 2-6-0 was introduced in 1911. Both of these became standard GWR freight locomotives, and continued to be constructed throughout the Collett era. These locomotives became staple power along the line from the end of World War I almost until the demise of steam in Britain. With the commencement of the withdrawal of the 'Aberdare' class in the 1930s, some of Collett's massive 2-8-2T of the '72XX' class were shedded at Oxley for a number of years for work over the line. In the meantime, several of Collett's numerous '57XX' class of 0-6-0PT were allocated to both Wellington and Gresty Lane sheds, and provided motive power for the local freight and shunting turns, as well as inevitably putting in an appearance on some of the lighter through workings.

During World War II, several members of Stanier's '8F' class of 2-8-0 were noted on the line, as these had been built as a standard wartime design. During these years, some of the US Army 'S160' class 2-8-0 were also seen on loan and before being sent to Europe after 'D-day'. Indeed, one of these is believed to have piloted a 'Castle' 4-6-0 into Wellington on an up Shrewsbury line express during the war, when the 'Castle' had failed near Walcot, and the 'S160' was commandeered from the nearby Allscott sidings to power the train forward. It is not known just how far the 'S160' continued in this role. The Riddles War Department 2-8-0 locomotives were regular visitors to the line, although more particularly in BR days. Also some of the LNER 'O4' class of Robinson 2-8-0 originally from the Great Central Railway were loaned to Oxley shed, which after the war usually had two or three of the same design that had been sold to the GWR after World War I.

Many of the locomotives from the former LNWR shed at Bushbury were transferred to Oxley shed in 1963, even before Bushbury officially closed in 1965, and so from this date more of the former LMS locomotives began to appear on freight workings along the line. Consequently, Stanier '8F' 2-8-0 engines once again appeared on these tracks, along with Stanier's 4-6-0 'Black Fives'. In the final days of steam, it was not unusual to find through freights powered by the BR Standard design of '9F' 2-10-0 and even 'Britannia' 4-6-2 engines. In fact, the doyen of the '9Fs', No. 92220 *Evening Star* was noted on the 2.00 pm Crewe to Banbury goods working on Christmas Eve, 1962. This locomotive was specifically allocated to Oxford shed in 1963 to work the Morris Cowley to Bathgate carflats, although other '9Fs' and even 'Britannias' were noted on these workings, as mentioned earlier.

Although the line was not open for very long during the diesel days, it did play host to most of the early main line designs, including English Electric type '4 ' (class '40'), Brush type '4' (class '47') BR type '2 '(classes '24' and '25') and English Electric type '2' (class '20'). Almost certainly, members of the English Electric type '3' (class '37') would have been used on the line, although this has not been confirmed. In addition Wolverhampton's Oxley shed hosted the newly-built North British 'Warship' class diesel-hydraulics (D600 series) and the Crewe-built 'Westerns' (class '52'), and these were tested over the line prior to their being accepted by the Western Region and sent to Swindon. Presumably the proximity to Crewe made the line a suitable venue for their running in, although this was not really applicable to the North British locomotives.

On the subject of unusual locomotive appearances, the Metropolitan Vickers gas turbine locomotive, No. 18100, also traversed the line. Upon completion at the AEI works at Trafford Park, Manchester on 15th December, 1951 it was sent to Swindon. However, its journey was undertaken at a leisurely pace, which included a layover of several hours at Gresty Lane, after which it continued through Market Drayton, to arrive at Swindon works the following morning.

Finally, it should be pointed out that through goods services by the NSR have not been included in the overall number of trains run on the line. Together with the NSR passenger services to Market Drayton, these will be examined more fully in the following chapter.

Operation of the halts

There is no doubt that the introduction of unstaffed halts was one of the GWR's most successful innovations, especially in an effort to stem the popularity of the rival road motor competition after World War I. The halts provided low cost provision for passengers and, in combination with the auto-trains or motor trains, a new flexibility of service. Actually, they were first introduced in 1905, although ground level halts had been in operation since 1903. The disadvantage of the ground level halts was that they required a cumbersome stepping mechanism to be fitted to the trains, which also limited the stock that could be used in conjunction with these low level facilities. The new type of halt, typically built with a timber facing (often of old sleepers) and an ash surface platform (to give a non-slip surface), could be provided for less than £300.

During the next 11 years 145 of these halts were installed by the GWR throughout its system. Their lengths varied from a minimum of 60 feet to around 120 feet, so that the longer motor trains of the 1930s, often of three carriages, could be accommodated. A further variation was the slightly more conventional 'platform' which, unlike the halt, was of more conventional construction, but still of utilitarian design and often staffed by a senior grade of porter. However, none of these appeared on our line. By 1939 all but 27 of the more than 150 GWR branch lines had at least one example of a halt or platform. It is a matter of record that in the period from 1903 until 1947, 347 halts and 34 platforms had been built with the average being one per week opening in 1905, the peak year of building. The independent companies absorbed by the GWR contributed another 40, and 10 more were opened by BR after Nationalisation on former GWR lines. The final total was 463 halts and platforms, of which none remain today. The concept was abolished by BR in 1969, and the last platform (Wootton Wawen) was declassified in May 1974.

Working of these halts required special operating rules and procedures. These are best illustrated by an extract from the Sectional Appendix to the 1960 Working Timetable relating to our line:

> Guards are required to collect excess fare books either at Wellington or Crewe before joining their trains, for the purpose of booking passengers at the various halts en route, as they are unstaffed. At each such halt, the enginemen are required to bring the vehicle in which the guard is travelling to stand at the platform (80 foot), and also that of the adjacent vehicle (100 foot). Passengers are to be advised by station staff at joining stations to travel in these vehicles (and by ticket issuing staff at Crewe and Wellington), and guards are to ensure that no-one alights or joins incorrect vehicles at these halts.
>
> Separate access to each platform is available from the public road at all halts, except Coole Pilate, where the only access is a public footpath, which crosses the lines by a footpath level crossing.
>
> Passengers' luggage is not labelled at the halts, and the guard must see that the luggage is labelled at the next station, up or down.
>
> Parcels traffic is not dealt with at the halts (except Ellerdine, where parcels put out at Peplow or Crudgington when Ellerdine is unstaffed, are later forwarded). In addition, parcels and milk traffic will be dealt with at Wollerton by special arrangement with the District Traffic Superintendent.
>
> Lamps at halts to be conveyed to the next station for servicing by the last train, and by the first, by the guard (except Ellerdine, where the goods siding porter is responsible for trimming, lighting and extinguishing lamps). Also, at Rowton there are two long burning lamps on the approach steps to the platform to be attended by Crudgington staff.

Ivatt class '2' 2-6-2T No.41204 enters Coxbank Halt with its two-coach train from Crewe in September 1963. The solitary passenger would have to pay the guard for her ticket.

R. Mulford

The station staff pose outside Market Drayton Station box, probably around 1900.

Shropshire Archives

Shelters were provided at all halts for the waiting passengers, and produced a variety of designs. One of the most well known was the 'pagoda' style, made from corrugated iron, although once again our line was never furnished with any of these. These lent themselves to prefabrication, and they were supplied to the GWR by an outside manufacturer in kit form. These useful buildings also saw extensive adaptation to a variety of uses such as bicycle sheds, lamp stores and other storage facilities, and were invariably painted in light and dark stone colours. However, once again our line mostly enjoyed wooden waiting shelters of perhaps even more austere outline, especially as they were painted black.

Signalling and Telegraph

We have seen that the line was fully equipped with signals and telegraph after its opening throughout in 1867. The signals were of the lower quadrant type fitted in slotted posts. The downward diagonal position of the arm signified a clear road, but the lamps were fixed separately, some 4 feet or so lower down the posts, and at that time white was the indication for a clear road. This was at a time when the more modern system of optical stepped lens was not available to give a pure white light. However, there were not likely to be many other extraneous lights in the vicinity of signals, from houses or street lights, to cause confusion. Thus the light given was that of an oil lit lamp, as the spectacle glass moved completely clear of the lamp when moved to the clear position. Around 1890 a new type of semaphore arm was introduced, in which the spectacle glass was incorporated. Then later, in 1895 a general decision was taken to adopt green (hitherto used to indicate caution) as the clear indication, although it was several years before this was adopted throughout the GWR system.

By the early 20th century the line was fully fitted with the familiar GWR lower quadrant signals that mostly survived until closure, although in a number of situations these had been replaced by the standard BR type of upper quadrant signals on metal posts.

It is believed that the time interval system of line traffic was used on this line until August 1891. This system was conducted at each station by the staff, who operated the signals to show 'danger' for five minutes after a train had passed, then 'caution' for the next five minutes, and then finally 'clear' after 10 minutes had elapsed. Under 'danger' no trains were permitted to proceed, but under 'caution' they could proceed at a reduced speed, being prepared to stop.

Included in the Railway Companies Bill of 1871 was a requirement to make compulsory the use of the absolute block system on passenger lines, in which each section of track was controlled at a signal box and the signals and related instruments linked by telegraph to the next one. However, this Bill was defeated by the railway lobby, as the railways would obviously have been exposed to a greater amount of expenditure. But eventually, with the passing of the Regulation of Railways Act, 1889 the use of the absolute block system was made compulsory for all lines having passenger traffic. Thus this system was implemented gradually, but quite quickly, from then on. The opening dates of some of the signal boxes around 1891 suggest that this was the date that the system was brought into use on the line.

The Stanier Moguls were a class of locomotive not often seen at Wellington. Here, No. 42980 is seen at the down Wellington platform with a Stafford to Shrewsbury passenger train on 6th July, 1951. The Station Hotel in the background is advertising Stone Ales, which have also disappeared. *Stephenson Locomotive Society*

Stanier 'Black Five' 4-6-0 No. 45190 arrives at Wellington with a stopping train from Stafford to Shrewsbury. A Fowler class '4' 2-6-4T is waiting in the bay platform with a working back to Stafford, 7th July, 1959. *Transport Treasury/Alec Swain Collection*

Chapter Seven

The Connecting Lines

The story of the line would not be complete without providing the reader with some idea of the history and traffic of the three connecting lines, especially as trains travelled the metals of the northern line onwards to Crewe, and to a lesser extent over the southern connection into Wellington. We will look first at the southernmost connection.

The GWR/LNWR Joint Line at Wellington

The line from Shrewsbury to Wellington was surveyed by Robert Stephenson and William Baker, as part of the Shrewsbury & Birmingham Railway (S&BR) and the plans were deposited at Shrewsbury County Court on 30th November, 1845. An enabling Act for the line received the Royal Assent on 3rd August, 1846. However, this line was backed by the GWR and involved the company in considerable legal costs in its efforts to win its line through to Birmingham against the might of the LNWR, which had been formed on 16th July, 1846 by the amalgamation of the London & Birmingham Railway, the Grand Junction Railway and the Manchester & Birmingham Railway. These legal costs amounted to something in the order of £190,000 and seriously depleted the reserves of the S&BR. It was therefore with some relief that the latter found a willing ally in the shape of the Shropshire Union Railway, which was planning its line from Stafford to Shrewsbury. They agreed that the line from Wellington to Shrewsbury would be constructed jointly. This plan was approved in the Committee Room of the House of Commons and the enabling Acts for both companies were amended accordingly. A new company for the construction of this railway was formed, to be known grandly as the 'Shrewsbury and Birmingham and Shropshire Union Railways and Canal Company'.

Sections 32 and 33 of the S&BR Act of 1846 required the formation of a 'Shrewsbury and Wellington Joint Line Committee' to oversee the construction of the line. At a meeting of this committee on 17th November, 1846 at the Swan Inn, Wolverhampton the committee appointed Robert Stephenson as Principal Engineer and William Baker as Chief Engineer for the line. The contract for the construction of the joint line was let by the committee on 16th April, 1847 to the firm of Hammond and Murray, whilst Thomas Brassey obtained the contract for building of the bridge over the River Severn at Shrewsbury station. Construction was completed in 1849, and the line opened on 1st June of that year, at the same time as the continuations to Stafford (for the Shropshire Union Railway) and as far as Oakengates tunnel on the S&BR. The 471 yard tunnel, and the Shifnal embankment further east were incomplete at this time, and so the line onwards to Wolverhampton was not fully opened until 12th November of that year.

Collett '56XX' class 0-6-2T No. 5690 takes the through road at Wellington on 7th July, 1959 with a down haul of mineral wagons, probably from Donnington yard.

Transport Treasury/Alec Swain Collection

Hawksworth '94XX' class 0-6-0PT No. 9472 passes Wellington , on 7th July, 1959 with a short class 'H' freight, which judging by the 'warflat' has probably originated at Donnington Ordnance Depot. *Transport Treasury/Alec Swain Collection*

Hawksworth 'Modified Hall' class 4-6-0 No. 7922 *Salford Hall* takes the down through line at Wellington with a northbound train, even though it is carrying the headlamp code for a stopping train, 14th May, 1951. *E.R. Morten*

Collett '57XX' class 0-6-0PT No. 9639 has just arrived in the bay platform at Wellington on 7th July, 1959 with a train from Much Wenlock. *Transport Treasury/Alec Swain Collection*

Meanwhile, the LNWR had been watching the activities of the Shropshire Union company, and had taken a lease of that company, authorized by an Act of June 1847. So by the time the railway opened, the LNWR was in effective control and actually ran the railway with its own stock and locomotives from the outset. Later, the S&BR was courted by the GWR and, as it had frequently been in bitter dispute with the LNWR (especially over its intended line into Birmingham), it succumbed to the advances of the GWR, no doubt with intense relief. The S&BR was absorbed into the GWR with effect from 1st September, 1854. Rivalry between the LNWR and the GWR over traffic on the joint line and especially for traffic continuing further south carried on for many years, despite the introduction of a joint traffic committee. Eventually, this gave way to a more co-operative mood, and both companies operated the line to their mutual satisfaction, particularly as regards rates and traffic flows.

The main traffic over this joint line was, of course, the through traffic from London to Shrewsbury and onwards to Chester and Birkenhead. Changes from broad gauge to standard gauge were generally made in Wolverhampton until 1st April, 1869 when the broad gauge lines were removed. However, such changes had been possible in Birmingham from 1856, when mixed gauge track had been laid northwards. The alternative route southwards was the standard gauge line of the OWWR, which nonetheless required a change of gauge at Oxford until 1861. Despite this disadvantage the route prospered, mainly because of the sheer volume of both passengers and freight to be gained in the West Midlands. Later, the opening of the Kingswinford branch, running from just outside Stourbridge northwards through Wombourn to join the S&BR line at a triangular junction just north of Oxley, did much to relieve congestion on the GWR route between Birmingham and Wolverhampton. This meant that through freight trains from Oxford, Worcester and South Wales to the North could be more easily routed to Wellington and thence along our line. Such services were noted in the earlier passages concerning freight traffic over the line. This continued until the Kingswinford branch closed entirely in 1965.

Passenger traffic from the south was important to our route, and this was reflected in the connecting services being properly timed at Wellington, as we have already seen. In addition, it will come as no surprise to learn that persons wishing to travel to Shrewsbury from any of the stations on our line, were persuaded to travel via Wellington, and thus complete their journeys throughout by the GWR.

As one of the major GWR routes, virtually all of the GWR main line locomotives could be found working along the line, except for the Collett 'King' class of 4-6-0 which was prohibited from working north of Wolverhampton until April 1959 after a bridge at Shifnal had been replaced. Into the BR days, locomotives were still principally GW types, with the occasional BR Standard 4-6-0, 2-10-0 or WD 2-8-0. However, after the transfer of the line to the London Midland Region in 1963 there were an increasing number of ex-LMS types to be found, although the variety was limited by the few remaining classes in service. Consequently, these comprised mainly Stanier 4-6-0 classes of 'Black Fives' and 'Jubilees', plus the Stanier '8F' 2-8-0 class, and occasional Moguls of the Hughes/ Fowler, Stanier and Ivatt designs. The Western Region's foray into

Collett 'Hall' class 4-6-0 No. 5933 *Kingsway Hall* rolls into Wellington on 14th May 1951 with a train of Southern Region stock, almost certainly being from Portsmouth or Southampton to Birkenhead. Note the headshunt on the right, used for releasing locomotives from trains arrived in the bay platforms. *E.R. Morten*

diesel-hydraulic transmission was well represented by the 'Warships', 'Westerns' and 'Hymeks', and by their replacements, the Brush type '4' (class '47'), and English Electric type '3' (class '37').

Although the line still performs its intended function, there are no major through passenger trains from Shrewsbury. Diesel multiple units perform the passenger duties, which are principally stopping trains. The through Shrewsbury to London trains were discontinued by BR in the 1980s, but later reintroduced after considerable lobbying. Subsequently, Virgin Trains have followed BR and most regrettably axed the service once again. Freight is a very small part of the traffic along the route, the most notable being several daily 'merry-go-round' coal trains to Ironbridge Power Station.

The North Staffordshire Railway branch from Stoke to Market Drayton

We have earlier seen how the GWR had promoted its Wellington, Drayton & Newcastle Railway in 1861 to link the towns of those names, and that the combined opposition of the LNWR and the North Staffordshire Railway had defeated it. The next year, 1862, saw the Shrewsbury & Potteries Junction Railway propose a railway from Whitchurch to Newcastle-under-Lyme via Market Drayton. Even though this proposal was also unsuccessful, it had gained a great deal of local support in the Potteries. Businesses in this area had become increasingly frustrated by the NSR, who not only had a complete monopoly on railways in the area, but also on the canals, as they had acquired the Trent &

Mersey Canal in 1848. Each of these new schemes gave local businesses an opportunity to have their raw materials delivered directly by rail without canal transhipment, and at rates that more properly reflected the movement of materials in the rest of the country. The GWR scheme was further promoted during 1863, once again without success. But the difference was that this time the NSR was forced to counter with a scheme of its own for the area, although the NSR Directors preferred to preface their scheme with the rather pompous announcement that 'it was impossible any longer to resist the claims of the Drayton district to the communication they had long sought with the Potteries'. Their idea was a line from their own at Silverdale as far west as Madeley, adjacent to the LNWR main line. From here they proposed that the LNWR would like to continue the line to Market Drayton, either as a joint line, or on its own. However, the LNWR was not interested and left the NSR to proceed with the entire line to Market Drayton, which it promoted in 1864 as the Silverdale, Madeley and Drayton Railway. This also countered a further bid by the S&PJR to access the area with a revised line from Shrewsbury to Hanley. Initially, the House of Lords suggested that the NSR scheme should be held in abeyance for a while, but when the S&PJR scheme was withdrawn, and the complete schemes of the GWR in the area were also withdrawn, the NSR scheme was left to pass unopposed through the Lords. Apparently, the NSR was only able to carry its support with the promise that it would substantially reduce its canal tolls, thus gaining the full approval of the Potteries Chamber of Commerce. It received its enabling Act, the North Staffordshire Railway (Silverdale, Madeley and Drayton) Act on 29th July, 1864, which included a connection at Madeley to the LNWR main line by a north-facing junction. The new railway company was authorised on the day with capital at £175,000 and loan powers of £58,000.

The NSR Engineer for the line was a Mr J.C. Forsyth, who, during construction of the line, complained of excessive demands for compensation for the land required. The contract for the construction of the line was awarded to William Field of Shrewsbury in December 1865. Progress was apparently slow, so that by the end of June 1868 work costing £87,772 had been completed. There seem to have been no major problems with the construction of the line causing this dilatory progress, which is therefore attributed to a shortage of money. Field had partnered Brassey in the construction of both the NMDR and the WDR, and so it seems that Brassey's style of generous but firm management had been adopted by Field, for whilst working at Norton-in-Hales it was reported that 'the quiet of this little village (has been) uninterrupted by a year's sojourn of navvies located in it'. On 27th January, 1870 Colonel Yolland inspected the line on behalf of the Board of Trade and reported that the line was satisfactory and ready for opening. The line opened to passengers and goods the following week, on Tuesday 1st February, 1870 and measured 12½ miles from its junction with the NMDR at Market Drayton to the junction with the NSR line at Silverdale. There were 29 bridges and 27 level crossings on this line. As with the WDR, there were no elaborate ceremonials accompanying the opening, and the *Wellington Journal & Shrewsbury News* limited itself to two rather short pieces on the completion and opening of the line. In the edition dated 29th January, 1870 the following item appeared:

> MARKET DRAYTON SILVERDALE RAILWAY [*sic*]
>
> On Thursday last [27th January, 1870 - *author*] this new line of rails was examined by Colonel Yolland, government inspector, accompanied by a staff of the North Stafford Railway Company, and several officials of the Great Western Railway. It is supposed that the report will be favourable, and the line will be opened very soon.

The following week's edition, dated 5th February, 1870 reported as follows:

> MARKET DRAYTON & SILVERDALE RAILWAY [*sic*]
>
> This line of rails was opened on Tuesday last (1st February, 1870 - author). There are at present four trains running each way between Stoke and Market Drayton. A public ball is advertised to take place on the 17th instant at the Assembly Rooms, Corbet Arms Hotel, in celebration of the opening of the line.

In addition, a commemorative dinner was held at the Chetwynd Arms Inn, Pipe Gate on 16th February. The *Staffordshire Sentinel* of 19th February, 1870 reported:

> About thirty sat down, including several Silverdale visitors. A beautiful spread was provided. Mr Goodall of Silverdale, the Chairman, suitably proposed the Loyal Toasts. Mr Williams, station master at Silverdale, proposed the toast 'to the health of the NSR Company' a number of toasts were proposed and several gentlemen of the party spoke of the convenience which the locality would enjoy by the running of trains along the new line. There was an intermixture of complimentary toasts and the company spent some pleasant time together.

Curiously, the more local newspaper, the *Newport and Market Drayton Advertiser*, failed to record the opening of the line altogether!

The terms of operation with the GWR provided for NSR running powers over the line to Wellington, although in practice this was only used by goods trains and the one passenger service between Market Drayton and Hodnet, as detailed below. The GWR, in turn enjoyed reciprocal running powers over NSR metals to Stoke, which again were only used for goods trains.

The initial passenger services comprised four weekday trains each way (leaving Stoke at 9.10 am, 12.35, 4.50 and 7.25 pm, and leaving Market Drayton at 10.30 am, 3.15, 6.10 and 8.20 pm). On Sundays there were two each way (from Stoke at 9.00 am and 7.20 pm and from Market Drayton at 9.55 am and 8.15 pm). Services in each direction took 45 minutes for the 16 miles to Stoke, calling at the intermediate stations of Norton-in-Hales, Pipe Gate, Madeley Road and Keele. However, the NSR soon withdrew its first weekday service each way, giving rise to considerable criticism in the local press. This must have been reinstated, as by 1898 the services (*see page 191*) totalled five trains each way, with a further return trip on Wednesdays, and an unbalanced working on Mondays from Stoke to Market Drayton. Sunday services remained at two each way. The 11.40 am arrival ran forward on alternate Tuesdays from 3rd May, 1898 from Market Drayton to Hodnet , so that passengers could visit the Hodnet Sale Day without having to wait for the next GWR train, which would otherwise have entailed a wait of over an hour. This train returned as empty stock to Market Drayton. By 1907 further NSR workings were made through to Hodnet, on Thursdays and Saturdays, leaving Market Drayton at 2.56 pm.

Silverdale Junction box, with the line towards Stoke curving off to the right. The Nantwich line passed around the back of the box, to the left, 4th February, 1967. *A.C. Baker*

The continuation of the Stoke line away from Silverdale Junction, with a number of five-plank wagons seemingly stored in the refuge sidings on the right. The signals on the left are the originals from the North Staffordshire Railway, 2nd February, 1967. *A.C. Baker*

It is fair to say that traffic was sparse from the outset, and the NSR did make some efforts to attract passengers. For example, as from 8th March, 1881 market travellers were allowed to take produce such as eggs, butter, fruit, etc. weighing up to 28 lb. free of charge. In 1908 ticket validity was extended to two days for local stations up to 20 miles apart, and eight days for those beyond. In the Summer of 1911, the boys of Market Drayton Grammar School were granted reduced fares. Half price contracts were also available to all under 12 years of age, and to pupil-teachers, scholars, students, apprentices, clerks and messengers up to 18 years.

By 1910 the NSR service had increased by one Saturday-only return trip, but the onset of World War I soon curtailed much of the passenger services, which were cut back severely as from 22nd February, 1915. The frequency returned to five down and four up weekday trains throughout most of the LMS era, with two return services on Sundays. However, some economies were made, with Madeley Road station closing on 27th April, 1931. The line was singled between Silverdale and Pipe Gate as from 7th October, 1934 proving to be no restriction to the line's capacity. By 1953, there were just three services in each direction on weekdays, rising to four on Saturdays, but none on Sundays. The last passenger train ran on Saturday 5th May, 1956 and was the 7.00 pm from Market Drayton to Stoke, hauled by Stanier 2-6-4T No. 42671 with a rake of four coaches.

The early four-wheeled carriages of the NSR soldiered on in use on the branch, being only slowly replaced by more modern six-wheelers, which themselves lasted well into the LMS days. Even then some of the NSR old side corridor bogie stock was often used. After World War II the standard coaching set was a rake of three LMS metal-bodied corridor or non-corridor stock.

The passenger services during the NSR days were generally handled by the Clare class 'A' 2-4-2T, and Longbottom class 'B' 2-4-0T. Of the former, NSR No. 35 (LMS 1455) was a regular, and of the latter class No. 48A (LMS 1446) was based at Market Drayton for a long time, possibly until its withdrawal in 1929. After this time, the standard LMS designs began to take over, as there were few of the original NSR locomotives left. In particular, the Fowler and Stanier class '4' 2-6-4T locomotives had a long association with the line.

Goods workings were never very numerous, and it seems that those given in the 1898 Working Timetable remained almost for the life of the line. There were four weekday workings, one GWR and three NSR with the engines of the respective companies working through. The GWR working left Shrewsbury at 3.30 am, Wellington at 4.50 am, calling at Hodnet (5.30) then Market Drayton from 5.45 until 6.30, at Pipe Gate (as necessary) at 6.50, passing Brampton at 7.15, Newcastle Junction from 7.38 to 7.55, and arriving at Stoke at 8.00 am. It returned at 10.30 am, passing Newcastle at 10.38, Silverdale at 10.44, and calling at Keele from 10.50 until 11.26, then at Pipe Gate from 11.40 until 11.50, Norton-in-Hales from 11.56 until 12.06 pm and Market Drayton from 12.15 until 2.50 pm. It then spent most of the afternoon calling at the goods sidings of Tern Hill, Hodnet, Peplow, and Crudgington before arriving in Wellington at 6.00 pm. From the 1930s this train left Shrewsbury at 3.45 am for the most part conveying cigarettes and other tobacco products from the W.D. & H.O. Wills factory at Bristol bound for the Potteries. The return working was handled in a similar

LMS Fowler class '4' 2-6-4T No. 2347 stands at the main down platform face at Market Drayton with a train for Stoke-on-Trent on 30th April, 1933. The locomotive is extremely clean, and features fully burnished smokebox fittings and front buffers. One wonders if it has been selected for special duties in the days preceding its appearance on this stopping train. *H.C. Casserley*

manner in reverse. The two NSR local goods arrived in Market Drayton at 5.05 and 8.10 pm respectively, returning to Stoke at 5.30 and 8.45 pm. A through NSR goods service ran from Stoke at 9.35 pm on weekday and Saturday nights, going forward from Market Drayton at 10.50 and arriving in Wellington at 11.35 pm without any intermediate stops. The return working left Wellington at 1.00 am and passed through Market Drayton at 1.40 am. Three daily goods trains then became the staple service on the branch until its final closure, although the times had changed somewhat by 1953, such that the up trains arrived in Market Drayton at 5.57, 11.26 am (11.41 am Saturdays) and 2.55 pm. The return workings to Stoke left at 6.33, 10.09 am and 3.45 pm. After the Grouping and into the nationalised days, engines working the goods services were changed at Market Drayton, so that the GWR engines kept to the GWR lines, and LMS engines worked the NSR line with the notable exception of the above through NSR working.

Goods trains were the province of the Clare class 'E' and Longbottom class '100' and '159' 0-6-0 tender engines. The first of the latter class, No. 159 (LMS 2351) was allocated to Market Drayton upon delivery from its makers, Nasmyth Wilson, in 1900. In 1927, one of the former NSR engines, Adams class 'L' 0-6-2T No. 89 (LMS 2258), returned to Market Drayton shed from the London area. Again, as the LMS purged the 'non-standard' designs from its locomotive fleet, the locomotive types from the early 1930s onwards tended to be the standard LMS design of '3F' and '4F' 0-6-0.

During the electrification work on the West Coast Main Line, it was decided to install trackwork on the embankment that had been built at Madeley to connect with the Market Drayton branch in 1870, but on which no track had ever previously been laid. This new link, the 'Madeley Chord' afforded another diversionary route for the many, mostly northbound freights passing over the Wellington to Market Drayton line, so as to arrive in Basford Hall Yard from the south. There is no doubt that this link provided a useful connection, and after completion of the work it was retained to provide a route for coal trains from Silverdale and Holditch collieries. Finally, the section between Madeley Chord and Market Drayton closed in August 1966 to all traffic, although not officially until 9th January, 1967. The main reason for the delay in closing the line was the indecision about the intention to open the new marshalling yard at Walcot (*see Chapter Five*). In any event, this proposal was not taken any further, thus sealing the fate of the branch.

The LNWR Shrewsbury to Crewe Line

The LNWR recognised in 1852 that the Shrewsbury & Hereford Railway would be bringing a great deal of extra traffic from South Wales to the North West, and foresaw that the GWR was well placed to gain the advantage of its onward movement via the Shrewsbury & Chester Railway. So it needed no further impetus to promote its own scheme to tap this lucrative traffic, and with a line centred on its hub at Crewe, was well placed to proceed. The Shrewsbury & Crewe Railway was authorized on 20th August, 1852 and plans for work were immediately put in hand. The Principal Engineer was Joseph Locke, and his Chief Engineer was John E. Errington. However, at Shrewsbury the proposed route into the new General station was not well regarded by the House of Lords, who in 1856 refused to approve the route, thus leaving the line outside the town amidst the fields. The LNWR was forced to reappraise its line, eventually adopting the very tight curve at the approach to Crewe Junction, that was to be a severe operating handicap in later years, and eventually the scene of a disastrous accident in 1907. The legal effect of these delays was overcome by the authorization of an Act in 1856 which extended the time for construction by one year. However, little construction could actually proceed until it was clear that the final authorization had been granted. The contract for the construction was awarded to Thomas Brassey, whose agent was a Mr Day. Daniel Climie of Shrewsbury was awarded the contract for the construction of the stations. The final cost of the line was £350,000 or £10,600 per mile.

Eventually, in August 1857 Errington reported that the half of the earthworks on the 26 mile section between Nantwich and Shrewsbury were complete, and that the section from Crewe to Nantwich was more advanced, with track actually having been laid. His report included one note of caution, that although most of the land had been acquired 'except some gardens close to Shrewsbury, where negotiations are still pending with the Great Western and other companies interested in the General Station, to obtain an entrance more convenient to all parties'.

Stanier 'Black Five' 4-6-0 No. 45060 ambles into Nantwich over the Shrewsbury Road level crossing with a stopping train from Shrewsbury to Crewe on 24th June, 1956. *J.M. Bentley*

Stanier 'Jubilee' class 4-6-0 No. 45553 *Canada* speeds through Nantwich station with an express for Shrewsbury on 30th September, 1952. *J.M. Bentley*

Collett 'Grange' class 4-6-0 No. 6847 *Tidmarsh Grange*, bearing only an 86A shed plate on its smokebox door, standing at the south end of Crewe's platform 2 on 27th October, 1963. From the position of its headlamp, it appears to have just backed on to the train, whose destination is not known. From the length of the train, it is unlikely be heading for Wellington, so it may be for Shrewsbury. *Kidderminster Railway Museum: W. Potter Collection*

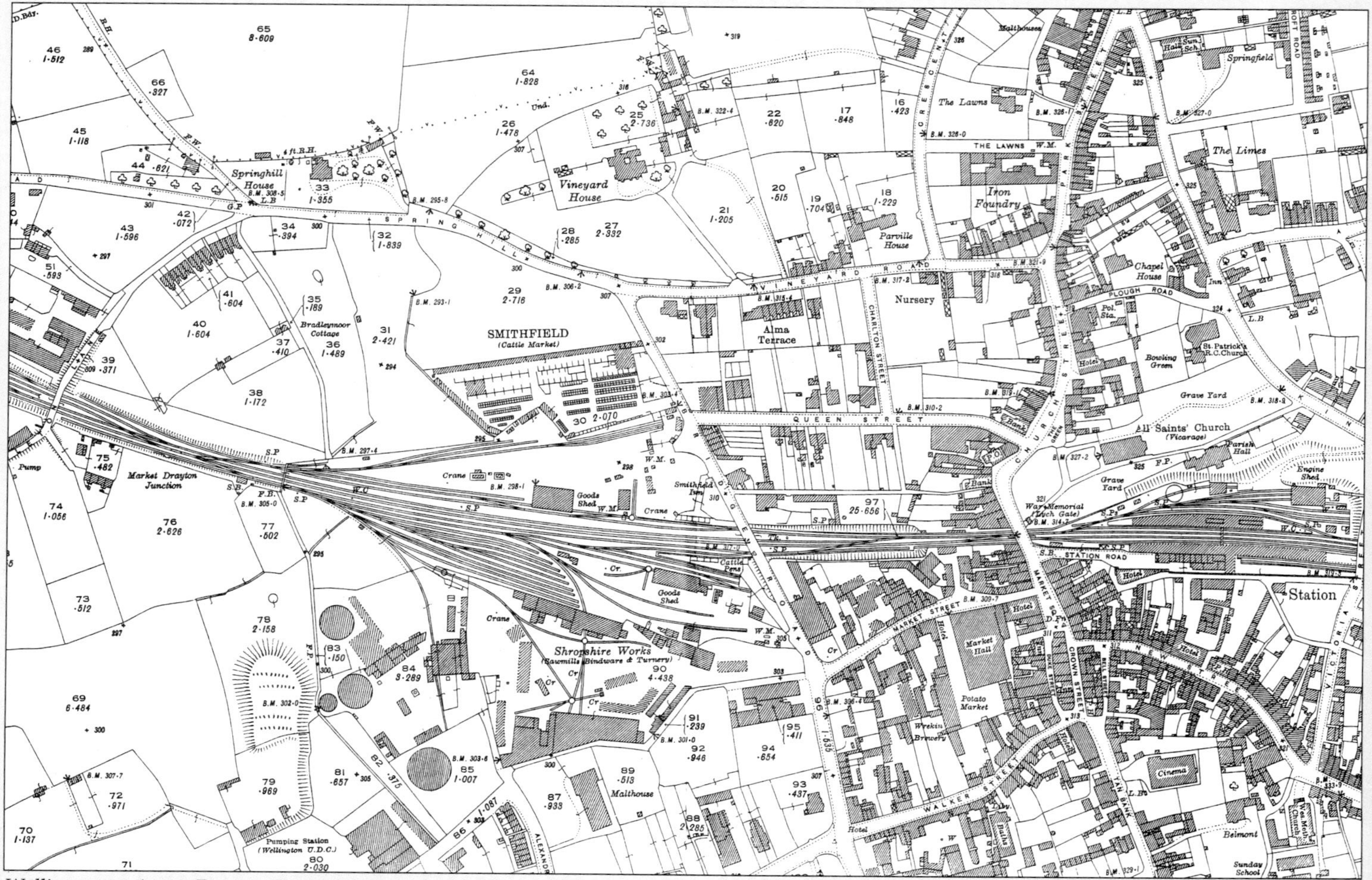

Wellington station to Drayton Junction.

Reproduced from the 25", 1925 Ordnance Survey Map

Collett 'Castle' class 4-6-0 No. 5022 *Wigmore Castle* stands in Wellington station with a six-coach express of Churchward and Collett corridor stock, around 1956. *R. Mulford*

An Ivatt class '2' 2-6-2T No. 41201 waits to leave Wellington with the 5.45 pm service for Crewe on 21st April, 1962. *Michael Mensing*

Looking west from the end of the down platform at Wellington, with the No. 3 signal box framed by the signal gantry. Note that the starter for trains leaving the platform is mounted unusually on the side of the gantry main support, along with a shunting signal. The extent of the brick-lined cutting through the town is clearly evident, 6th September, 1969.

M. Priestley

Churchward Mogul No. 6368 with an up freight train from the Crewe line passes Wellington No. 4 signal box on 4th July, 1959. *Michael Mensing*

depot. Both goods depots were equipped with 10 ton loading cranes. The GWR depot was served by a complex of sidings, which also served the substantial timber yard and premises of Richard Groom, Sons & Co. Ltd. This eight acre site was originally established by John Dickson in 1852 as his engineering works called Shropshire Works, producing a wide range of railway products including rolling stock and served as the base for his railway contracting business. At this time he was building the S&BR Madeley branch, and later built the Wellington & Severn Junction Railway from Ketley to Lightmoor, which opened in 1859. His contracting business expanded, but he was scandalised by some very shoddy work, especially on the Whitby, Redcar & Middlesbrough Union Railway in Yorkshire and was bankrupted for the third time by the early 1870s. The site was taken over by R.G. Groom (1818 to 1892) who had started a basket making business in New Street, Wellington around 1841. His son Richard developed the business on its new site to include sawmilling and turned wooden ware and bendware. The rail connection was retained for incoming timbers. On the western side was the Wellington Gas Company's works, which again was rail connected, being supplied with coal for the making of town gas.

Nearby, Wellington No. 4 signal box controlled the western end of these goods yards and the nearby Drayton Junction, where our line swung off in a general northerly direction. This signal box was always kept continuously open. There were runaway catch points on the up branch line located 600 yards before the home signal. Also, an up refuge siding was provided before the junction, with capacity for 36 wagons plus engine and brake van.

Nearby was the scene of a puzzling but tragic accident on 9th September, 1950, when the body of John Laurence Mundy, aged 27, a railwayman of nearby Ellerdine, was found at the side of the line near to the Pheasant Bridge, Admaston. He appeared to have been run over by the train that he had fallen from, the 9.28 pm Wellington to Crewe, and at the inquest held in Shrewsbury, the guard, John Davies of Crewe, was reported in the *Wellington Journal & Shrewsbury News* of 16th September as recalling the events as follows:

> At Wellington, Mundy got into the guard's van with his bicycle. Mundy was his normal self. He and Mundy stood at the door of the van till the train had passed No. 4 signal box. The window was open. He moved away and left Mundy by the door. He heard a noise like the sound of a door, turned round and saw that Mundy was missing. Davies stated that he himself had closed the door safely at Wellington, but when he turned round and missed Mundy the door was slightly open.
>
> A relief porter at Wellington, John Caddick, said he saw the train leave Wellington, and the door was closed with the handle in the locked position.

As soon as the train stopped at Longdon Halt, the train crew returned down the line to search for Mundy. The driver, James Shipperbottom of Wigan, found the body at the side of the line, lying on his back. He had suffered severe injuries, and died later in the Royal Salop Infirmary, Shrewsbury. Asked how the train could have run over Mundy, the driver replied that it was a mystery. The police investigation came to the conclusion that the door must have sprung open, and that Mundy must have clutched at it, or some part of the carriage, which in turn swung him beneath the wheels of the train.

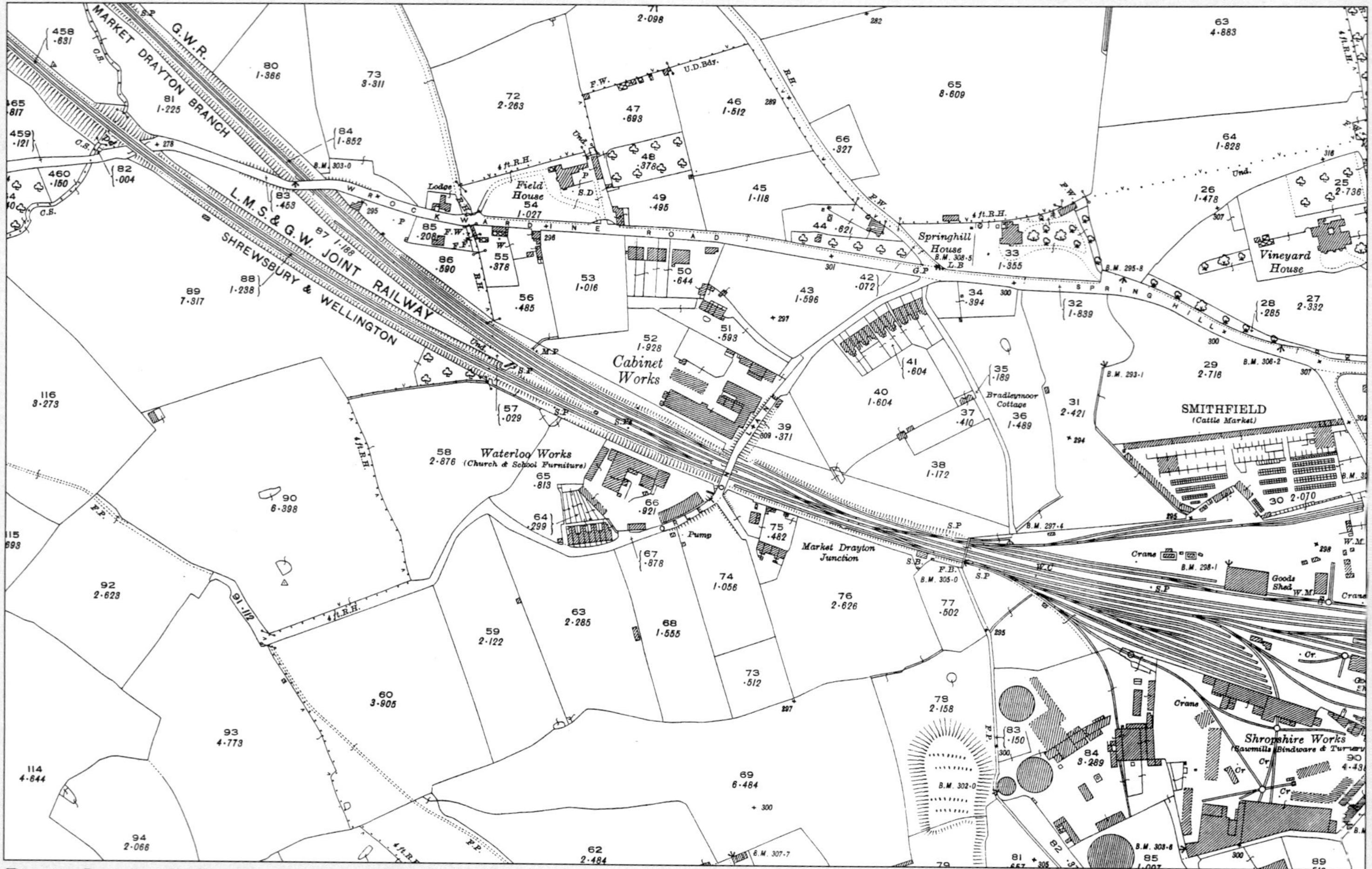

Drayton Junction, Wellington.

Reproduced from the 25", 1925 Ordnance Survey Map

'28XX' class 2-8-0 No. 2856 approaches Drayton Junction with an up freight on 27th August, 1962. *Michael Mensing*

Ivatt class '2' 2-6-2T No. 41204 passes the village of Admaston as it works the 5.45 pm local passenger train from Wellington to Crewe on 27th August, 1962. The Admaston village's railway station was on the Wellington-Shrewsbury Joint Line. *Michael Mensing*

Longdon Halt was located on a slight curve, and featured the familiar wooden waiting shelters. In this view, looking north, it can be seen that pedestrian access to the down platform was via a short set of steps from the lane at the left-hand side, whilst the up platform was accessed using a steep flight of steps adjacent to the road overbridge.

J. Maden Collection

The line had been level from Wellington station, but the ruling gradient for the next section is falling at 1 in 104, as the line passed in a cutting round the eastern side of Admaston and headed into open country on a low embankment to Longdon Halt (2 miles 61 chains or 2¾ miles), which was authorised by the GWR on 4th October, 1934 and opened on 20th October following. This halt was located south of an overbridge which was also the site of a crossroads between the road from Wellington to High Ercall (now B5063) and a minor lane. It comprised black wooden waiting shelters on each of the 100 ft-long platforms constructed of timber facings with ash surfaces. The estimated cost had been £290. Lengthy paths led from each side of the road overbridge to the platforms. No facilities for goods traffic were provided here.

There were a number of RAF airfields in this part of North Shropshire during World War II, and this subject will recur during the course of this story. At Longdon, the significance was that there was a nearby airfield at RAF Bratton from 1940 to 1945 and so the servicemen stationed and visiting here would have used this modest halt on their way to and from periods of leave, and for access to Wellington and Market Drayton for evenings out.

This location was memorable to Don Houlston for an entirely different reason, as he recalls how when firing trains past here, he regularly dropped off a lump or two of coal by the permanent way hut adjacent to Longdon Halt for his father-in-law to collect. However, on one occasion when he was firing a tender locomotive, he managed to drop a lump larger than normal, whilst travelling at around 40 mph. The lump bounced like a Barnes-Wallis invention and demolished the door of the hut, which faced the direction of travel, for although these huts were stoutly built from old sleepers, the doors were normal thin wooden affairs. Don was unaware of what had happened, as by the time of impact he was some distance away. It was fortunate that the hut was not occupied at the time of this incident.

The line continued over gently undulating farmland, and crossed the remains of the Shrewsbury Canal, which had been opened in 1796, but by the mid-1930s was virtually abandoned, and was closed officially by the wartime 1944 LMS Act. Shortly after, it crossed a minor river, then headed to Crudgington (4 miles 55¼ chains or 4¾ miles), where just before the station it crossed the River Strine on a fine brick-built three-arch bridge, just before where this river flows into the River Tern. The station, which opened with the line, was located south of the overbridge carrying the Newport to Shrewsbury road, and was of a pleasingly ornate style. The two-storey station building on the down platform was in red brick with ornate cream brickwork around the windows and beneath the roofline, and could be described as being of a vaguely Italianate style. A fairly simple red brick shelter with a wooden awning was provided on the down platform. The goods yard was located behind the station building, and included a single road goods shed of similar design to the station building, but entirely of red brick. This was equipped with a 1½ ton loading crane. The sidings, in order away from the running line, were the Straight Siding (into a bay at the side of the down platform that also had two loading docks), Short Dock Siding (with access to the cattle dock), Coal Siding and the New Siding. This latter opened in 1929 and forked off north-eastwards at an angle to the other sidings. It was officially an up refuge siding, having a capacity of 39 wagons plus engine and van. The signal box was situated on the south end of the down platform, and opened in 1893. In 1898 the signal box was only closed between 5.30 am on Sunday until 7.30 am on Monday.

Crudgington station from the up platform looking north in 1962. The steps leading from the road overbridge to each platform are clearly visible, these being the only (official) means for passengers to get from one platform to the other. This was particularly necessary if, having purchased a ticket at the station building on the up platform, one was then travelling north from the down platform. *R. Mulford*

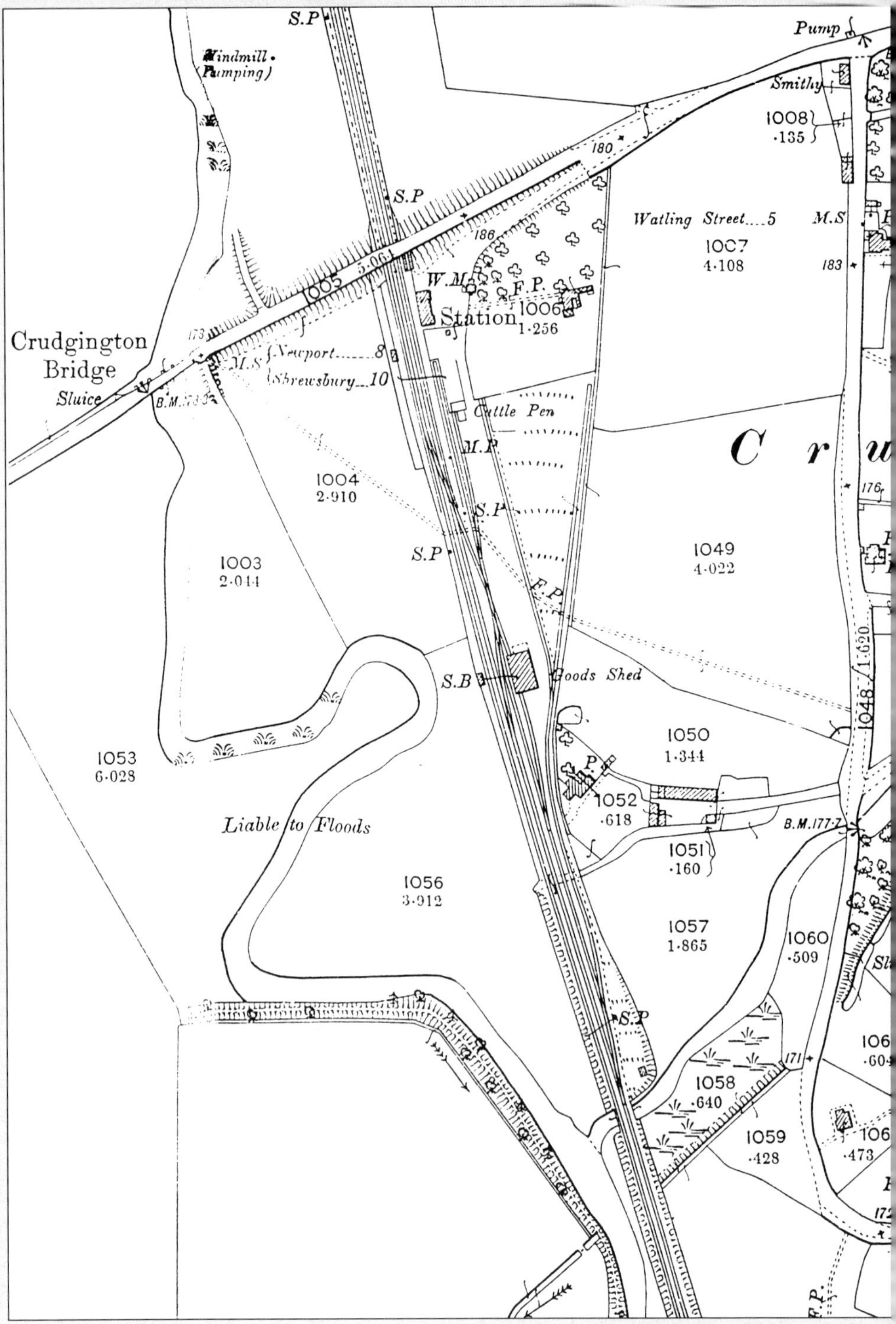

Crudgington station. *Reproduced from the 25″, 1901 Ordnance Survey Map*

Wellington's Collett '5101' class 2-6-2T No. 4120 has just arrived at Crudgington with the 12.50 pm Wellington to Market Drayton on 15th April, 1958. A mobile crane is busily unloading coal wagons stabled on the mileage siding. *M. Priestley*

The up platform at Crudgington, viewed from an 'SLS Special' headed by Stanier class '4' 2-6-4T No. 42482 of Walsall shed heading northwards on 31st May, 1958. This train was photographed shortly after at Market Drayton. The steps leading from the road overbridge are clearly visible, and the milk churns on the up platform lend a period charm. *M. Priestley*

Ivatt class '2' 2-6-2T No. 41232 bustles into Rowton Halt with a train from Crewe to Wellington around 1961. Note that this locomotive retained its original early BR emblem on the tank side. The steep steps from the road overbridge can be seen in the background. *J. Maden Collection*

Ellerdine Halt looking north in its later days. The waiting shelters here were of corrugated iron construction. Access to both platforms was from the lane running across the overbridge. *J. Maden Collection*

This signal box was the scene of an unfortunate incident, similar to that at Longdon, when the driver and fireman (Alf Astbury and Alf Wedge) were carrrying out the time honoured custom of dropping off some coal for the signalman, as they approached the box. Unfortunately, the lump of coal was rather large, and the timing of the drop was not well judged. The coal went right through the wooden panelling of the box considerably damaging the interlocking equipment inside. Little could be done to cover up the incident, and all three railwaymen were reprimanded.

At the other side of the road overbridge, a farmer's co-operative dairy was set up in the 1920s, which sent milk to London in the Winter, and made cheese in the Summer. It became a true creamery, collecting only cream for butter making, and was taken over by the Milk Marketing Board in 1935. The dairy has since expanded considerably and continues in use today. Additional produce consisting mainly of tomatoes and cucumbers was shipped out from Crudgington, originating at the Roden nurseries, and bound for the Co-operative Wholesale Society in Manchester.

Northwards the line climbs on to another embankment to cross the River Tern and then enter a shallow cutting wherein is located Rowton Halt (5 miles 71¼ chains or 5⅞ miles). It was located south of the road overbridge carrying a lane from the hamlet of Sytch Lane to the small village of Rowton, and from which paths and steps led to each of the platforms. This halt opened on 29th June, 1935 and was smaller than most of the others, at only 80 feet and cost £272 to construct. It comprised the usual timber and ash construction platforms, whereon were black wooden waiting shelters, whose roof lines were cantilevered towards the platform so as to provide rudimentary canopies. Again, no goods facilities were provided.

This was another halt regularly used during World War II by service personnel, this time from the large fighter squadron airfield at RAF High Ercall (1942 to 1962), and the army camp in Rowton itself, at High House farm. At various times, USAAF aircraft and crew were also stationed at the RAF airfield, so it is eminently possible that they too used the halt. It can well be imagined that they would have considered such facilities to be decidedly quaint.

It was a short distance then across further slightly rolling open countryside to Ellerdine Halt (7 miles 13 chains or 7⅛ miles). Just before the halt was located the single goods siding at Ellerdine, which was opened on 28th February, 1928. Access was made via a loading bank edged with stone, and at least in later years a grounded van body was situated nearby to act as a porter's room and goods lock-up. The key for unlocking the ground frame to operate the siding points was kept in this building. As the siding was a trailing one from the down running line, and there was no crossover from the up line, only down trains could access the siding. So traffic from the north had to be worked on to Crudgington, and then back by the next down local goods train. Conversely, traffic from the siding to go south had to be worked to Peplow or Market Drayton, and then back south as services permitted. It was the responsibility of the Ellerdine porter to advise Crudgington of any traffic requirements. The halt was opened later than the siding, on 7th July, 1930, and was of the usual timber and ash construction, and was 100 feet long. The waiting shelters were of black

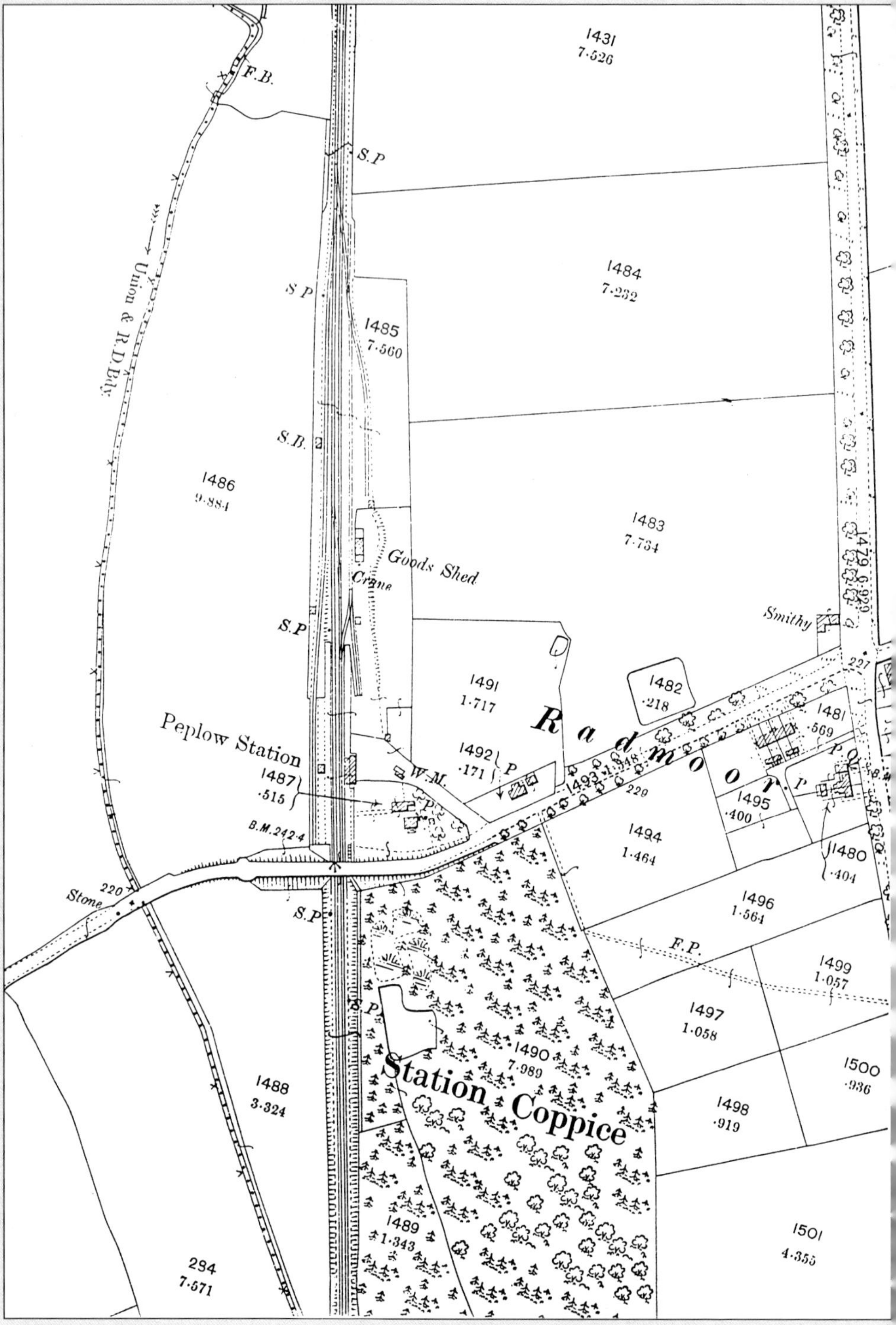

Peplow station. *Reproduced from the 25", 1901 Ordnance Survey Map*

corrugated iron, and a path led to the down platform, whilst steps led from the road overbridge north of the halt to the up platform, supplemented by a separate slope for the handling of milk churns.

After Ellerdine, the line ran into a small cutting then crossed the Platt Brook and proceeded on a rising ruling gradient of 1 in 594 into slightly more wooded countryside at the approach to Peplow (8 miles 67½ chains or 8⅞ miles). After passing beneath a road overbridge the line entered the station, whose main buildings were located on the up side, consisting of a single-storey building in red brick, with a wooden cantilevered canopy over the platform. A small red brick waiting shelter was sited on the down platform. The station was apparently constructed at the request of the ironmaster Francis Stanier of Silverdale and Apedale ironworks, who had purchased around 7,000 acres in the vicinity and had taken up residence at Peplow Hall, near to the station site. This enabled him to travel to Market Drayton, then on the NSR (of which he was a Director from 1865 until his death in 1900) to Silverdale, where he would complete his journey to his works in a private saloon hauled by one of his own locomotives. The opening of the station is believed to have been on 14th November, 1870 as it first appeared in the timetables of the local *Wellington Journal* and of the *Shrewsbury News* on 12th November, 1870. Prior to this time, goods sidings had already been provided at Peplow from the opening of the line, consisting of an up loop line with access from both directions, and serving a cattle dock and loading bank. This was later furnished with a 1 ton loading crane, which by 1933 had been uprated to 1½ tons capacity. In 1894, the layout was extensively remodelled, giving a down refuge siding, having a capacity for 50 wagons plus engine and brake van. The goods yard on the up side was given two further sidings, and a new, longer cattle dock was sited alongside a bay platform on the northern end of the up platform. A weighbridge was installed in the goods yard, and a wooden goods shed (not rail served) was put up nearby. A new signal box in red brick was also installed at this time, north of the down platform. It is probable that prior to this, all movements were controlled by a ground frame in the station building. Also at this time the platforms were lengthened. By 1898 the signal box was unmanned each evening between 8.00 pm and 7.30 am, and at weekends from 8.00 pm on Saturdays until 7.30 am on the Monday morning.

Peplow was another station frequently used by service personnel, as RAF Peplow airfield (1941 to 1949) was nearby, actually near to Childs Ercall. This airfield had the distinction of including gliders among its aircraft. So popular was the railway service from here, that a metal bicycle rack was provided by the RAF at the station for the servicemen whilst they enjoyed their nights out in nearby towns.

The area around Peplow was a major producer of sugar beet, and many wagons were loaded here for transport to the British Sugar factory at Allscott, just west of Wellington, adjacent to the Shrewsbury line and with its own extensive internal railway system. The siding behind the down platform was often used in later years for the storage of redundant wagons, and carriage stock.

The line now entered much more wooded, but rather flat countryside, and passed beneath the Wellington to Whitchurch road (now A442) before reaching

Peplow station looking towards Hodnet. The long siding behind the down platform on the left was used for storing a variety of vehicles over the years, but latterly seems to have held redundant 16 ton metal-bodied mineral wagons for some years. The GWR station nameboard is retained on the down platform. *J. Maden Collection*

From the state of the platform surface here, it is evident that Peplow station did not see a great deal of patronage at this date, 30th May, 1961. The siding behind the down platform is interesting in that it is at a higher level than the running line. It is not known why a string of three former LMS carriages is stabled on this siding, behind the brick-built waiting shelter. The vehicle nearest the camera is an open saloon, built around 1930.The signal box can be seen in the background. *Transport Treasury/Alec Swain Collection*

Hodnet signal box pictured around 1905, with the proud staff posing for their portrait.
R.S. Carpenter Collection

Hodnet (11 miles 1½ chains) which opened with the line. First, the single-road red brick goods shed was passed on the west side of the down line, set in the midst of the five down side sidings. On 25th January, 1928 the siding nearest the down main line was altered to provide a refuge siding accessible by either a down train (35 wagons plus engine and van) or an up train (42 wagons plus engine and van). The cattle dock and loading bank were positioned near to the station, and a hand-operated crane was sited in the goods yard near to the goods shed. This crane was initially of 4 ton capacity, but by 1933 had been replaced by one of 6 tons. The station building was a single-storey red brick building on the down side enlivened with the use of cream edging bricks. The waiting shelter on the up side was of wooden construction with a small canopy, mounted on a short (around 3 ft 6 in.) red brick base. The platforms were extended in 1891. As at Peplow, no footbridge was provided, it being assumed that passengers would use the adjacent road overbridge, north of the station. However, it is likely that most used the wooden-sleepered 'barrow crossing' provided for the benefit of railway staff to cross the line.

By 1960 the station was unstaffed after 6.30 pm on weekdays, so the guards of the last up trains had to extinguish the platform lamps and convey them to Peplow. In the down direction, the lamps were conveyed to Tern Hill. These were returned by the first trains in each direction on the following morning. The signal box, located on the up side, almost opposite the goods shed, was opened in 1891, but by 1898 this was switched out between 11.00 am and 6.00 pm on Sundays.

The line continued over gentle country, never far from the River Tern, on a ruling downward gradient of 1 in 220, until reaching Wollerton Halt (12 miles 5¾ chains). This halt was adjacent to the very small village that it served. Pedestrian access to the up platform was from a short lane, and from near to the adjacent road overbridge by a path to the down platform. The 100 ft platforms

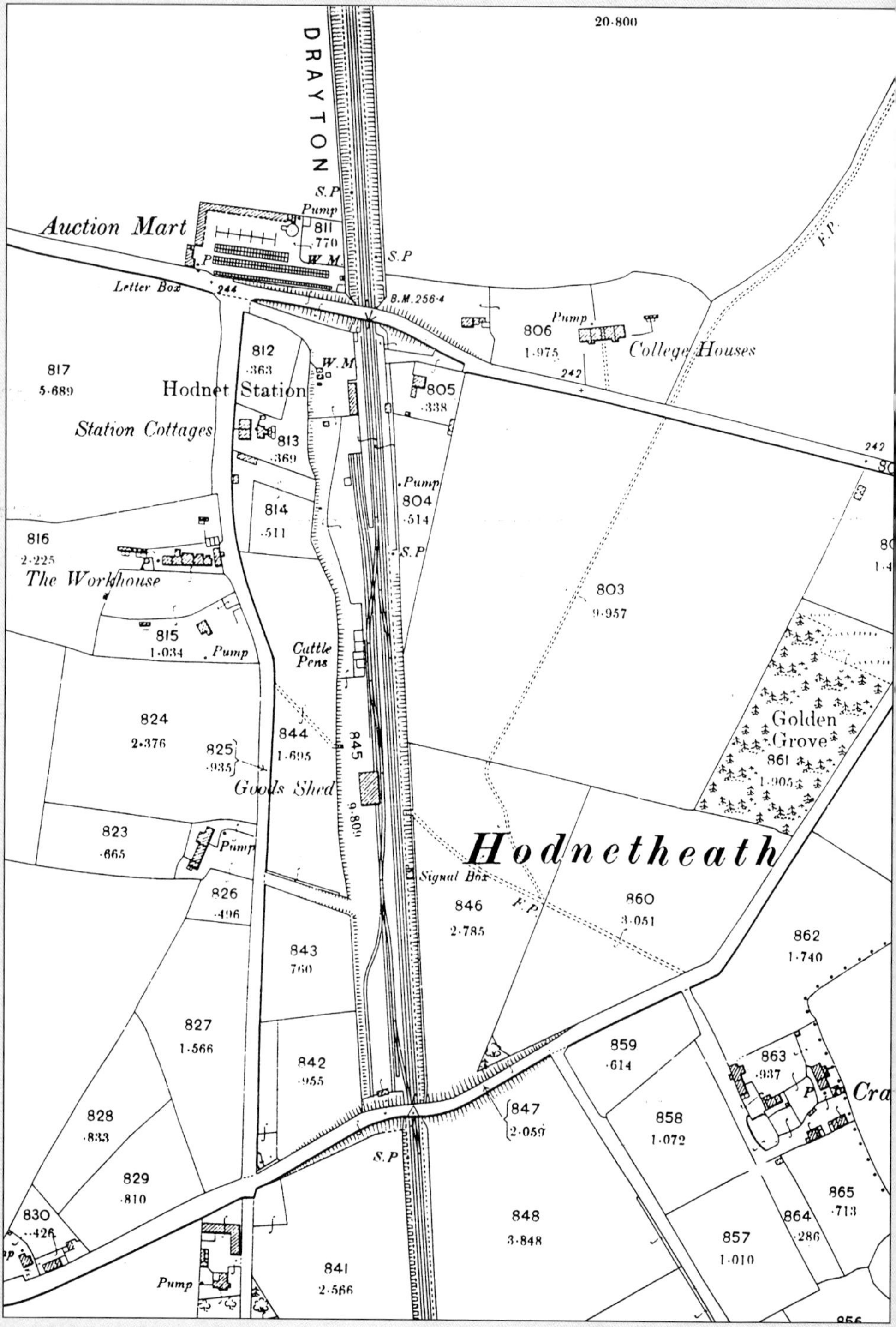

Hodnet station.

Reproduced from the 25", 1901 Ordnance Survey Map

The signal box and goods shed are clearly seen in this view at Hodnet as Ivatt class '2' No. 41201 arrives with the 5.45 pm Wellington-Crewe passenger service on Easter Monday, 15th April, 1963. *Michael Mensing*

'Hall' class 4-6-0 No. 4943 *Marrington Hall* arrives at Hodnet with the 12.15 pm Wellington-Crewe service on 15th April, 1963. *Michael Mensing*

Collett 'Grange' class 4-6-0 No. 6844 *Penhydd Grange* threads its way through Hodnet station with a string of class'F' empty mineral wagons bound for Crewe on 1st May, 1962.

M. Priestley

Wellington's Ivatt class '2' 2-6-2T No. 41241 arrives in Hodnet with the 1.02 pm from Crewe on 1st August, 1962. The station staff were evidently keen to cultivate the rambling roses on the fencing of the down platform. *M. Priestley*

Wollerton Halt looking north to Market Drayton. The waiting shelters here were of corrugated iron, and the glass in the small windows appears to have suffered the attentions of vandals by this date, around 1962. *J. Maden Collection*

were of the familiar timber and ash construction, were estimated to have cost £270 to construct, and the halt had opened on 2nd November, 1931. The waiting shelters were built of corrugated iron.

After passing beneath the road overbridge, the line proceeded across several meadows and then crossed the River Tern twice, on three-arch red brick bridges. The ruling gradient was now rising at 1 in 220 before passing over the Newcastle to Shrewsbury main road (now A53) and entering Tern Hill (13 miles 60 chains or 13¾ miles). Here goods facilities were provided from the outset, although the passenger station did not open until 3rd April, 1899. The original siding leading from the down goods loop was removed in 1870, and not replaced until 1895. A siding near to the later site of the station was furnished with a loading wharf, and is believed to have been in connection with the loading of timber. In this connection, supplementary instructions were in force at least from 1898 and certainly until 1960. These required:

> When timber is being loaded in the siding adjacent to the up main line, the signal box must be switched in, and the Foreman Timber Loader must obtain permission from the signalman to proceed with the loading. Signalman is to send 'Blocking Back Inside Home Signal' 2-4 and be acknowledged by Market Drayton station box, or other box in the rear of the section, and the up line signals placed at danger. When it becomes necessary to accept an up train, loading must cease, and 'Obstruction Removed' Signal 2-1 sent, when signalman has seen that the loading has ceased and the line is clear. Loading may not recommence until the train has left Tern Hill.

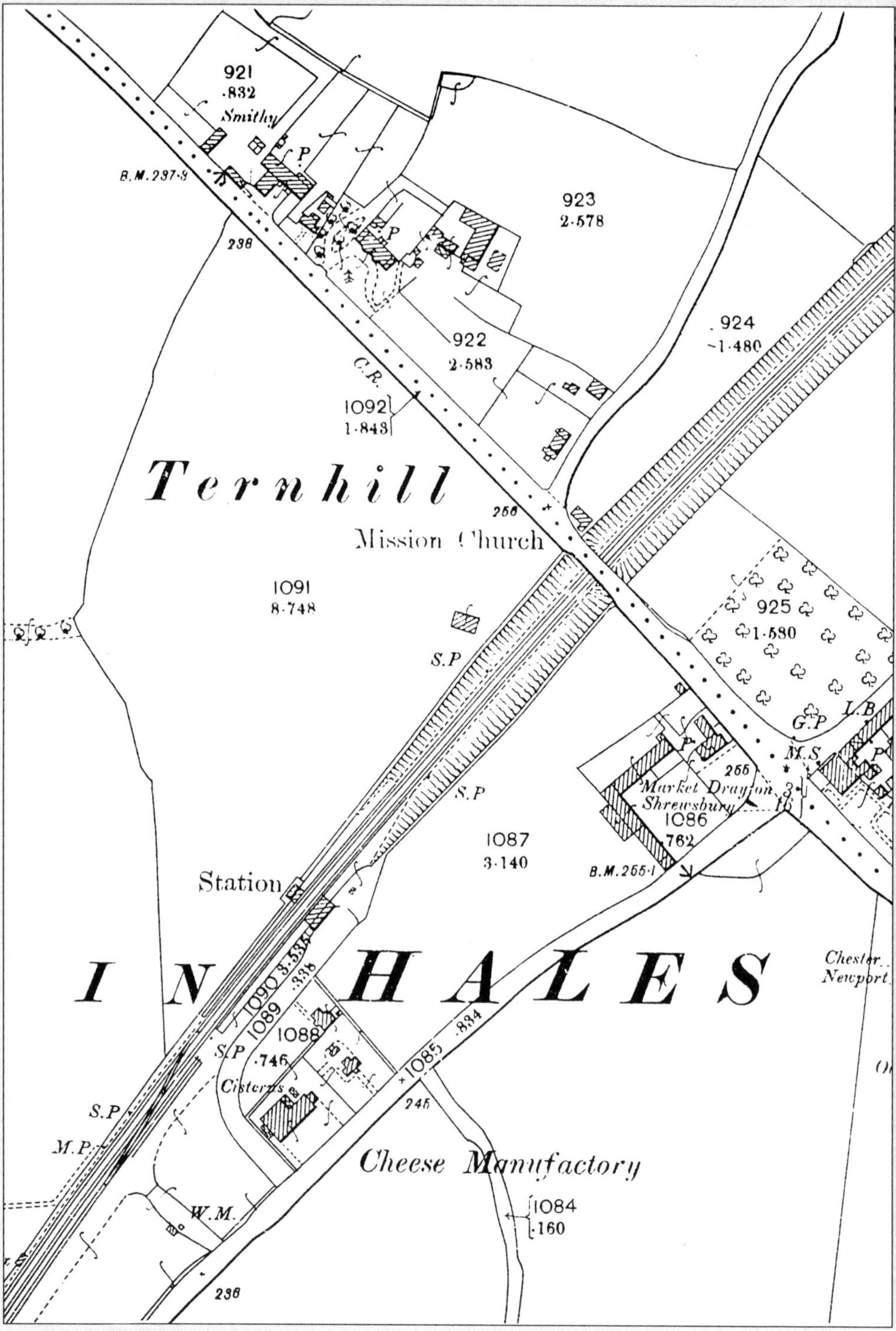

Tern Hill station.

Reproduced from the 25", 1901 Ordnance Survey Map

Evidently, there was concern that timber being loaded could swing and foul the up running line.

A further siding was installed in 1915 in connection with the movement of materials to the nearby airfield (*see Chapter Nine*), and afterwards used as a mileage siding.

The single-storey station building on the up platform was of a later standard GWR design in red and blue brick, with additional staff buildings in wood. A wooden waiting shelter with a red brick base was positioned on the down platform, but was available to passengers only from the up platform, initially presumably over a boarded crossing. Later, during 1942, an open steel footbridge was erected, almost certainly to reflect the increased number of passengers, and probably after one or two near misses, especially during the black-out. At the time of the station opening, the *Newport and Market Drayton Advertiser* of 8th April, 1899 commented:

> A large number of passengers made use of the station on the opening day. The new station will be of great utility to the residents generally and the agriculturists of the district in particular. It has been used as a goods station for some time, and the result we understand, has been satisfactory to the Railway Company.

The station was used during World War II, not only by service personnel on their way to and from RAF Tern Hill, but also by aircrew at another nearby airfield RAF Hinstock. This was actually located at Ollerton and during the war years was an inland airfield for the Royal Naval Air Service, better known as the Fleet Air Arm, who designated the base as HMS Godwit. It was a naval instrument flying training base, opening in October 1941 and closing in April, 1946. The large numbers of service personnel, civilian workers and visitors using the station in the years before, during and after World War II are indicated in the history of RAF Tern Hill, described in Chapter Nine. Morevoer, there was a considerable traffic in new engines, propellers, wing and fuselage parts, and much other equipment in connection with the repair and refurbishing of the wide variety of aircraft out at the RAF maintenance unit, which formed part of the base. Indeed, an RAF crane often spent much of the day unloading wagons at the goods dock. Therefore because of the restricted space, the regulations above concerning goods being unloaded and passing passenger trains, were brought into effect. This meant that the signal box, which was usually switched out, had to be manned. This was normally performed by one of the senior porters, who then received a signalman's hourly rate - and mostly for very little work. Small wonder then, that this was a very popular duty.

A pre-cast concrete store was also furnished in the goods yard, for the use of the BOCM fertiliser and agricultural feedstuffs company. This surprisingly remains at the time of writing.

From here the line turned into a north-westerly direction and the ruling gradient changed to rising at 1 in 165 on its way into Market Drayton, first of all calling at the short lived Little Drayton Halt (approximately 16 miles) which was authorised on 25th July, 1935 at an estimated cost of £240, and opened on the following 14th September. It was relatively short lived, closing as part of the

A full complement of station staff in this portrait at Tern Hill station, looking towards Market Drayton, believed to be from 1929. Note the sighting board for the down starter signal.
D. Houlston Collection

This 1929 shot of Tern Hill station is looking towards Wellington, with the signal box in the distance on the right.
D. Houlston Collection

Tern Hill station is fairly distant in this view taken from the A41 road overbridge east of the station on 28th July, 1964. Passenger services had been withdrawn the previous September.
J.M. Bentley

The down platform at Tern Hill, illustrating the wooden waiting shelter that had evidently been recently refurbished. The metal footbridge dating from World War II presents a rather stark contrast to the scene. *Transport Treasury/Alec Swain Collection*

Collett '57XX' class 0-6-0PT No. 9630 of Wellington shed passes through Tern Hill with an up short local goods on 4th November, 1957. The station staff have evidently turned out to watch the passage of this train. *M. Priestley*

wartime economies on 6th October, 1941. The halt was virtually invisible from neighbouring roads, and few people knew of its existence, so it is not surprising that it attracted few passengers. It is presumed to have been of the usual timber and ash construction, and it is difficult to see what economies could have generated by closing this unstaffed halt. Perhaps there were other reasons. At any rate, it was not dismantled immediately, and in 1943 one of the two black wooden waiting shelters was moved to Tern Hill and positioned on the down platform, to supplement the existing otherwise rather small shelter. Some time after the war, this black wooden shelter was removed. Nearby, the Rush Lane level crossing was replaced by an overbridge around January 1920.

It is interesting to record that juvenile acts of vandalism are nothing new, as the *Newport and Market Drayton Advertiser* of 3rd November, 1944 carried the following story:

> Stone throwing at a passing train at Little Drayton on August 24th led to the appearance of three children at Market Drayton Juvenile Court on Tuesday [31st October - *author*]. Two, a brother and sister aged 10 and 12, were summoned for throwing stones, and a 10 year old boy was summoned for doing wilful damage to the window of a guard's van.

There is no record of the sentences passed, but it is reasonable to assume that at that time, their parents would have dealt swiftly and with some effect to curb future behaviour of this sort!

Passing beneath the Adderley Road overbridge, we arrive at Market Drayton (16 miles 52 chains or 16⅝ miles). The station was originally furnished with one up and one down platform, with the main station buildings being on the up platform. However, with the opening of the NSR line in 1870 it was remodelled to make the down platform into an island platform, from the outer face of which the NSR trains thereafter arrived and departed. The line on this platform face terminated at the south end, i.e. it did not form a complete loop. An agreement of 31st December, 1877 with the NSR allocated the NSR share of the station cost and running expenses since their arrival as £4,141 8*s*. 8*d*. Presumably, the delay in arriving at this settlement was the result of much bargaining rather than attempting to account for it all. A small signal box was positioned on the up platform, just to the north of the station building, and the control over the junction was handled by the Silverdale Junction box, located on the down side opposite the fork of the two lines. The same 1877 agreement included the operation of this box, which although constructed to a GWR design and manned by GWR personnel, was financed by the NSR.

There were major changes to the buildings and layout during the period from 1880 to 1900. The main station buildings were replaced by a standard single-storey GWR design often referred to as 'French Renaissance' style with ornamental ironwork to embellish the roof ridges, and a square topped pavilion at each end. The waiting room on the island platform was substantially constructed in red brick, and a covered GWR pattern footbridge gave access between the platforms. The track on the outer face of the island platform was linked to the down main running line, thus completing the loop around the island platform. The layout of the goods yard to the west of station, which formerly contained four loop lines and one terminal siding was altered around 1890 to two through lines and three terminal sidings, and an additional mileage siding was added at the extremity of the company-owned land. In later years, further warehouses were provided on the land between this siding and the main group of sidings.

The view westwards from the Adderley Road bridge in Market Drayton with the track still *in situ*, around 1967. The pale coloured water tank seen to the right of the running line is at the water pumping station. *M. Temple*

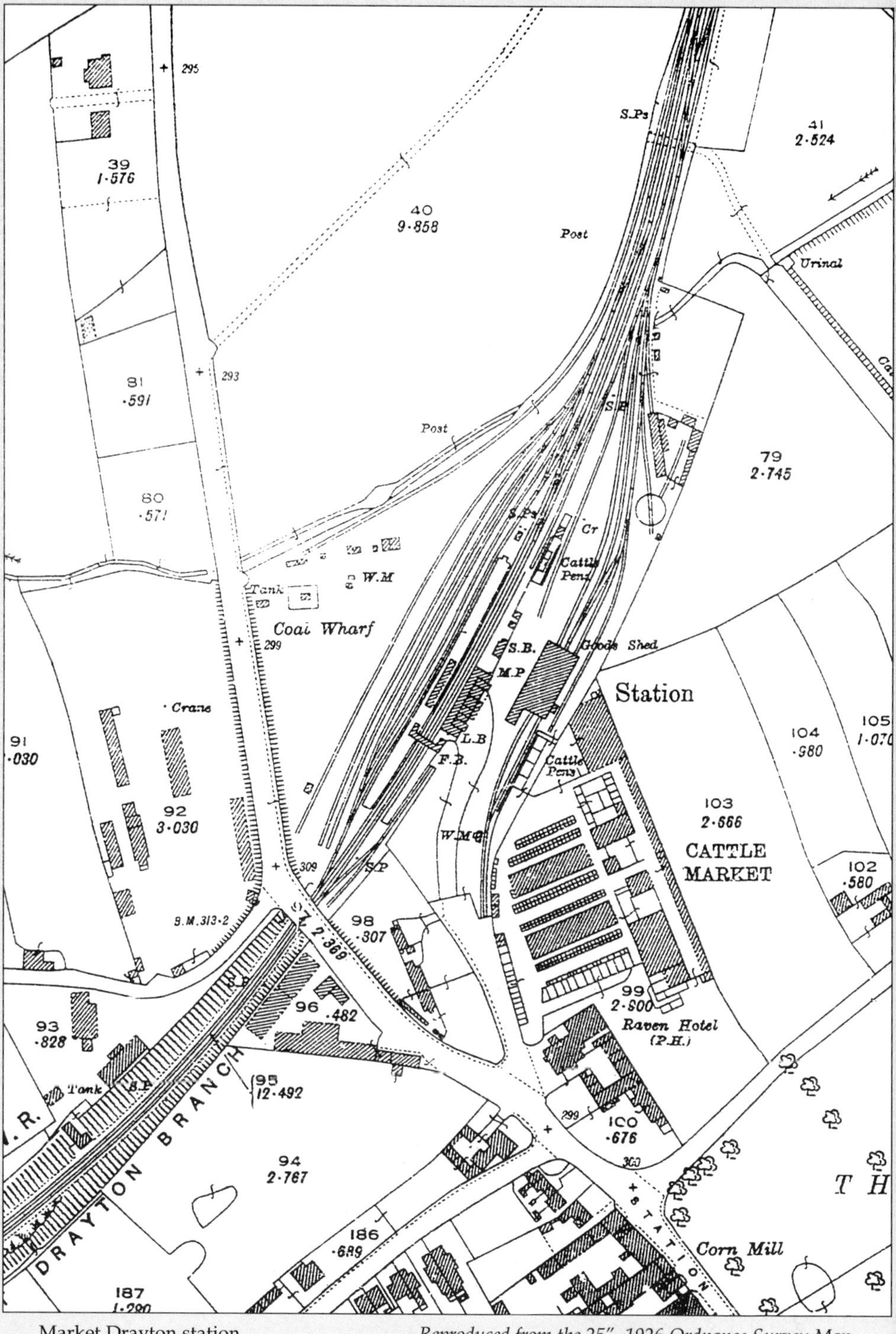

Market Drayton station.

Reproduced from the 25", 1926 Ordnance Survey Map

A date of 1893 has been determined for the installation of the new signal box ('Market Drayton Station') which was erected on the north end of the up station platform. In 1898 the Station box was switched out between 11.00 am and 6.00 pm on Sundays, and the Junction box between 10.30 am and 6.30 pm on Sundays, then again from 9.20 pm on Sundays until 6.00 am on Mondays. Access to both refuge sidings required reversal from the main running lines; for the up line, just north of the Silverdale Junction, and for the down line (opened 1893) between the station and the junction. Both had a capacity of 44 wagons plus engine and brake van.

The short bay platform adjacent to the up platform at the south end was generally used for parcels vans, and other such commodities, although horse boxes were also loaded here. An unusual arrangement for access to this bay, and other sidings at this end of the station was that a gong was affixed to the abutment of the adjacent road overbridge, and was to be used during shunting operations. Use of the gong alerted the signalman in the Station box. The following codes were used:

	No. of rings
Up main to down main, and vice versa	1 - 2
Up main to horse dock siding, and vice versa	2 - 2
Up main to bay	2 - 3
Up main to No. 2 siding, down side, and vice versa	2 - 4
Up main to No. 1 siding, down side, and vice versa	2 - 5

On the up side, a new two road goods shed was constructed around 1890, principally in brick, to replace the original single-road wooden affair, and the engine shed was enlarged, virtually doubling its length, but remaining single road. An additional road led northwards from the turntable to facilitate engine stabling. The adjacent cattle dock was itself positioned near to the cattle market which, although it had been authorised by statute in 1865, was delayed until the coming of the through railway. The loading crane adjacent to the goods shed was listed as being of 5 ton capacity in 1904, but by 1933 had been downrated to 4½ tons.

Mark Temple was employed in the goods department from 1962 to 1964, latterly as a road driver. His transport was usually a Scammel three-wheel tractor, with a 3 ton trailer, although he also had a Bedford 4 ton unit, and then one of the larger Bedford 4½ ton units. If there was any upsurge in demand for road deliveries, additional units were obtained on loan from Shrewsbury.

The only other major alteration to the station during the 20th century was the removal of the covering from the footbridge connecting the platforms, sometime in the mid-1960s and not long before the station closed.

After passing Silverdale Junction, the line returned to its northerly direction, and ran in close company with the Shropshire Union Canal on its eastern side for many miles, across the soft, gently undulating countryside that provided such rich farming land. There was little otherwise of note until reaching Adderley (20 miles 11½ chains or 20⅛ miles). The ruling gradient had been rising at 1 in 220. This station had also opened with the line, and comprised a blue brick single-storey building with a wooden platform canopy on the down side, south of a minor road overbridge. The platforms had been extended further

Market Drayton station around the turn of the 20th century with the proud station staff posing for the photographer. *Courtesy Shropshire Star*

From the footbridge, looking south at Market Drayton, the line disappears through the portal of the Adderley Road bridge, 1st July, 1962. *J.M. Bentley*

A roadside view of Market Drayton station on 1st July, 1962 illustrating the neat standard GWR building, which by this time had lost its cast-iron decorations to the towers. *J.M. Bentley*

Looking south from the up platform at Market Drayton on a sunny 1st July, 1962 with the footbridge still complete and flowers on the down side island platform. *J.M. Bentley*

An unidentified Collett 'Manor' class 4-6-0 takes water at the column on the up platform at Market Drayton around 1960. The footbridge still retains its covering at this time, and the goods yard in the background seems still to be quite busy. *F.W. Shuttleworth*

Market Drayton Station box on 4th February, 1967. *A.C. Baker*

Looking northwards from the up platform at Market Drayton on 1st July, 1962 at which time the station was still in good order. *J.M. Bentley*

Looking northwards along the up platform at Market Drayton, it is noteworthy that the former GWR lower quadrant signals, present in 1962, have been replaced by BR standard upper quadrants by 4th February, 1967. The waiting shelter on the down island platform is also looking past its best, being devoid of passengers for over four years. *A.C. Baker*

Right: A Scammell 'Scarab' with open platform trailer in the driveway leading to Market Drayton station in 1963. Mark Temple drove this vehicle whist employed in the goods department there.

M. Temple

Below: A Bedford 3½ ton flatbed lorry, also at Market Drayton, and used by the goods department.

M. Temple

Looking back from Silverdale Junction towards the station and goods yards at Market Drayton on 4th February, 1967. Even at this late date there were still a fair number of goods vehicles in the up and down yards. *A.C. Baker*

Silverdale Junction signal box at Market Drayton on 4th February, 1967. *A.C. Baker*

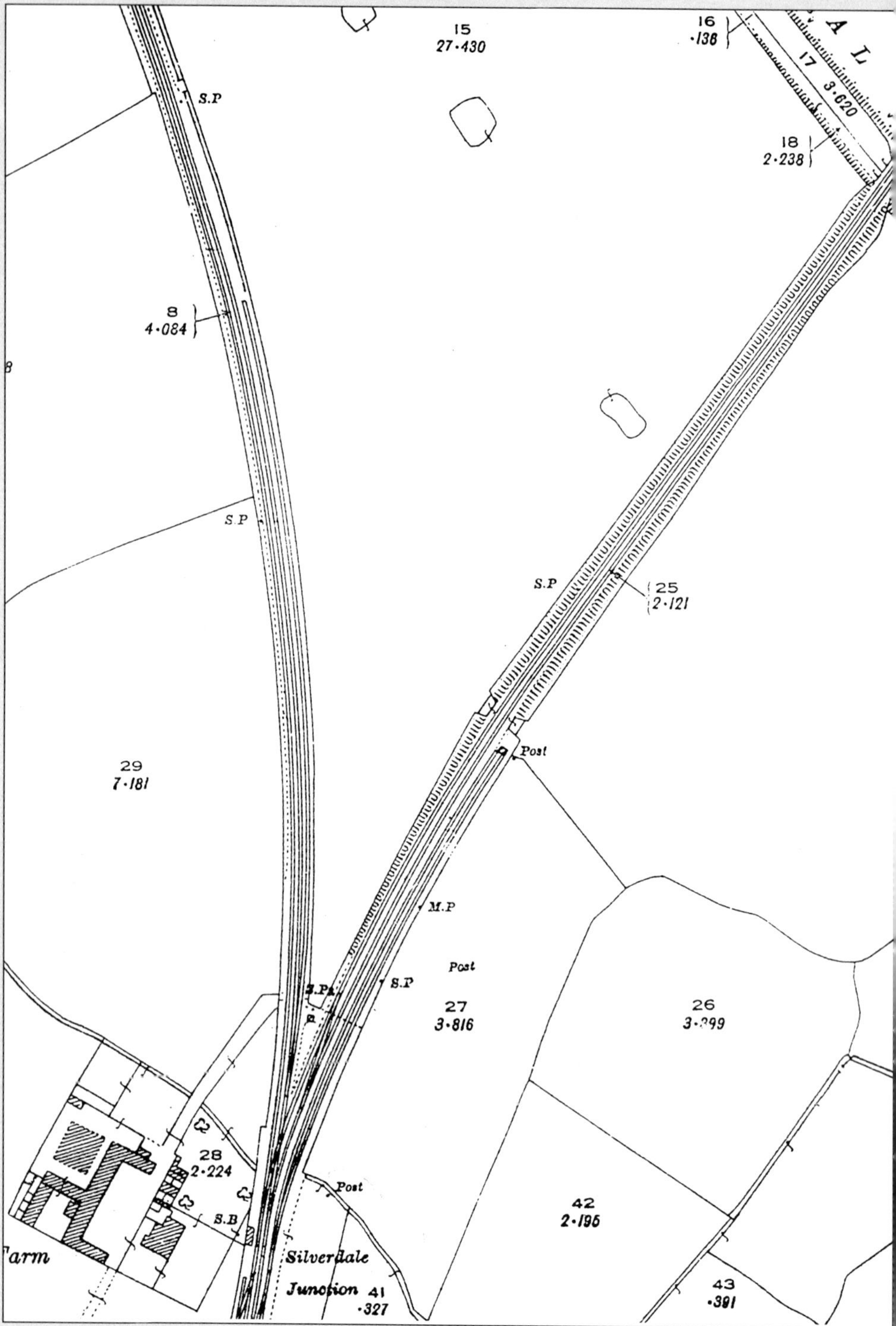

Silverdale Junction.

Reproduced from the 25", 1926 Ordnance Survey Map

south during 1891. A waiting shelter also constructed in blue brick was positioned on the down platform. Living accommodation for the station master was provided in a two-storey building behind the station. The signal box was also of blue brick, and was sited on the down platform next to the station building. A goods yard with three sidings was provided behind the signal box, but there was no goods shed. A cattle dock and loading platform were also behind the signal box, and next to the down platform. This made for a very compact area, that presumably could be worked with the minimum of staff. So it is not surprising to learn that, by 1960, staff were only in attendance here from 7.45 am until 4.25 pm Mondays to Fridays, 7.45 am until 1.25 pm on Saturdays, and on Sundays only for when the 9.15 am from Wellington and the 8.35 am from Crewe called. However, by 1962 even these trains no longer called. Even in 1898, the signal box was only opened when trains called to pick up or put off vehicles, or when an engine required to use the crossover from one running line to the other.

Leaving Adderley, the line continued through this rather undulating countryside until reaching Coxbank Halt (21 miles 27 chains or $21\frac{3}{8}$ miles), where it had just passed over the border into Cheshire. The usual timber-faced, ash-surfaced platforms were 80 feet long, and sited north of the overbridge that carried a minor lane from the Market Drayton to Audlem road (now A529) to the small village of Coxbank. As usual the road overbridge gave access to each of the platforms, which were each furnished with wooden waiting shelters, latterly painted black. It is recalled that this halt, and the one at Coole Pilate, which we shall see later, were opened as the result of lobbying by a Mr G.P. Tapley, who was on the local GWR permanent way staff, and also an Audlem parish councillor for many years. He put in the first pegs for the engineer's theodolite. The halt was then erected by one joiner with the help of local labour. The GWR authorised the construction of this halt on 31st May, 1934 with an estimated cost of £368, and it opened on 23rd June of that year.

Less than a mile later we come to Audlem (22 miles 7 chains or $22\frac{1}{10}$ miles). This was a pleasant small market town of some history and importance in this rural area. The substantial station was again executed in blue brick. The main building was on the up side, with a wooden cantilevered canopy, and a small waiting room was provided on the down platform. Both platforms extended over the main road (the A529 from Market Drayton) and supported by iron girders. The blue brick single-road goods shed was situated adjacent to the station, on the up side, and on a siding furthest from the running line. In between were two additional sidings, which ran from the up refuge loop to either side of a loading bank combined with cattle dock. A loading crane of 1 ton capacity was provided here, which by 1933 had been increased to $1\frac{1}{2}$ tons. This loading crane has been preserved outside the 'Shroppie Fly' public house alongside the Shropshire Union Canal in Audlem, as a replacement for the canal's own loading crane which was regrettably scrapped. The signal box was of red brick and sited at the south end of the down platform, but was taken out of use as from 23rd June, 1957 and replaced by a ground frame to give access to the goods yard sidings, sited at the south end of the up goods refuge loop. Earlier, on 7th August, 1955 the crossover from the up to down running lines,

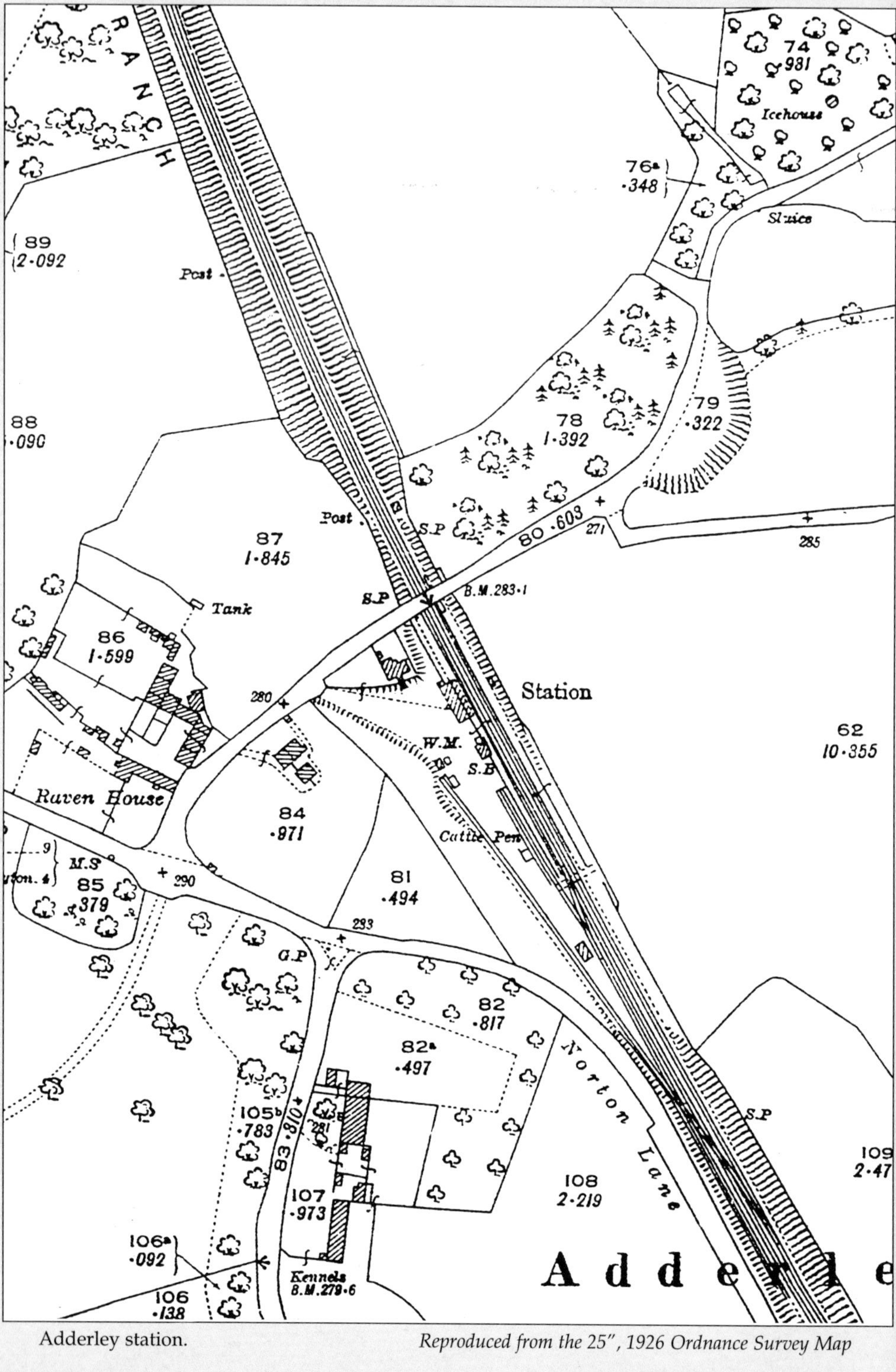

Adderley station. *Reproduced from the 25", 1926 Ordnance Survey Map*

Adderley station and yard on a rather wet day, 9th April, 1959. The view is towards the south, and illustrates the closeness of the signal box to the station building, the compact goods yard, and the rather small waiting shelter on the up platform. *M. Priestley*

Looking north along the down platform at Adderley, with the signal box and station building in clear view on 30th May, 1961. *Transport Treasury/Alec Swain Collection*

The down platform at Coxbank Halt, showing the rudimentary wooden waiting shelter, on 30th May, 1961. *Transport Treasury/Alec Swain Collection*

Coxbank Halt with the village of this name in the background, and just beyond, the town of Audlem. This neat halt featured wooden waiting shelters with cantilevered roofs. *J. Maden Collection*

Looking south from the end loading dock at Audlem, with the cattle dock on the left, on 9th July 1961. *J.M. Bentley*

The up side of Audlem station on 9th July, 1961 complete with rambling roses on the fencing. The platform can be seen to pass over the road bridge, whose abutments and girders can be seen on the left. *J.M. Bentley*

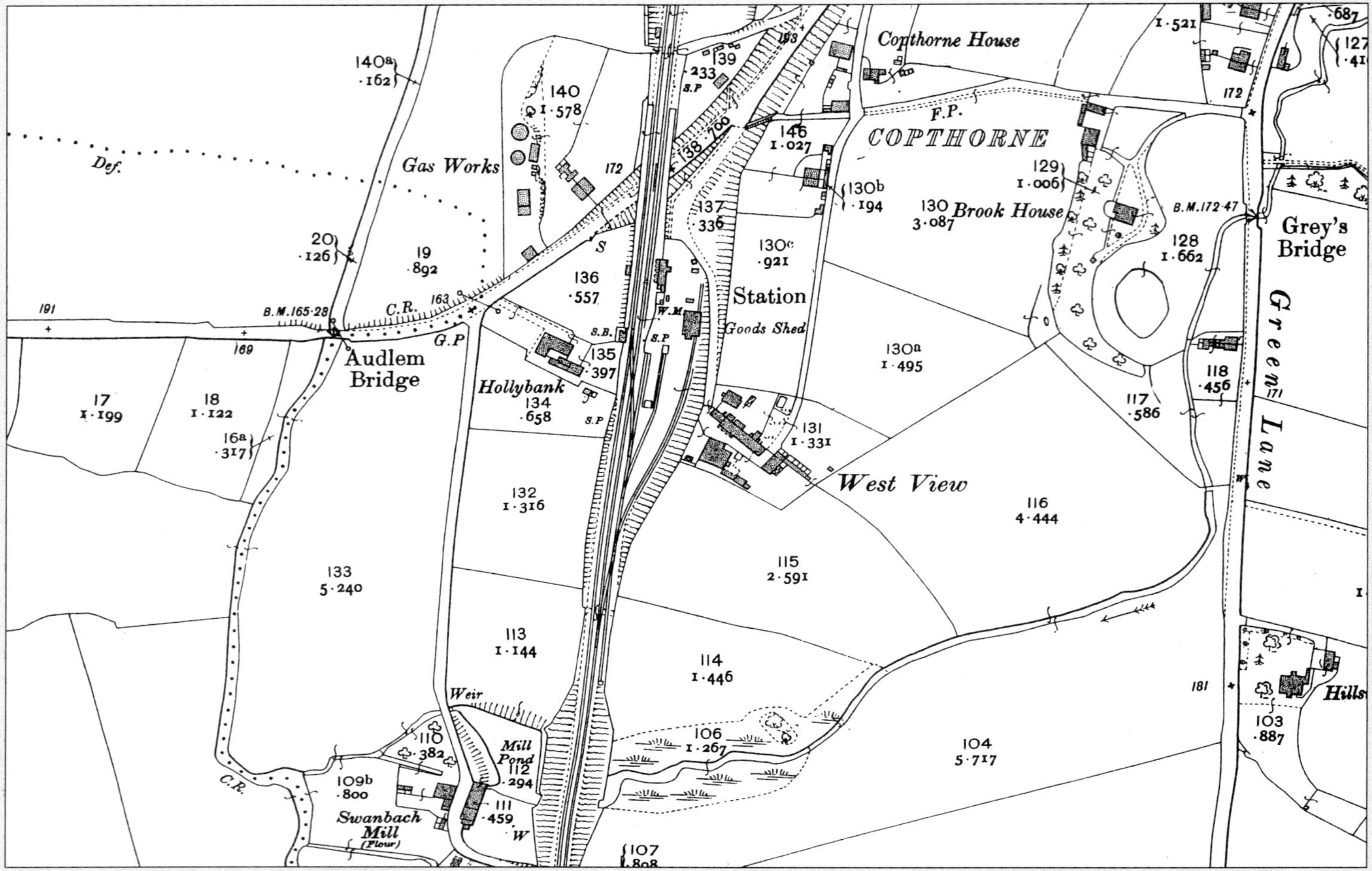

Audlem station. *Reproduced from the 25", 1909 Ordnance Survey Map*

The single-road goods shed at Audlem on 9th July 1961, with its attendant delivery lorry. By this time there was little goods traffic here. *J.M. Bentley*

A roadside view of the station building at Audlem on 9th July, 1961 with the adjacent weighbridge and its wooden hut. The car parked at the front of the station would have been old even at that time. *J.M. Bentley*

The down side platform at Audlem, with its small brick built waiting shelter. Again the abutments and girders of the road underbridge can be seen alongside the platform to the right, 9th July 1961. *J.M. Bentley*

sited near to the signal box was taken out, so that thereafter only up trains could call at the goods yard. In 1898 the signal box was closed on Sundays from 10.00 am until 7.00 pm.

Continuing northwards, the line proceeded with a ruling falling gradient of 1 in 150 and then crossed the River Weaver near to Moss Hall. This historic residence was reputed to have three subterranean passages, which entered the hall through concealed doors. These were reputed to be places used by the family living at the hall to hide from Cromwell's army during the Civil War of the 17th century.

The line had been fairly closely parallel and to the west of the course of the Shropshire Union Canal since we left Market Drayton, but just before arriving at the intriguingly named Coole Pilate Halt (24 miles 20¼ chains or 24¼ miles) it crossed the canal on a skew bridge supported by abutments in the familiar blue brick. This halt obtained its name from a nearby farm, which itself was named after two local families who had become united through marriage. Construction was authorised on 27th June, 1935 at an estimated cost of £275, and it opened shortly afterwards on 17th August. The halt was different from the others in that it was built on a piece of level ground, and was entirely of wooden construction, including the staging for the platforms and the waiting shelters. At the northern end of the halt was a footpath level crossing (actually more of a cart track) from which passengers gained access to the platforms. As usual no goods facilities were provided.

From here the line continued in almost a dead straight northerly direction, across level fields with no earthworks at all until reaching the LNWR main line. But first, there was a level crossing over a minor lane at Hack Green. There was

The down side of Coole Pilate Halt on 22nd August, 1963 displaying the timber construction of the platform stage and waiting shelter. Beyond is the boarded crossing that gave access to the house in the background and also served as a means of access between the platforms.

F.W. Shuttleworth

The up side of Coole Pilate Halt on 22nd August, 1963 with a family in conversation with the guard, having presumably just alighted from the train. *F.W. Shuttleworth*

An unidentified Stanier '8F' 2-8-0 storms towards the level crossing at Hack Green around 1966. The signal box design is typical of those constructed by BR in the early and mid-1950s. The box controlling the crossing became necessary because of anticipated increased use by military authorities. *J. Maden Collection*

a ground frame here so this is likely to have controlled the gates, but as from 23rd June, 1957 a red brick and concrete signal box was opened to control movements here, and a crossover put in. To the uninitiated this must have seemed rather strange in this remote location. However, it was only in more recent times that the reasons became clear.

Going back to 1942, a site some ½ mile west of this level crossing was selected as a 'decoy target' for enemy bombers to distract them from Crewe. Later it was converted into a radar station, and from 1945 it became a Defence Radar Station. During the mid-1950s the ground floor was massively reinforced with concrete, and two further underground levels were added, to give a total of 35,000 square feet containing a radar and communications network, BBC studio, technical support facilities, administrative offices and offices for Government ministers and local government, as well as living accommodation. It had thus become one of the secret Regional Seats of Government in the event of a nuclear war, although from 1966 it reverted to its former role as a radar station. It was finally declassified in 1993, and has since become a (very worthwhile) tourist attraction, even if it seems rather illogical to have brown 'tourist signs' giving the direction to a 'Secret Bunker'!

So the reason for the signal box, which was finally taken out of use on 6th March, 1967 shortly before the line closed, and the associated track work becomes clear. There is no indication of any means of transferring materials and equipment from rail to road here during the construction work at this site, so such work must presumably have been performed by Army handling units. During the mid-1950s the signalman here was believed to have been one of the two surviving locomotive crew from the disastrous accident at Harrow and Wealdstone in October 1952. He was apparently transferred here afterwards, 'on light duties'.

The remaining two miles crossed fairly flat and uneventful countryside with no earthworks, other than an overbridge carrying the Nantwich to Whitchurch road (now A530). Then the line curved towards the north-west, and joined the LNWR main line at Market Drayton Junction (27 miles 39 chains or 27½ miles). This was a double track junction, controlled by the LNWR signal box sited opposite on the down side. The original box had been replaced in 1884 by a typical LNWR wooden box with red brick base, and this continued in use until destroyed by fire during the evening of 16th/17th January, 1967. It officially closed as from 23rd July, 1967 some two months after the closure of the branch, so some temporary form of control must have been established for the short period in between, although there was likely to have been little traffic in the meantime.

Having joined the LNWR Shrewsbury to Crewe line, trains now crossed over the River Weaver by an attractive skew bridge of plate and girder construction with a span of around 50 feet. About 200 yards later, the Shrewbridge level crossing is negotiated, which was controlled by Shrewbridge signal box on the down side and within view of Nantwich station box. This latter was a busy signal box, as it also controlled the major level crossing of Wellington Road immediately at the western end of Nantwich station (27 miles and 71 chains or 27⅞ miles). This was an attractive station with the main red brick buildings on the downside, and brick waiting rooms on the up side. Both were furnished with substantial wooden canopies supported by cast-iron pillars on the platforms. The large wood and lattice footbridge, with glass panelling from shoulder height, was fully enclosed and sited midway along the two platforms so that it connected the waiting areas on each platform. Adjacent to the level crossing an open metal lattice footbridge was available for pedestrians to use when the level crossing was closed against the road traffic. Beyond the station, six sidings served the goods yard and single-road goods shed on the down side, with a crossover from the up running line. A single refuge siding was located on the up side, with a capacity for 33 wagons plus engine and brake van. Nantwich Goods Yard signal box controlled the movements here.

The Domesday Book records the ancient name for this town as 'Wych Malbeng'. The earliest market recorded here was in 1283 when King Edward I granted a right of fair on the feast of St Bartholomew. Cheese, grain and salt were traded here from early days, and tanning became an established local industry from medieval days. As a result, glovemaking became an ancient cottage industry practised by 'the poor incapable of following any other employ'. Later, cotton spinning and boot and shoe manufacture took over as major industries. The Great Fire of 1583 destroyed nearly 600 timber houses in the town, the fire lasting for 20

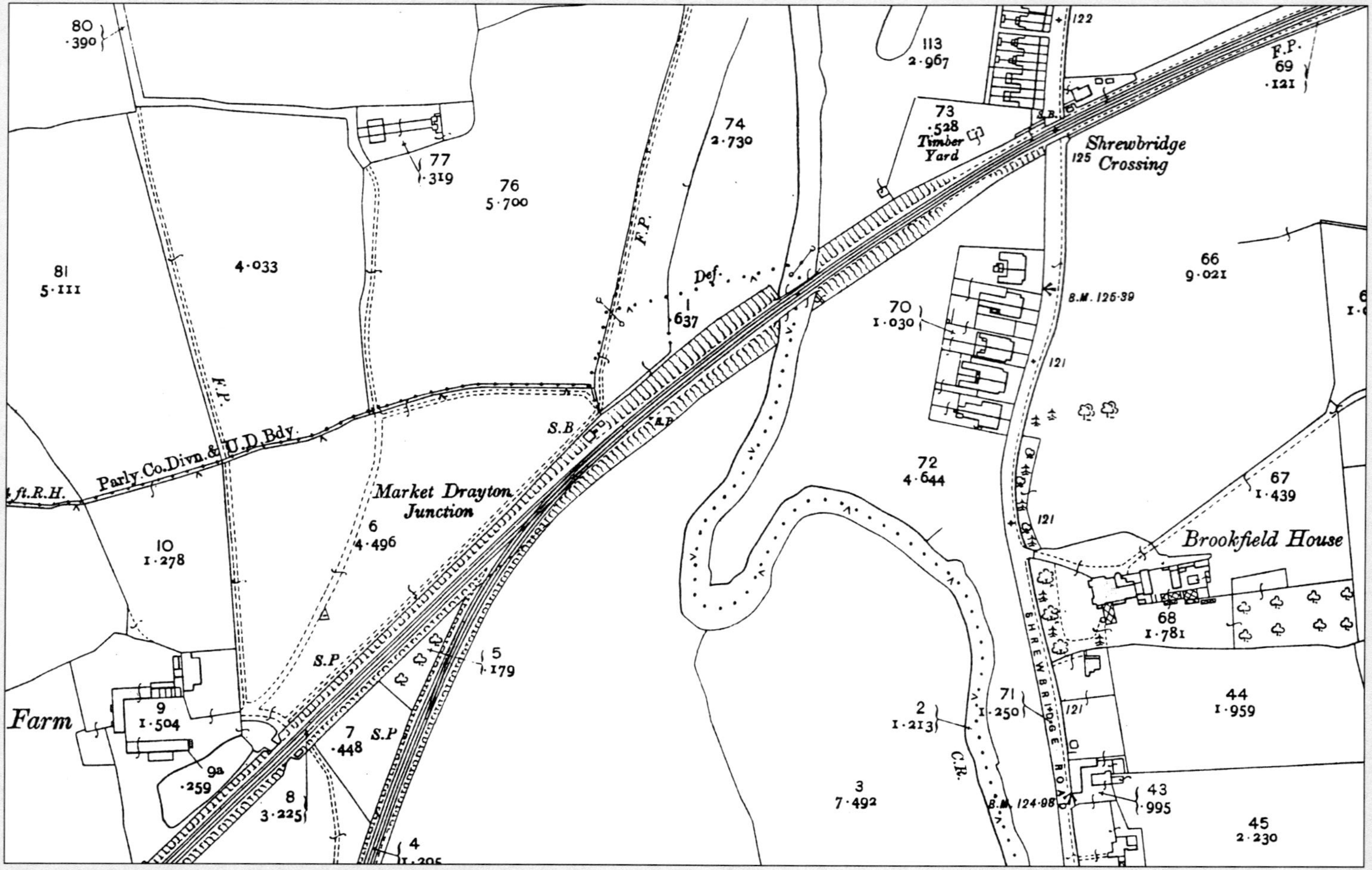

Market Drayton Junction, Nantwich.

Reproduced from the 25", 1909 Ordnance Survey Map

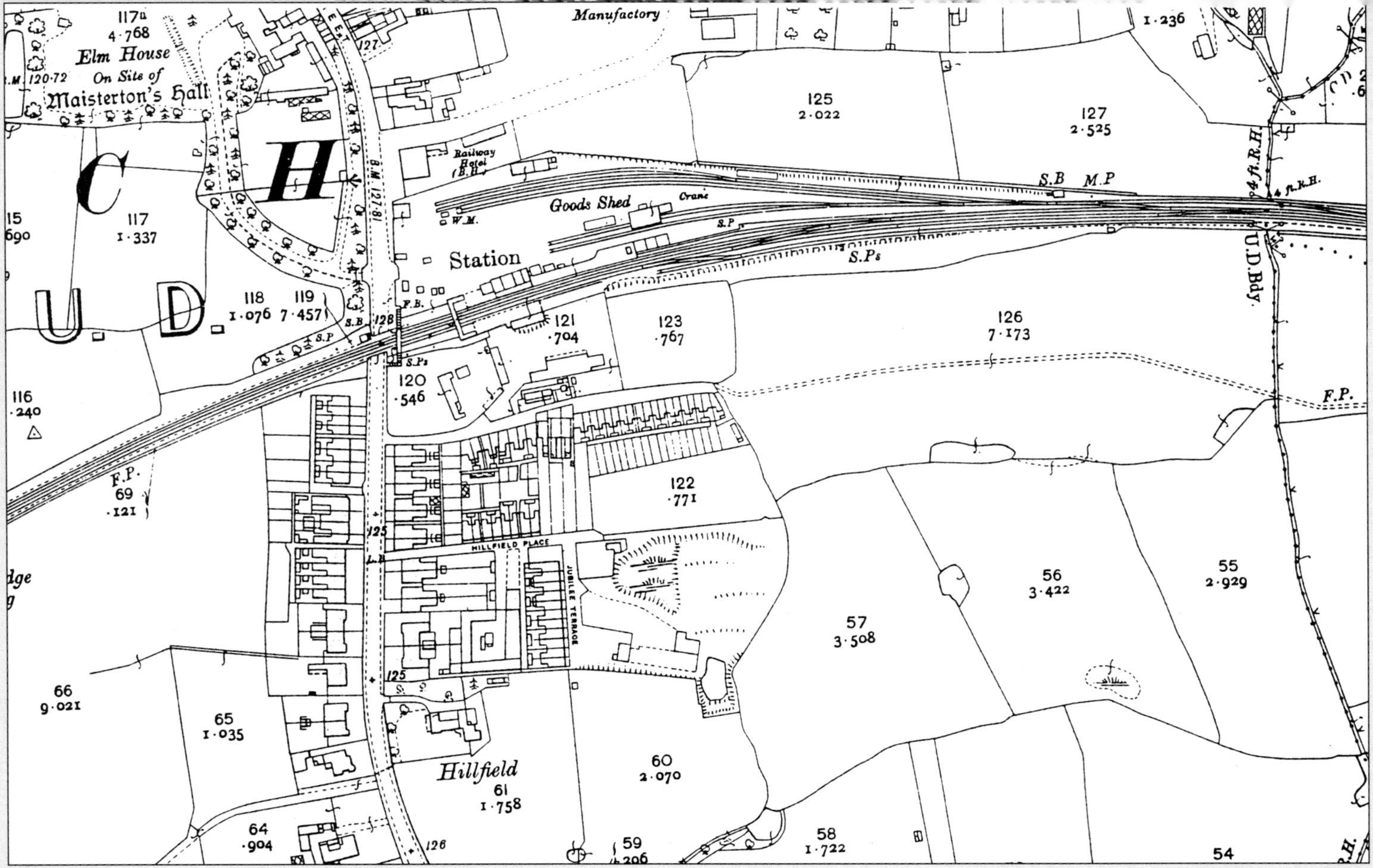

Nantwich station.

Reproduced from the 25", 1909 Ordnance Survey Map

Nantwich station around 1900 looking towards Crewe, with the station staff posing for the photographer. The cast-iron canopy supports on both platforms are particularly noticeable in this shot. *D. Houlston Collection*

Looking east along the down platform of Nantwich station on 30th September, 1952 showing the LMS style running-in board and the fully glazed and enclosed station footbridge. *J.M. Bentley*

The view westwards from the up platform at Nantwich on a very pleasant Spring day, 30th May, 1966. The level crossing gates over Shrewsbury Road are firmly closed against rail traffic and protected by the Nantwich Station signal box, just beyond. The curve of the line and the large enclosed station footbridge necessitated the provision of the tall up platform starter, with a repeater at a lower level. *M. Priestley*

A fine view of Nantwich Station signal box on 30th September, 1952. *J.M. Bentley*

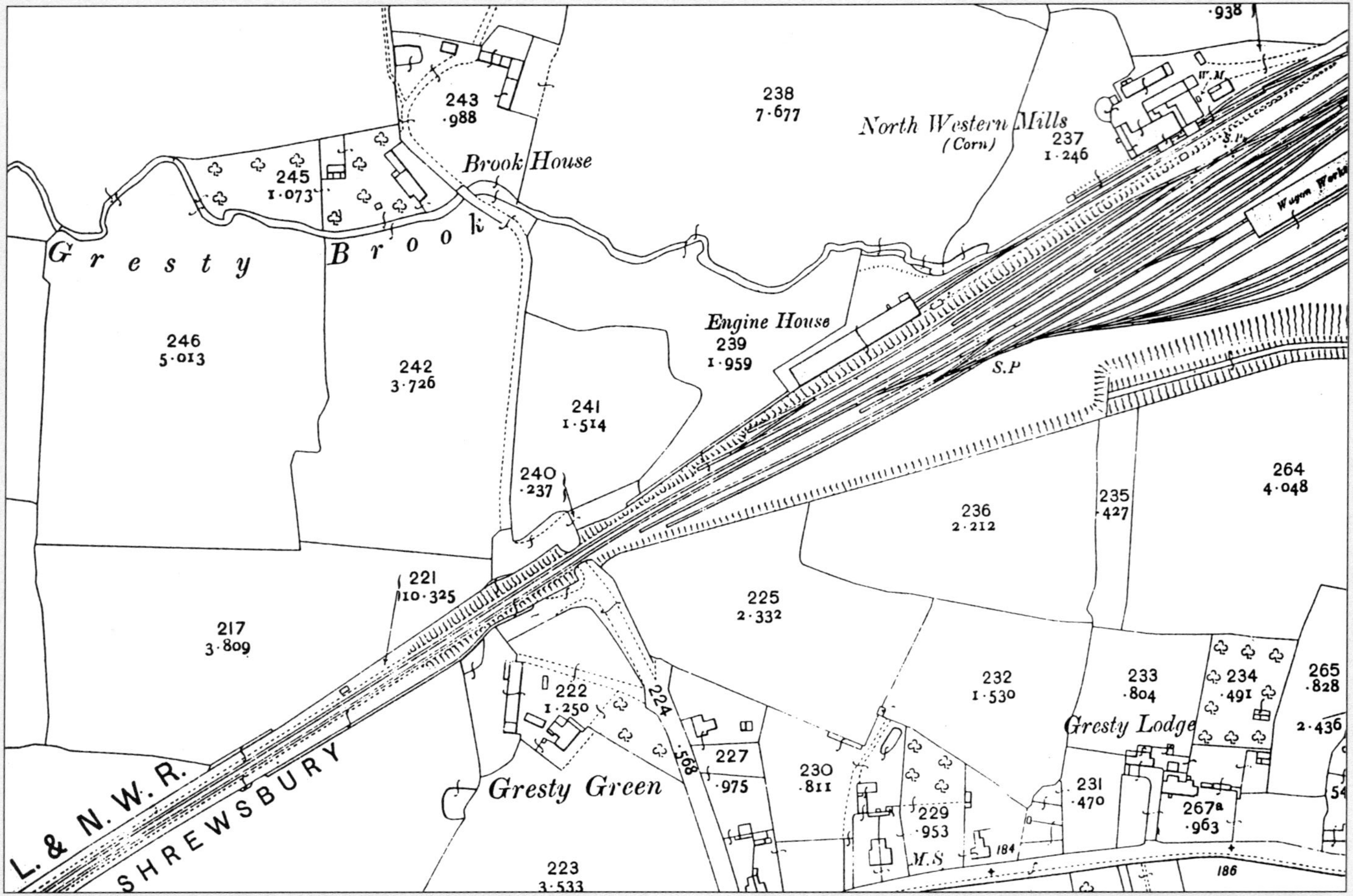

Crewe Gresty Lane engine shed.

Reproduced from the 25", 1910 Ordnance Survey Map

days. This was followed by a plague in 1586 during which 140 were buried, and again in 1604 over 400 died in the six months that it lasted. In the Civil War, the Parliamentarians took the town, and garrisoned over 2,000 soldiers here, holding out against Royalist attacks. After the industrial revolution, the town became even more annexed by Crewe, with whom it had always been considered as a twin, and finally in 1973 the Borough of Nantwich and Crewe was formed.

Now heading almost due east, the line continues around the south side of the town, and crosses the Newcastle to Nantwich road (now A52) on the level . This was originally controlled by Newcastle Crossing signal box, adjacent to the crossing. All of the signal boxes in Nantwich were latterly of the standard wooden LMS design.

Just over a mile further, the line entered Willaston (29 miles and 70 chains or 29⅞ miles), immediately beyond the level crossing over Wybunbury Road, which was again controlled by its own signal box. The station building was a two-storey brick-built affair, located on the down side. This station closed on 6th December, 1954.

After passing under Ropegreen Bridge, the line passed between the goods yards at Gresty Lane and the locomotive shed on the down side. Passing Gresty Lane Nos. 1 and 2 signal boxes the line swung northward once more and into the busy environs of Crewe South Yards and then to the station itself. Trains from Wellington normally terminated and started in the southern bays of platforms 2 and 3.

Ivatt class '2' No. 41232 waits to leave Crewe with the 5.20 pm to Wellington on 23rd September, 1961. *Michael Mensing*

A general view of the hangars at Tern Hill during World War I. *RAF Museum, Hendon*

One of Tern Hill's several Handley Page 0/400 bombers, stationed here during World War I, and seen in front of one of the original hangars. *RAF Museum, Hendon*

Chapter Nine

RAF Tern Hill

We have seen that the erstwhile country station at Tern Hill was boosted by the construction of Tern Hill airfield, and in later years by the constant passage of aircrew, recruits and trainees along its platforms. For that reason, it seems logical to devote one chapter to the story of this airfield.

The first inclination that powered flight was destined for this rather remote corner of Shropshire occurred on 22nd August, 1906 when a balloon piloted by a Major Atcherley, which had ascended at Shrewsbury, landed in one of the 20 acre fields belonging to Mr Goodall at Stroke Grange, just half a mile south of Tern Hill. This caused consternation and excitement throughout the locality for quite some time after.

The First Airfield

The site at Tern Hill was first selected as an airfield for the newly formed Royal Flying Corps by the Government during World War I, when land was purchased at Stoke Grange in the Autumn of 1915. The airfield and camp were to be sited on the south-western side of the hill, and work began early in 1916. Fields were cleared and levelled using Foden steam tractors, and the site was prepared for the buildings and equipment to follow. The runways for the airfield were at this time of grass.

Soon wooden huts and portable Bessaneoux hangars were erected. However, conditions for the early recruits in the huts were somewhat spartan, as these contained few furnishings, the beds were hard and the only source of heating was a single coke stove in each hut. There was no hot water, no proper kitchens, nor permanent kitchen staff and so the meals were generally prepared (often from frozen meat) by the recruits themselves until 1st December, 1916. From this date the first electricity supply was installed at Tern Hill, being generated at the airfield station by a single cylinder horizontal paraffin engine (with another in reserve). Thereafter, permanent hot water was available for baths, showers and general ablutions.

Work had proceeded smoothly up to this time, with the notable exception of a gale on 6th October, 1916 which almost destroyed two hangars, and injured several persons. The number of personnel on the site gradually increased during 1917 and 1918 to around 1,000 and there were nearly 50 aircraft in the hangars.

The original occupants of the station were Flying Units Nos. 34 and 43R, and Training Squadrons Nos. 30 and 33. However, these were replaced during 1918 by No. 13 Training Depot Squadron, just prior to when the Royal Flying Corps joined with the Royal Naval Air Service to become the Royal Air Force.

During World War I the aircraft at Tern Hill had mainly comprised Sopwith Camels and Dolphins, Handley Page 0-400 Bombers, Avro 504s and at least one captured Albatross D1, which was used by the RFC for training purposes.

After the cessation of hostilities the station continued in its training role, and seemed to be set for a fairly relaxed existence. Unfortunately, during March 1919 a fire in one of the small wooden huts spread rapidly and gutted two of the main hangars, further spreading to most of the station. Four of the Handley Page Bombers and several Avro 504s were destroyed. Much of the damage was never repaired, and as a result the station never really recovered from this body blow. Eventually the decision was taken to sell off the station and airfield, and in 1920 it was turned over to its new owners for stabling and training racehorses. Those buildings that had not collapsed of their own accord were either demolished or converted into stables, and the airfield became a training racetrack. Gradually over the next 15 years, much of the airfield not used as a racetrack became infested by rabbits, whose subterranean excavations were to prove a hazard later.

The Second Airfield

During the 1920s and 1930s the RAF had been gradually reduced in size and number of personnel, so that by 1934 it was operating at minimum strength. But the political climate in Europe was changing, and eventually the Government recognised the desirability of improving the RAF capability in order to respond to any untoward threat. So it was that the Tern Hill site was purchased in 1935 to regain its original role as an RAF station. The last of the racehorses left Tern Hill in the Summer of 1935, and civilian contractors arrived to determine the requirements for building a more permanent station at the old airfield. The whole airfield had to be scoured, resurfaced and grassed to eliminate the years of burrowing by the resident rabbits. Initially, temporary wooden huts were erected for the civilian workers and the first influx of service personnel, who had to endure conditions not unlike those of the early RFC personnel when they first arrived at Tern Hill in 1916. The first service personnel to arrive were one stores officer and 15 other ranks on 15th December, 1935 to take charge of materials and equipment that started to arrive. On 1st January, 1936 the first Station Commander, Group Captain C.C. Darley arrived in a Bristol Bulldog, and on the same day a civilian adjutant arrived. From this date the No. 10 Flying Training School came into existence, and the first course of pupils arrived on 1st February, 1936. As weather permitted, the first of the 44 aircraft then also began to arrive, using the runways which were still of grass at this time. The aircraft comprised Avro Tutors, Hawker Harts, Hawker Audax, and Gloster Gauntlets, and were then divided equally between the Flying Training School, and an Advanced Training Squadron. One of the most distinguished pupils to emerge from the training programme was later to become Wing Commander Guy Gibson, VC, the leader of the 'Dambusters'.

Autumn 1938 saw almost a repeat of the March 1919 fire, when an overbanked fire in one of the wooden huts started a fire which practically wiped out the whole of the domestic accommodation. As a result, for several weeks afterwards, many people slept in the offices where they worked. Happily on this occasion, the buildings were repaired and by 1939 the building programme was complete, so that the station emerged largely as it is today. With the storm clouds gathering over Europe it was decided in 1939 to camouflage the hangars and airfield, and this was completed by the Summer of that year. Thick black lines were painted over the whole of the airfield, which gave the appearance from the air of a patchwork of small fields. The outlines of the hangars and other buildings were camouflaged so as to merge with the surrounding trees.

Empire Air Days

Returning to the Summer of 1936, much of the station building programme was well under way and Tern Hill was opened to the public for Empire Air Day on 23rd May, 1936. This type of open day was repeated at many airfields throughout the country, in an effort to explain where much of the country's taxes were being spent, and to encourage a pride in the country and its armed forces. Around 15,000 visitors arrived to watch the flying displays and to view the aircraft at close quarters on static display. Many special trains were laid on, from Shrewsbury, Wellington and Crewe for the benefit of people wishing to attend.

This event was repeated the following year, on Saturday 29th May, 1937. The local newspapers reported enormous crowds, and people attending from a wide area once again. Spectators were thrilled by the aerobatics displayed, and in particular by the high speed dives of a Gloster Gauntlet single-seater fighter aircraft. Other manoeuvres displayed included formation flying, bombing, air drill and message collecting. There were a large number of static exhibits showing aircraft under repair as well as in operational order.

The following year, on Saturday 28th May, 1938 the show was presented once again. This time the attendance was estimated at over 20,000 people. Refreshments were apparently provided in the hangars, and it appears that the provision of seating for spectators was probably an innovation. The following is part of a report included in the *Wellington Journal and Shrewsbury News* of 4th June, 1938:

> Of the new features of the programme a 'dummy' parachute descent and the introduction of anti-aircraft guns, the latter at one period being brought into action to defend the station against 'enemy bombers' drew considerable attention. During an interval a demonstration of gliding was given by the North British Aviation Co. This was another new feature.
>
> Aerobatics, blind flying, formation flying, dive bombing, and attacks by fighters on a target attached to another plane were also included in the programme, and there were many side-shows. Various types of aircraft were on view, stripped aircrafts were to be seen in the repair section, there were demonstrations of firing a machine gun forward through the propeller arcs, a gas chamber was open throughout the afternoon, and demonstrations were given by the Shrewsbury air raid precautions department.
>
> Musical items were played during the afternoon by the Royal Air Force Band, Tern Hill. The officer commanding is Group Captain, G.E. Livock, DFC, AFC, RAF, who, with other officers, had gone to considerable pains to entertain the crowd.

Don Rowland can recall visiting this show, arriving on a train from Crewe. However, to accommodate all of the spectators, the GWR had strengthened the train at Crewe with additional coaches. At Tern Hill the train was much longer than the

Aerial views of RAF Tern Hill during its construction prior to the start of World War. II The biplanes lined up in neat rows are probably Avro Tutors used for training purposes.

(Both) RAF Museum, Hendon

platform, and it seems that the station staff at Tern Hill were not warned to expect a longer train. Furthermore, the engine crew evidently could not decide what to do, so that the passengers had to jump down on to the trackside from the last few coaches.

The last occasion that the air show was held before hostilities began was on Saturday 20th May, 1939. A report in the *Shrewsbury Chronicle* of 26th May estimated that the total attendance had grown to around 35,000. It particularly commented on the drill performed by nine bombers, which was due to commence at 2 pm, and that it was all the more remarkable that the aircraft arrived low over the airfield at exactly 2 pm! The remainder of the programme appears to have been similar to previous years, but mention is made of some of the types of aircraft appearing, such as Avro Anson, Hawker Hurricane, Hawker Fury, North American Harvard (reckoned to be the loudest aircraft of the day), and a lone Spitfire.

World War II

The possibility of war was being taken seriously, as late in August 1939 a company of gunners arrived to take over guard duties and station defence. Then on 1st September, 1939 a signal was received confirming General Mobilization. Simultaneously, 10 Whitley aircraft of No. 78 Squadron arrived from Dishforth, North Yorkshire on dispersal orders. This required that large concentrations of aircraft were to be avoided, as they presented too much of a potential target for enemy action. Eventually, at 11.00 am on 3rd September, 1939 war was declared. The next phase has been described as the 'phoney war', when for nearly six months nothing very much happened. During this time at Tern Hill the defence of the station was planned, reinforcements continued to arrive, and exercises continued, especially for air raid precautions, and perimeter defence. The No. 10 Flying Training School continued in its work, although the activity was naturally increased to reflect the demand for aircrew, and consequently a more intensive flying programme was instituted. The Whitleys of No. 78 Squadron remained, but were used on operational sorties, usually in support of Coastal Command.

Late in the Summer of 1940, Tern Hill began to receive a rota of fighter squadrons, sent for rest periods during the Battle of Britain. This included members of the Free French Air Force. However, few managed to receive much rest, as they were called out on operational sorties in defence of the city of Liverpool. As a result many were shot down over the Irish Sea, and in the Welsh mountains. As Tern Hill's training programme had to continue at this time, it can be imagined that life became somewhat hectic with conflicting requirements at the airfield. But however much operational sorties were given priority, new pilots were required even more now. So it was that in November 1940 the No. 10 Flying Training School was closed down and moved to Moose Jaw, Canada where it was reformed as No. 32 Flying Training School, and training could logically proceed unabated in the calmer air of North America. However, back at Tern Hill the No. 5 Flying Training School was formed to provide advanced training, which from April 1942 was reformed as No. 5 Advanced Flying Unit. This provided the acclimatisation for newly qualified pilots to adjust to European flying after their spell in Canada. Many hundreds of airmen passed through this school during the remaining war years.

In the meantime, tragedy had struck during the morning of 16th October, 1940. Bristol Blenheim night fighters were stationed here at this time, and after returning from a long night it had become customary for them to 'beat up' the station before landing (i.e. to fly in low over the airfield and buildings). However, on this morning, what was first though to be a Blenheim doing precisely this turned out to be a Junkers 88. He came in low, at about 250 feet, from the south-east and flew straight over the airfield, then turned and came in on his bombing run. He released a stick of high explosive and incendiary bombs on the south-west side of the station, in line with the main three hangars. The first bomb fell between the two most easterly hangars, and destroyed a wooden tower, which had ironically been erected as a bombing trainer. The remaining bombs smashed through the roof of the most easterly hangar, hit the concrete floor and bounced back into the roof before exploding. The roof and upper parts of the walls were completely demolished, leaving only the flight offices intact. Ten aircraft were completely destroyed. After his bombing run, the Junkers 88 made another tight turn and began strafing the mess rooms and domestic quarters. Casualties must have been considerable, but no details are known. Curiously, this strafing run was broken off suddenly, and the German aircraft flew off towards Newport. It is believed that this aircraft was never intercepted, and that it returned to its base in France intact. The hangar was never rebuilt, and became known as the 'Sunshine Hangar', for obvious reasons. The flight offices remained in continual use as part of the Station Flying Wing.

By early 1942, the two main runways had been hard surfaced, and were complete, so that they could then take much larger and heavier aircraft. The station boundaries were also pushed further outwards, so that groups of hangars could be erected for aircraft repair and maintenance. It had become apparent that even this relatively quiet part of Shropshire was not immune from attack, so it made sense to ensure that aircraft were dispersed even when on one site. At Stoke Heath, towards the south-west of the station was 'A' site, where Spitfires and Lancasters were repaired and refurbished. A little further east, on the site of the present day HM Prison at Stoke Heath, was the 'B' site, known as 'Spitfire Corner', solely concerned with the rebuilding of Spitfires. South-eastwards and across the Wolverhampton to Chester road (now A41) was the 'C' site, comprising two hangars used for the storage of Fairey Battles and De Havilland Tiger Moths. Adjacent to the married quarters, and to the east of the airfield was 'D' site, which was used for the storage of requisitioned civilian aircraft. These were used for transport of equipment, stores and personnel between RAF stations, and also when considered expendable, for use at 'decoy' airfields, to tempt the Luftwaffe into attacking spurious targets. By this time, there were around 2,000 civilian and service personnel at Tern Hill, including approximately 400 women.

The following aircraft types are known to have been stationed at Tern Hill during World War II, excluding those sent for repair, refurbishment and storage:

Airspeed Oxford	Bristol Blenheim	Miles Master
Armstrong Whitworth Whitley	De Havilland Tiger Moth	North American Harvard
Hawker Hurricane	Avro Anson	

After World War II

Despite the excellent reputation earned for its pilot and flying school, in 1946 the No. 5 Advanced Flying Unit was declared redundant, and subsequently disbanded. However, a new pilot training unit, No. 6 Flying Training School was opened, and started training as from 15th May, 1947. Unfortunately, the first day was marred by two accidents. This new unit incorporated all levels of training, from the initial stage right up to 'wings' standard, using Tiger Moth, Harvard, and later on, piston-engined Handley Page Provost aircraft.

With the increasing presence of jet aircraft in the RAF during the 1960s, the future of Tern Hill took a surprising turn. The airfield was considered too small for jet aircraft training, and so in 1961 a decision was taken to move the No. 6 Flying Training School to Acklington in Northumberland. In its place, the Helicopter Wing of the Central Flying School moved from RAF South Cerney, Gloucestershire to Tern Hill in late 1961. In January 1963 the Officer Command School also moved here. The Helicopter Wing comprised two squadrons, which were equipped as follows:

No. 1 Squadron - Bristol Sycamore, Sikorsky Sioux, Saunders Roe Skeeter, Westland Dragonfly.
No. 2 Squadron - Westland Whirlwind Mk. 2 and Mk. 10.

In 1971 the similar elements of each of these two squadrons were combined to form new Nos. 1 and 2 Squadrons. The instructor elements of each were combined into a new No. 1 Squadron, using Whirlwinds and Sioux helicopters, whilst the pilot training elements were formed into a new No. 2 Squadron, designated as Advanced Training Flying School, using Whirlwinds. In August, 1973 Westland Gazelles arrived at No. 1 Squadron to replace the Sioux and Whirlwinds, and had become standard by 1974.

It should be further mentioned that during the post war period Tern Hill hosted a considerable number of short term residential training courses for the Air Training Corps. This body comprised young persons of school age and into their later teens interested in a career in the RAF, and, as such, played an important role in the recruitment of personnel for the RAF.

Although there was no 'Open Day' at Tern Hill in 1946, one was held at nearby RAF High Ercall on Saturday 14th September, 1946. There are no details of this event, but it must have been a fairly modest affair, bearing in mind the availability of staff and equipment at this time, which was still finding its way back home. Tern Hill's first 'Open Day' was held on Saturday 20th September, 1947 and, again, the local press gave no details of the event. However, this became an annual event once more, but this time referred to as 'Battle of Britain Display' in recognition of the third Sunday of each September that had become designated as 'Battle of Britain Day'.

The final two events were widely reported, and some mention of the attractions is worthwhile. On Saturday 19th September, 1964 a crowd totalling 48,500 attended, and was rewarded with aerial displays by the 'V-bombers': Handley Page Victors, Avro Vulcans, Vickers Valiants, as well as a Bristol Britannia transporter, at least five English Electric Canberra bombers, an English Electric Lightning fighter, and several De Havilland Vampires. The Fleet Air Arm sent a De Havilland Sea Vixen, and the United States Army Air Force was represented by a North American F-100 Super Sabre fighter, a

Three Hunting Provost T.1 piston-engined trainers from the No. 6 Flying Training School in formation in the skies above Tern Hill. *RAF Museum, Hendon*

A Provost T.1 trainer of the No. 6 Flying Training School in front of one of the hangars at RAF Tern Hill during the 1950s. *RAF Museum, Hendon*

McDonnell F-101 Voodoo fighter and two Boeing B66 bombers. Aerial acrobatics were performed by the Red Pelicans display team from the Central Flying School at RAF Little Rissington using six Hunting T-10 Jet Provosts. Tern Hill's helicopters were on ground display, and there were further ground displays of ATC gliding, Mountain Rescue teams and gymnastics. A planned parachute fall was cancelled due to high winds.

The following year the event was not referred to as 'Battle of Britain Display', so that presumably this commemorative day had been dropped by then. Nonetheless the 'Open Day' was once again well attended, with 50,000 spectators turning out. High winds once more caused the cancellation of a parachute display, this time by the SAS 'Sky Divers'. Similarly, the aircraft supplied by the USAAF were not permitted to fly because of the conditions, although there was no description of these aircraft. However, the eight-strong team of the RAF's 'Red Arrows' put on a terrific display of aerial acrobatics and formation flying with their Folland Gnat jet trainers. From World War II, a lone Supermarine Spitfire made several passes over the airfield, as later did a De Havilland Mosquito (one of the twin-engined, wooden-framed fighter bombers famed for its outstanding speed). Tern Hill's helicopters showed their paces in the air-sea rescue demonstration, and combined with the Royal Artillery and the Shropshire Yeomanry in an Army co-operation excercise. Further aerial flypasts were made by English Electrics Lightnings (apparently a deafening sensation when on full burn), a Hunting Jet Provost trainer, a De Havilland Comet transporter, an Avro type 696 Shackleton (a multi-role aircraft used by Transport Command, Coastal Command and even by Bomber Command), and several English Electric Canberra bombers. The climax of the show was stolen by two ageing aircraft. The first was a Gloster Gladiator (the last biplane built for the RAF, in the mid-1930s); and a Miles Hawk monoplane (used by the RAF as a trainer around 30 years earlier) which was piloted by Wing Commander Geoff Cairns from Tern Hill. Further aircraft were available for inspection on the ground, and hundreds queued for some time to see inside a Douglas Dakota of the USAAF, that workhorse of World War II, of which many thousands were built. Engineering and technical displays were provided inside the hangars, and there were numerous other amusements available around the site.

The following year, 1966, it was announced that there would be no such show that year, although an Open Day was to be held at Shobden airfield, near Hereford. This was the start of severe cuts in defence spending, and no further shows were held at Tern Hill.

* *

The story of Tern Hill has thus taken us beyond the life of the railway, and can be concluded by mentioning that from 1976 to 1986, the site was more or less unused, but the buildings were protected on a care and maintenance basis, until taken over by the Army at that time. Since that date, the Army has been in residence, and whilst various units have resided here, training in Army helicopters has continued right up to the present day.

It is not known whether the cause of this accident to Provost T.1 No. WV488 was pilot error or a component failure, as it lies on the airfield at Tern Hill. *RAF Museum, Hendon*

The present day site of RAF Tern Hill, with the eponymous hill in the background. The site is now occupied by the Army as a barracks, and is used for helicopter training. *Author*

Chapter Ten

Locomotive Sheds

Wellington

The locomotive shed was constructed jointly by the Shropshire Union Railway and the Shrewsbury & Birmingham Railway for the opening of the joint line as a two-road goods shed, with one road passing through to the rear. It was built in brick with a gabled slate roof, and was situated on the north side of the up platform. Up to 1867, GWR locomotives had been stabled in fairly primitive conditions at Ketley. However, with the building of the WDR, it was realised that there would be further locomotives to require servicing and stabling. This would be an ideal opportunity to improve the existing facilities in Wellington. So, in July 1867 the Joint Line Committee (consisting of representatives of the GWR and LNWR) agreed to convert the goods shed into a three-road locomotive shed, as its use had been made redundant by the opening of the separate GWR and LNWR goods depots further west in the town. The conversion work was completed at a cost of £635 5*s*. 8*d*. by April in the following year, not long after the opening of the WDR. The shed building measured 85 feet by 50 feet. One of the shed roads passed through the shed to a stop block at the rear, near to the separate stores, fitting shop and a wooden building for the shed foreman and his clerk. The enginemen's mess room for many years was actually the coach body from a broad gauge carriage, but was eventually replaced by conversion of a World War II air raid shelter. The foreman's office was replaced by a pre-cast concrete building after World War II. A well was situated at the rear of the shed, near to this collection of small buildings, and this supplied the 14,000 gallon tank mounted over the pump house, sited between the shed and up the running road.

For most of its life, Wellington shed was the property of the GWR, supplying locomotives for local shunting and freight turns, plus passenger duties on the Severn Valley and Crewe lines. In the mid-1950s the shed received a small mechanical coaling hoist, protected by a structure of corrugated asbestos and sheet steel, as a replacement for its ancient coaling stage, which utilised a bucket and hoist coaling mechanism. This protective structure also hopefully reduced the amount of coal dust blown on to the passengers waiting on the nearby northern face of the up island platform of Wellington station. At around the same time, the turntable provided from the outset (and believed to have been of only 45 feet diameter) was removed.

The locomotive allocation for around 70 years comprised representatives of the various classes of 0-6-0ST and 0-6-0PT built at Wolverhampton, and as mentioned earlier, became well known for the various 2-4-0 and 4-4-0 classes seeing out their days, principally working over the line to Crewe. Another interesting veteran to appear here was GWR No. 92, which arrived in July 1942 for use as a stationary boiler. This long-lived locomotive had an especially interesting history. It had been built by Beyer, Peacock in 1857 (Works No. 51) as an inside-framed, inside-cylinder 0-4-2ST with open splashers, along with a sister engine, No. 91.

An interesting view of permanent way works being carried out on the approach roads to Wellington shed around 1920. Although the ballast wagons are lined up right back inside the locomotive shed, the Dean pannier tank in the background is not isolated whilst the work proceeds, as there was another track passing behind the coaling stage. The platform face used for Market Drayton and Crewe trains is on the right. *Author's Collection*

Wellington shed on 3rd June, 1951 with Collett '5101' class 2-6-2T No. 4154 in the foreground, surrounded by the shed's allocation of the ubiquitous '57XX' class 0-6-0 pannier tanks.
Kidderminster Railway Museum: P. Bingham Collection

Dean '3206' class 2-4-0 No. 3223 on the turntable at Wellington shed during the 1930s. This class were also known as 'Barnums', and had a long association with the line. This particular engine was withdrawn from Wellington shed in May 1936. *Stephenson Locomotive Society*

Originally built as an 0-4-2ST by Beyer, Peacock (Works No. 51) in April 1857 for the GWR as its No. 92, this engine was converted to an 0-4-0ST at Chester in December 1878, and was further reconstructed at Wolverhampton in October 1893. It was transferred to Wellington just before World War II for use as a stationary boiler, and after final withdrawal in June 1942 its boiler continued in use for steam raising purposes for a few more years there. *Author's Collection*

Churchward '44XX' class 2-6-2T No. 4400 is serviced at Wellington shed on 13th November, 1948. Locomotives of this class allocated to Wellington were used almost exclusively on the workings to Much Wenlock and Craven Arms.The old coaling stage can be seen behind the locomotive, and at this time is evidently in poor condition.

W. Potter/Kidderminster Railway Museum

Wellington shed on 7th July, 1959 showing a Collett '5101' class 2-6-2T at the later coaling stage, and a bevy of '57XX' class 0-6-0PTs, Nos. 9630, 5765 and 4605 standing in front of the shed. The siding on the right appears to contain the two-coach set and a van for the next Crewe service.

Transport Treasury/Alec Swain Collection

Above: Collett '57XX' class 0-6-0PT No. 3749 awaiting its next turn of duty outside Wellington shed on a sunny day in 1956. Note that the ends of the shed roof have already succumbed to the combined effects of exhaust steam and soot by this date.
R. Mulford

Left: 'Dukedog' 4-4-0 No. 9014 stored out of use at the back of Wellington shed. The locomotive still carries its Croes Newydd (84J) shedplate, 14th February, 1960.
Transport Treasury/Alec Swain Collection

However, No. 92 was rebuilt at the GWR works at Saltney, Chester in December 1878 as an 0-4-0ST. It was again rebuilt, this time at Wolverhampton in 1893, with a shortened wheelbase, new wheels, modified frames, closed splashers and a new boiler. It now also sported a new cab complete with a roof supported by front and rear spectacle plates. This locomotive spent most of its life in the Wrexham colliery district, but was transferred to South Wales in 1933, spending time at Severn Tunnel Junction and Radyr sheds before its arrival at Wellington. It disappeared for scrapping soon after the end of the war, having somewhat surprisingly accumulated a total mileage of over 785,000.

As indicated above, the site of the shed meant that such activity as there was could be leisurely viewed from this platform. During 1961/62 several interesting locomotives were stored at Wellington shed. One of the 10 Stanier 0-4-4 tanks, No. 41900, which had been tried unsuccessfully on the Much Wenlock branch was stored here until removed for scrapping. Around the same time, the last three GWR 4-4-0 'Dukedogs', Nos. 9004, 9014 and 9018, were stored here too.

Under the GWR, the shed was numbered 184, and the code painted on locomotives on the front end of the running plate near to the buffer beam was always WLN. But in February 1950 under BR it became 84H in the Wolverhampton Motive Power District of the Western Region. In February, 1963 it became part of the London Midland Region and the code was changed to 2M on 9th September, 1963.The shed closed on 10th August, 1964 and was subsequently demolished. The site is now in use as the station car park.

Market Drayton

A locomotive shed and 35 ft turntable was provided here, from the opening of the NMDR in 1863. It was sited just north of the station and on the up side of the line. The building was of wooden construction on dwarf brick walls, with individual smoke vents in the gabled roof. It measured approximately 50 feet by 18 feet, with a water tank housed above the 10 feet by 10 feet office at the rear. The shed appears to have passed to the NSR when it opened its line through to Market Drayton in 1870, and on 8th April, 1873 estimates were prepared, ostensibly for a new shed. However, the estimate of £146 does not seem sufficient for a replacement structure, and it is generally accepted that this was in fact for the enlargement of the existing shed but there does not seem to have been any major work carried out at this time. Furthermore, the NSR engineer was instructed in February 1880 to enlarge the shed. The exact date that this was accomplished is not known, and probably it involved dismantling the existing building in order to rebuild it to double its previous length, although at 50 feet by 15 feet the extension was some three feet narrower. At around this time, the original single-road wooden goods shed was replaced by the two-road building constructed in brick. It is therefore tempting to speculate that some of this original building may have been incorporated into the rebuilt locomotive shed. In 1889 the turntable was replaced by a larger 40 ft unit, and a further siding added off the turntable to pass along the rear of the shed, sufficient to hold two engines. Further alterations costing £100 were approved in 1920, relating to the

Market Drayton engine shed, the timber construction and dwarf brick walls can be clearly seen. *W.H. Whitworth*

doors. This is likely to have been the result of many similar such incidents at locomotive depots involving shed doors and locomotives!

No coaling facilities appear ever to have been provided, and so it is assumed that any such coaling as may have been required was effected directly from an adjacent coal wagon into the locomotives. A curiosity was that the water column was located inside the shed building. Such positioning of the water column may have resulted from the rebuilding of the shed, or it may have been desired to protect the column from freezing temperatures - not an unknown practice.

Water was pumped from a well situated north of the line, about 300 yards west of the station and the Adderley Road bridge. In fact the only access to the pumping station was from a lane leading off this road just north of the overline bridge. The water was pumped from the storage tank along the mains buried alongside and beneath the trackbed to the two platform water columns at the station, and to a further water tank located in the up side goods yard, from where water was distributed to the locomotive shed, the station and goods shed for non-potable use.

There was a succession of intriguing locomotive boilers used here for pumping water. The first known was from Shrewsbury & Chester Railway 2-4-0 No. 6, which was built by Longridge and started work in January 1847. This locomotive was taken into GWR stock when the Shrewsbury & Chester was absorbed as from 1st September, 1854 as GWR No. 6, and continued in use until withdrawn in August 1868 after which date the boiler was installed in Market Drayton. The next boiler was from the Birkenhead Railway inside-cylinder 2-4-0 No. 25 *Birkenhead,* which was built by Robert Stephenson (Works No. 871) in January 1853. This locomotive became GWR No. 99 when the Birkenhead Railway was jointly vested

The turntable at Market Drayton remained *in situ*, and the two-road goods shed (abbreviated from three roads at some time in the past) intact on 28th January, 1970. *A.C. Baker*

Collett '5101' class 2-6-2T No. 4120 standing at the entrance to the two-road shed at Gresty Lane, Crewe. The front part of the shed roof appears to be in terminal decline at this time. *J. Maden Collection*

in the GWR and LNWR as from 1st January, 1880. It only lasted until February 1880 after which the boiler came to Market Drayton. Finally, we come to Shrewsbury & Birmingham Railway long boiler 0-6-0 No. 13, which had inside cylinders, inside frames, a Gothic firebox and was built by Longridge and delivered in June 1849. Upon absorption of the S&BR by the GWR as from 1st September, 1854 this became GWR No. 47, and was rebuilt at Wolverhampton in June 1868 as an 0-6-0ST with the short type of saddle tank. In August 1875 it was again rebuilt at Wolverhampton, this time with a domed boiler and ordinary firebox. It was finally condemned at Wolverhampton in August 1889 and its boiler used here. It is presumed that these boilers were put to successive use, and so as a new one was installed the previous one was disposed of.

No further boilers have been traced for subsequent use, although the pumping plant continued in use, evidently by other means, until closure of the line. The 1960 Sectional Appendix to the Working Timetable gives the following instructions:

> An indicator showing whether the water in the tank is high or low, and an alarm bell to call the signalman's attention are provided in the Silverdale Junction box. The bell can be stopped by pressing the plunger provided. If low, or because of failure, notice must be sent to the District Outdoor Machinery Engineer at Crewe, and to Control at Crewe, Stoke, and Shrewsbury.

The normal allocation before the Grouping of 1923 was a tank locomotive for passenger work, and Longbottom 0-6-0 No. 159 for goods work, in particular the nightly goods to Wellington.

The shed was unable to weather the strict economies necessary in the 1930s, and closed officially on 8th December, 1934, although it may have gone out of use earlier. It was demolished very soon after.

Crewe, Gresty Lane

This shed was sited on the north side of the LNWR Shrewsbury line, about a mile west of the station, and just beyond the Gresty Lane underbridge. The site was at a lower level than the Shrewsbury running line, and was adjacent to Gresty Brook. Consequently, the shed did not receive a great deal of direct sunshine, and with its proximity to the brook was frequently a damp and rather unpleasant place. It was actually owned jointly by the LNWR and the GWR, but was of a very clear GWR design. It was of a brick construction with a slated roof and individual roof ventilators, and is believed to have been erected around 1870. No reason has been established why the LNWR would wish to part own this shed, as it certainly never made use of it. The only possible reason is that, as the GWR was only in Crewe by virtue of running powers over the LNWR, it did not wish the GWR to feel too much 'right' to be there.

Notwithstanding the logic of its action, the LNWR shared the cost of an enlargement in 1899 with the GWR. This entailed doubling the amount of engine accommodation, such that the final dimensions of the shed were 220 feet by 30 feet, with offices measuring 60 feet by 10 feet. A single line ran from the

Crewe Gresty Lane shed on 29th May, 1960 with Ivatt class '2' 2-6-2T No. 41231 being watered, and an unidentified GWR 4-6-0 in the other shed road. The main line from Shrewsbury to Crewe ran on the top of the embankment to the left. *F.W. Shuttleworth*

Ivatt class '2' 2-6-2T No. 41201 standing over the ash pit at Gresty Lane shed, Crewe around 1962. This locomotive appears to have lost its 'SC' plate from beneath the shedplate. *J. Maden Collection*

down running line, after serving the sidings of the North Western Corn Mills, and divided in front of the shed. Ash pits were placed on both shed roads, and a typical GWR 'parachute' type combined water tank and column was positioned alongside the southernmost track, adjacent to a small coaling stage, which involved manual coaling of locomotives.

No turntable was ever provided. Consequently, until Crewe South shed opened in 1897, any tender locomotives requiring turning had to travel to Crewe North for this purpose. Indeed, the practice continued even after 1897, for passenger tender locomotives that had run into the through platforms at Crewe station. Generally, the tender locomotives arriving at Crewe from our line were working on freight turns, and did not always use the turntable at Crewe South, preferring to use the triangle arranged as part of the running lines in the area after the reorganization of 1927.

The allocation varied from a maximum of seven in the 1930s to two just before absorption as a sub-shed in 1951. During 1921 the only locomotives allocated here were Gooch double-framed '131' class 0-6-0 No. 312 and Armstrong '360' class 0-6-0 No. 366 - both considerable veterans at that time. From the 1930s onwards the allocation generally consisted of two of Collett's '5101' class 2-6-2T and one of the ubiquitous '57XX' class 0-6-0PT, although some of the 4-4-0 classes still lingered.

Into the BR days, the use of GWR types continued, but for passenger duties these were gradually replaced by the Ivatt class '2' 2-6-2T from Crewe North's allocation.

The shed was listed as GWR shed number 74, and although a sub-shed of Wellington was coded independently as CEW, retaining this coding after Nationalisation until February 1950 when it officially lost its own allocation of locomotives, which had in any case dwindled by then. In July 1951 it was placed into the London Midland Region of BR for administrative purposes, but for the most part there was little change to the workings. The one effect was that shunting of the Gresty Lane sidings became an LMR duty for Crewe South shed, and was generally performed by one of their diesel shunters. In April, 1953 the shed became part of the Crewe Motive Power District, and was officially classed as a sub-shed to Crewe North. The shed was officially closed on 17th June, 1963 but for some time prior to this date visiting locomotives had increasingly gone to Crewe South for servicing, and the shed building had become rather dilapidated by this time. It remained empty for some time, but was demolished by 1990, and the site is now covered by industrial development.

Details of the locomotive allocations at Wellington and Crewe Gresty Lane sheds at various time intervals can be found in *Appendix Eight*. Market Drayton was really only an out-station of Stoke, so never had its own official allocation of locomotives, even if certain ones did become the regular branch motive power.

An unidentified Brush type '4' (later class '47') appears to be setting back into the up refuge siding at Market Drayton on 4th February, 1967. This must have been a special working as the train reporting number shown does not appear in the working timetable from this date. The Stoke line leads off to the right in the foreground. *A.C. Baker*

Stanier 'Black Five' 4-6-0 No. 45240 is standing in the down goods yard at Market Drayton on 28th April, 1967. It had just worked in from Crewe with the full brake seen here, and was clearing the yards of rolling stock in order that track removal could commence. *M. Temple*

Chapter Eleven

Closure and the Line Today

Closure

We have seen in a number of instances that the volume of passengers never reached an acceptable level. For example, it is recorded that in 1872 a typical day saw only 19 tickets issued at Audlem. In September 1874 receipts at Audlem for the month totalled only £12 4*s.* 10*d.* for 60 tons of goods sent out. The amount of cash received here on Saturday 29th January, 1881 was £8 0*s.* 3*d.* for passengers, goods and parcels. In fact, £5 was a more normal daily amount. With this sort of background, the celebrated GWR innovation of providing halts can be seen as an effort to attract more passengers, rather than to prevent the passengers defecting to road transport. This is one of the reasons why auto-trains were never introduced on the line. However, this too never really achieved a satisfactory result. So it was that thoughts of closing the line to passenger traffic were considered after World War II, but it was left to the infamous 'Beeching Cuts' of the 1960s to provide the final impetus. Consequently, the line from Wellington to Nantwich was closed to passengers as from 9th September, 1963. This event did not seem to have caused much local concern, as, despite considerable efforts, the author has been unable to find any reference to the closure in any of the local newspapers of the time.

Freight traffic was still healthy at this time, but as mentioned earlier, the line was of strategic rail importance during the electrification work on the West Coast Main Line between Euston and Crewe, which was completed on 6th March, 1967. It was estimated that during this period over 10,000 tons of freight was passing over the line each week. Unfortunately, it was coincidental that at the conclusion of this work BR decided to concentrate on bulk freight, and that also at this time there was in any event a distinct move away from railways for the transport of freight. This was certainly linked to the considerable improvements being made in the country's roads, with the first of the motorways being opened, and thus facilitating door to door movement of goods without transhipment. The final nail in the coffin for the line was the decision not to proceed with the Walcot marshalling yard. So freight traffic too was withdrawn, and the line was officially closed to all traffic as from 8th May, 1967.

Lifting of the line did not commence immediately, but was in any case completed during 1970, as the accompanying photographs show. The Cheshire County Council was keen to utilise disused trackbeds as public walks and planned several such as Country Parks. But in the case of the trackbed within Cheshire, i.e. from Nantwich south to Audlem, it was felt that the countryside was too flat and rather monotonous, and so the idea was never adopted here.

View through the stone-built Adderley Road bridge towards the abandoned Market Drayton station around 1967. *M. Temple*

Track removal had started as Sulzer class '2' Bo-Bo No. D5002 arrived in the up side goods yard at Market Drayton with wagons to collect the redundant rails. *M. Temple*

Market Drayton station and yards in the Winter of 1970/71. The track has been removed, but the snow covers its absence, and the presence of the water crane at the platform end make the railway scene appear to be more complete than was actually the case. *M. Temple*

A snow-covered trackbed disguises the absence of rails in this view westwards from the Adderley Road bridge in Market Drayton. The curved roof of the building to the right of the line is that of the water tank, surmounting the water pumping station referred to in the text. *M. Temple*

Market Drayton station, viewed from the south, on 28th January, 1970 with the goods shed on the right was still substantially complete at this time, even though the track and the footbridge had gone.

(Both) A.C. Baker

The rather ornate level crossing gates, and the brick base of the signal box at Hack Green, after removal of the track: 28th January, 1970. *A.C. Baker*

Audlem station buildings and up platform on 28th January, 1970. *A.C. Baker*

Inside Silverdale Junction signal box, most of the levers were still intact, even if the instruments had gone by 28th January, 1970. *A.C. Baker*

Today

Wellington station remains substantially complete, although the outer face of the up island platform is no longer used by trains, and of course the engine shed has long gone, the site now being used as the station car park. The familiar brick and concrete Wellington No. 2 signal box, on the up side adjacent to the station disappeared as recently as December 2002, and the accompanying semaphore signals in the station area went at the same time. Fortunately, most of the signals were rescued by the Telford Steam Railway, where they will be installed at a future date. Otherwise the line is still open, although both the GWR and LNWR goods depots have also disappeared, and in both cases the sites are now occupied by supermarkets with their inevitable car parks. The most northerly of the two former bay platforms has been reinstated, albeit somewhat shorter than before, for use by diesel multiple units operating between Walsall and Wellington. However, this service is currently threatened with withdrawal.

The point at which the Nantwich line diverged can be easily discerned from a nearby overbridge, although here too commercial development has encroached upon the trackbed. The course of the line through the eastern part of Wellington towards Admaston can be followed and part has been converted into a footpath. Out into the countryside, the route can be picked up easily although at the site of Longdon Halt the overbridge has been removed, so that the crossroads now sits on the former trackbed which is difficult to find at this precise point. At Crudgington, the station master's house remains, now in private use, but the rest of the station buildings and goods shed were demolished in 1978. The dairy north of the station has continued to expand, such that it now reaches across the former trackbed. At Rowton Halt, only the road overbridge remains, with no signs of the halt. However, the site of Ellerdine Halt can be traced to its earthworks, and even the stone-faced former loading bank exists, complete with the old grounded van body used as a parcels store.

Across the countryside, the embankments and cuttings mostly remain, giving direction to the route, and at Peplow the remains of the down side waiting shelter are now in the gardens of a house that was once that of the station master. All the other railway buildings have gone. Further north, the road overbridge crossing the A442 Telford to Hodnet road has been removed so as to straighten the road alignment, and the trackbed at this point is difficult to find. However, on reaching Hodnet, one is at last rewarded by the former goods shed. This has been completely renovated and put into use as Hodnet Pumping Station of the Environment Agency's Shropshire Groundwater Scheme. Even in its new role, the building is largely unaltered, and looks fine. Regrettably, there is no trace of any of the other railway buildings here.

At Wollerton the earthworks of the halt can be found, including some of the timber platform facing amongst the undergrowth. But north of here there has been a recent (2003) road diversion scheme of the A53 towards Tern Hill that has used part of the trackbed, although the arches of one of bridges over the River Tern are still extant.

At Tern Hill the station buildings have been replaced by commercial development, and the A41 road overbridge was removed many years ago in

A Central Trains class '158' diesel multiple unit enters Nantwich with a stopping service from Shrewsbury to Crewe in June 2003. Note that the up starter signal is nowadays that of a BR standard pattern semaphore, and no longer has the tall repeater arms, necessary in the days when the station footbridge obscured the sighting of the lower arm on the curve of the line westwards into the station. *Author*

Nantwich station looking eastwards, with the remainder of the station building on the down platform now painted black, and in use as a Tandoori Restaurant. A 'bus shelter' is provided on each of the platforms for the benefit of intending passengers: June 2003. *Author*

Looking west from Nantwich station, with the Nantwich Station box in the foreground, which controls all three level crossings in the town. The Shewbridge Road level crossing can just be seen as the line curves to the left towards the top of the photograph, June 2003. *Author*

The site of Ellerdine Halt on 1st August, 2003 looking south towards Wellington. The earthworks of the down side halt platform can be seen centre right, whilst towards the centre of the picture is the original stone built loading bank which was adjacent to the single siding provided here, and the original goods van body which functioned as the goods storage depot. *Author*

The bridge abutments are still existing near to Coole Pilate Halt where the line crossed the Shropshire Union Canal. The extent to which this skew bridge caused a severe restriction on the canal can be clearly seen in this view, looking south on 1st August, 2003. *Author*

The former single road goods shed at Hodnet on 1st August, 2003 now completely refurbished, and in use as the Hodnet pumping station of the Environment Agency's Shropshire Groundwater Scheme. The line ran behind the building, to the right, where the trees have since sprung up. *Author*

order to flatten the approach to a nearby roundabout. However, a precast concrete building adjacent to the loading bay remains, in dereliction, as does a small weighbridge office. Eastwards of here, the line has returned to agriculture and only intermittent overbridges act as pointers. Actually, the A53 Market Drayton by-pass now runs on part of the route, just as it passes the massive and well known Mueller dairy products factory. In towards the centre of Market Drayton much of the line has been lost to housing development. In the centre of the town the stone-built overbridge on Adderley Road still exists, but from there where one would once have gazed into the station and goods yards, the vista today is of a supermarket, petrol station and other retail outlets. No trace whatsoever remains of the bustling rail activity, nor of the Silverdale Junction site. In fact it is also difficult to trace the line northwards from the town as much has again been returned to agriculture. The approach to Adderley is however, easy to trace and although some remains of the platforms can be found, the station building has gone, but not the station master's house, which is now a private residence. Curiously, the road overbridge at this point was also recently (2003) completely renovated rather than being removed.

At Coxbank Halt, only the vague outlines of the platforms can be seen from the overline bridge. However, this is more than can be found at Audlem, where the entire station and goods yard site were completely replaced by housing in 1986, and even the abutments of the nearby road underbridge (A525) have been removed.

At Coole Pilate, the abutments of the blue-brick bridge over the Shropshire Union Canal remain, inconveniently narrowing the width of the canal at that point, but all traces of the wooden halt have gone. As mentioned earlier, north of here the land was relatively flat, and so little remains of the trackbed, as it was long ago easily returned to agriculture. Surprisingly, the earthworks of the embankment at the approach to Market Drayton Junction, Nantwich have also been removed making it difficult to determine the precise alignment of the junction.

From here we join the still open Shrewsbury to Crewe line, and cross the River Weaver over the fine skew bridge at the approach to Nantwich, which still boasts its three level crossings, now all controlled from the original wooden signal box at Nantwich station. Although the station remains open, it has been reduced to bus shelter style waiting accommodation. Most of the original station building on the down side remains, now painted all over in black, and currently in use as an Indian restaurant. Of course, the platform canopies and station footbridge have gone, but the steel lattice footbridge next to the Wellington Road level crossing is still used by pedestrians. The goods yard has been taken over by commercial development.

At Willaston, only the station buildings remain, adjacent to the level crossing over Wybunbury Road, although now a private residence. And so into Crewe, where the former Gresty Lane sidings are now used by permanent way equipment, so retaining at least some of their railway heritage. The site of the engine shed has been included in the expansion of the nearby flour and corn mills.

The original station building at Willaston, on the down side facing towards Crewe, and now in use as a private residence. The platforms were between the building and the present day trackbed, which has been slightly amended. The level crossing, over Wybunbury Road is now protected by automatically-operated barriers, January 2004. *Author*

Wellington station, looking west on 10th February, 2004. The Arriva Trains class '158' is about to depart for Shrewsbury and pass into the brick-lined cutting. The Station Hotel is on the left, and it will be seen that the four-track formation has been retained at this point. *Author*

Wellington station with a Central Trains class 158 dmu arriving with a Shrewsbury to Birmingham stopping service on 10th May, 2004. One of the two former bay platforms (*left foreground*), unused for many years has been revived in a truncated form, for a new Central Trains service operating from Wellington to Walsall. *Author*

The future

The Market Drayton Railway Preservation Society was formed a number of years ago, with the intention of restoring a section of the line north of Market Drayton to working order and eventually to operate steam trains over the restored track. Apparently, a number of railway relics and parts of suitable buildings have been acquired and are in private storage away from the intended site. However, little has been accomplished on the intended trackbed, and the society would seem to face a considerable challenge with their aims. I wish them every success, and look forward to the time when their labours can be enjoyed.

Appendix One

Prospectus of the Nantwich & Market Drayton Railway

NANTWICH AND MARKET DRAYTON RAILWAY,

TO BE INCORPORATED BY ACT OF PARLIAMENT,

CAPITAL £60,000, IN 3,000 SHARES, OF £20 EACH.

DEPOSIT, £2 PER SHARE.

NO FURTHER CALL WILL BE MADE UNTIL THE ACT OF PARLIAMENT IS OBTAINED, AND THE LIABILITY OF EACH SHAREHOLDER WILL BE LIMITED TO THE AMOUNT SUBSCRIBED FOR.

PROVISIONAL DIRECTORS:

H. R. CORBET, ESQ., ADDERLEY, SHROPSHIRE, CHAIRMAN.
SIR J. N. L. CHETWODE, BART., OAKLEY, STAFFORDSHIRE.
RICHARD CORBET, ESQ., 40, PORTMAN SQUARE, LONDON, AND ADDERLEY, SHROPSHIRE.
WILLIAM TAYLEUR, ESQ., BUNTINGSDALE, SHROPSHIRE.
THOMAS TWEMLOW, ESQ., PEATSWOOD, STAFFORDSHIRE.
E. W. HARDING, ESQ., OLDSPRINGS, STAFFORDSHIRE.
CHARLES TOWNSHEND, ESQ., CHESTER.
MR. GEORGE TUNNICLIFFE, WILLOUGHBRIDGE, STAFFORDSHIRE.
MR. WILLIAM RODENHURST, MARKET DRAYTON, SHROPSHIRE.
MR. WILLIAM HARPER, MARKET DRAYTON, SHROPSHIRE.
MR. JOHN BENYON, MARKET DRAYTON, SHROPSHIRE.

WITH POWER TO ADD TO THEIR NUMBER.

ENGINEER:

JOHN GARDNER, ESQ., 18, Adam Street, Adelphi, London.

SOLICITORS:

MESSRS. WARREN AND ONIONS, Market Drayton.

SECRETARY pro tem:

G. H. WICKHAM, ESQ., Market Drayton.

BANKERS:

THE MANCHESTER AND LIVERPOOL DISTRICT BANKING COMPANY.

PARLIAMENTARY AGENTS:

MESSRS. PRITT, JONES, AND CO., London.

PROSPECTUS.

The object of this Railway is to connect the Town of Market Drayton and surrounding districts, with the Nantwich Station, on the Shrewsbury and Crewe Railway, and thus to open a communication with Liverpool,

Manchester, and the Potteries. It is brought forward with the support and co-operation of the London and North Western Railway Company, who have agreed to work the line upon fair and proper terms.

Market Drayton, with a population of 5,000, is situated in the centre of a rich Agricultural District, and the area to which the proposed line will afford accommodation is upwards of 95 Square Miles, a district without Railway communication almost unequalled in extent in this country, considering the fertility of its soil.

The report of the Engineer states the length of the line to be Ten Miles and Six Furlongs. Also that accurate Plans and Sections have been prepared, with detailed Estimates of Cost; and that the Parliamentary Plans and Sections for deposit on the 30th of November are in a forward state.

The line selected is one particularly easy of formation, being free from Tunnels; there are also but few Roads to cross, and no Mansions or Ornamental Grounds interfered with. The Curves and Gradients are all unexceptionable, there being no Curve of a less Radius than three-quarters of a mile (excepting at the Terminus where there is a Curve of half a mile Radius), and no Gradient steeper than One in One Hundred and Ten, a fact which ensures the economical working and maintenance of the line, and which is of still further importance when considering the position occupied by the proposed line upon the Railway Map of England, as it is evident that at no distant period an extension either to Newport or to some other point to the South will be carried out, and in the event of this being done, the proposed line will become one of the Trunk Lines of the Kingdom.

The proposed Railway will connect the highly productive Agricultural Districts around Market Drayton, with the great consuming Districts of the Potteries, Staffordshire, and the North. The whole of the traffic, consisting of corn, cheese, and cattle, from Market Drayton and its Neighbourhood, will pass over the proposed line, and a traffic in return of coal, lime, manure, and general merchandise, may be relied upon, in addition to which there is the Passenger traffic from the Towns of Market Drayton and Audlem, and the Villages of Adderley, Norton, and other places on and near the proposed line.

The experience of the last few years has shewn that no Railways constructed, even through a country purely Agricultural, when the traffic has been fully developed, produce less than £10 to £15 per mile, per week, equal to £520 to £780 per mile per annum gross traffic, and a mileage traffic of only the former amount per week, would yield a dividend of five per cent. upon the proposed outlay, after allowing even as much as 50 per cent. for working expenses; and it is anticipated from the character of the works and Gradients, the working expenses will be below 50 per cent.

The Stations proposed are frequent, so as to give the fullest accommodation to the district, and are as follows:—Market Drayton, Adderley, and Audlem.

Upwards of 2,050 Shares have already been subscribed for by persons locally interested, and residing in the district, a fact in itself bespeaking the importance of the project, and the favourable opinion entertained of it.

Application for the remaining Shares to be made in the annexed form to the Secretary, Solicitors, or Bankers.

Appendix Four

Working Timetable, 1865

All trains are passenger trains, and run Monday to Saturday only.

	C		C		WO
	am	*am*	*pm*	*pm*	*pm*
Market Drayton	8.30	11.50	2.45	5.50	10.20
Adderley	8.40	12.00 *noon*	2.55	6.00	10.30
Audlem	8.45	12.05 *pm*	3.00	6.05	10.35
Nantwich	9.00	12.20	3.15	6.20	10.50

	C		C		WO
	am	*pm*	*pm*	*pm*	*pm*
Nantwich	9.30	12.50	4.05	7.00	11.00
Audlem	9.45	1.05	4.20	7.15	11.15
Adderley	9.50	1.10	4.25	7.20	11.20
Market Drayton	10.00	1.20	4.35	7.30	11.30

Notes

C Also conveys goods traffic.
WO Runs on Wednesdays only.

Working Timetable, January to June 1870

Up trains - Weekdays		*Goods*	*Goods*	*Pass.*	*Goods*	*Pass.*	*Goods*	*Goods*	*Pass.*	*Pass.*	*Local Goods*	*Pass.*	*Pass.*	*Goods*	*Goods*
		MO			RR			MX							
		am	*pm*	*am*	*am*	*am*	*am*	*noon*	*pm*	*pm*	*pm*	*pm*	*pm*	*pm*	*pm*
Leeds			8.35												7.35
Manchester (London Road)						8.40			11.45	1.30		4.15	5.15		
Manchester (Liverpool Road)			*am*						*pm*					6.30	9.05
Crewe	*dep.*	1.10	3.50	7.45	8.45	9.40	9.50	12.00	1.08	3.05	3.50	5.15	7.05	8.45	11.40
Nantwich			5.50	7.55		9.50			1.17	3.16	4.25	5.24	7.15		
Audlem				8.09		10.03				3.31	4.45		7.28		
Adderley				8.15		10.08		*pm*		3.38	4.55		7.33		
Market Drayton	*arr.*		6.40				10.45	1.05			5.10				
	dep.		6.50	8.22	CR	10.16	10.50	1.40	1.35	3.46	5.47	5.42	7.41	CR	CR
Hodnet			7.15	8.34		10.28				3.57	6.05		7.52		
Peplow Siding											CR				*am*
Crudgington			7.45	8.50		Thur				4.12	CR		8.07	10.05	1.10
Wellington	*arr.*	2.50	8.00	9.05	10.30	10.50	11.45	2.30	2.05	4.25	6.45	6.12	8.20	10.10	1.20
	dep.	3.00	8.25		10.40		12.00				7.00			11.00	
Oxley Sidings		4.00	9.25				1.10				8.10				
Wolverhampton (Victoria Basin)					12.20										
Worcester															5.55

Up trains - Sundays		**Pass.**	**Goods**	**Pass.**
		am	***am***	***pm***
Manchester (London Road)				4.15
Manchester (Liverpool Road)				
Crewe	*dep.*	7.10	9.30	6.10
Nantwich		7.20		6.20
Audlem		7.34		6.34
Adderley		7.39		6.39
Market Drayton	*arr.*		10.25	
	dep.	7.47	10.30	6.47
Hodnet		7.59		6.59
Peplow Siding				
Crudgington		8.15		7.15
Wellington	*arr.*	8.30	11.20	7.30
	dep.		11.30	
Oxley Sidings			12.35	

Notes

MO	Mondays only.
MX	Mondays excepted.
RR	Runs as required.
CR	Conditional request (calls to stop if the train has not a full load on).
Thur	Calls on Thursdays only.

Down trains - Weekdays

		Goods	Goods	Goods	Pass.	Goods	Pass.	Pass.	Local Goods	Pass.	Goods	Pass.	Local Goods	Pass.	Goods
		MX	MX	MX		MX									
		pm	*am*	*pm*	*am*	*am*	*am*	*am*	*am*	*pm*	*pm*	*pm*	*pm*	*pm*	*pm*
Paddington Goods				9.50											
Bordesley Junction		10.45													
Worcester															7.39
Wolverhampton (Victoria Basin)			2.30												
Oxley Sidings		*am*		*am*		7.30			10.00		2.50		8.00		
Wellington	*arr.*	1.55	4.00	5.50					11.00		3.50		8.55		11.20
	dep.	2.00	4.10	6.00	7.50	8.40	9.46	11.55	11.20	2.25	4.00	5.25	9.05	8.20	11.30
Crudgington					8.06				11.35	Thur		5.38			
Peplow Siding									CR						
Hodnet					8.21			12.15	12.20	R		5.53		8.40	*am*
Market Drayton	*arr.*	2.50	5.10					12.26	12.35		4.50				12.20
	dep.	2.55	5.20	CR	8.33	CR	10.07	12.34	12.50	2.55	5.00	6.04	CR	8.51	12.25
Adderley					8.41				1.00	R		6.12			
Audlem					8.46				1.15	3.05		6.17		9.03	
Nantwich					9.00			12.49	1.45	3.15		6.30		9.15	
Crewe	*arr.*	3.40	6.20	7.30	9.10	10.15	10.36	12.58	2.00	3.25	5.55	6.40	11.00	9.25	1.45
Manchester (Liverpool Road)		6.55		10.10		2.55							2.55		4.40
Manchester (London Road)					11.05		11.45	2.00		4.25		7.45		10.55	

Down trains - Sundays

		Pass.	**Pass.**
		am	***pm***
Wellington	*dep.*	9.00	7.55
Crudgington		9.15	8.10
Peplow Siding			
Hodnet		9.31	8.26
Market Drayton	*arr.*		
	dep.	9.43	8.38
Adderley		9.51	8.46
Audlem		9.56	8.51
Nantwich		10.10	9.05
Crewe	*arr.*	10.20	9.15

Notes

MO	Mondays only.
MX	Mondays excepted.
R	Calls as required.
CR	Conditional request (calls to stop if the train has not a full load on).
Thur	Calls on Thursdays only.

GWR Working Timetable, May 1898

WELLINGTON, MARKET DRAYTON AND CREWE.

DOWN TRAINS. WEEK DAYS.

Distance from Wellington. M	C	STATIONS.		1	2	3	4	5	6	7	8	9	10	11	12	13	14	15	16	17	18	19	20	21	22	23
				B	F	B	B	B	B	B	A	Spcl B RR	A	C	A	B	D	A	A	A		F	B		A	
				B'dsly, W'hton & Y'kshr Exp. Goods.	Wstr, L'pool & North Express Goods.	N.S. Goods Train.	W'hampton L.&Y. Express Goods.	L'd'n&S'thptn Exp. Goods to M'nch'r & N'th	3.30 a.m. Goods from Shrewsbury.	Birm, Wolver-h'mptn&North Express Goods.	Passenger.	Cattle Train	Passenger.	W'ster&Crewe thro' Goods.	Passenger.	W'ster &Crewe thro' Goods.	Local Goods.	Passenger.	Passenger.	Passenger.		Broccoli Train.	Goods.		Passenger.	
M	C			P.M.	P.M.	A.M.	P.M.	P.M.	A.M.	A.M.	A.M.	A.M.	A.M.	A.M.	A.M.	A.M.	A.M.	A.M.	A.M.	P.M.		P.M.	P.M.		P.M.	
		London	dep.	....		....	....	9 50	....	....	....	....	....	....	6 30	....	....	9 50	9 45	....	....	....	....	....	1 30	....
		Basingstoke ..	,,	..	Returns at 11.45 p.m. ex Crewe.		..	9 30	..	..	..	..	..	..	—	..	..	—	—	..	..	..	M	..	—	..
		Reading	,,	....			....	9 55	....	....	....	....	....	....	7 46	....	....	—	11 0	....	....	....	....	....	—	....
		Oxford	,,	..			..	12 10	..	..	..	MO	..	..	8 42	..	..	11 13	11 48	..	..	RR	..	..	2 53	..
		Bordesley Junction	,,	7 35		Worked by N.S. Engine over G.W. Line.	....	A.M.	....	....	....	..	....	M	—	MO	....	—	—	....	....	....	H	....	—	....
		Hockley	,,	—			..	—	..	..	..	....	..	..	—	..	..	—	—	..	..	..	..	..	—	..
		Worcester	,,	—	8 25		....	—	....	....	....	....	....	2 15	—	5 15	....	—	—	....	....	....	....	....	—	....
		Victoria Basin ..	,,	—	—		11 20	3 15	..	.	..	..	..	—	—	—	9 0	—	—	..	..	2 0	2 35	..	—	..
		Oxley Siding	arr.	9 58	11 0		11 25	3 25	....	....	....	....	....	5 30	—	9 50	9 5	—	—	....	....	2 10	2 45	....	—	....
			dep.	11 5	11 45	M	12 20	3 55	..	4 40	..	..	..	8 30	—	10 30	9 30	—	—	..	..	2 40	3 0	..	—	..
		Wellington	arr.	11 55	12 30	....	1 10	—	....	5 30	....	....	....	9 45	—	11 30	11 45	1 40	—	....	....	3 25	4 25	....	—	....
—	—	**Wellington** ..	dep.	12 5	12 45	1 0	1 20	4 40	4 50	5 40	7 38	..	9 50	10 0	11 40	12 10	12 30	1 50	2 55	..	..	3 40	4 50	..	5 45	..
4	55½	Crudgington	,,	F	A.M.	—	—	—	—	—	7 47	....	L	—	11 49	—	12 55	2 1	3 4	....	....	—	5 10	....	5 54	....
8	67½	Peplow	,,	—	—	—	—	—	—	—	7 56	..	—	—	11 59	—	1 10	2 11	3 13	..	..	—	—	..	6 3	..
11	1½	Hodnet	,,	M	M	—	M	M	5 30	M	8 2	....	10 9	—	12 7	—	1 45	2 20	3 19	....	....	—	5 30	....	6 9	..
		Tern Hill	,,	—	—	—	—	—	—	—	—	RR	—	—	—	—	O R	—	—	..	..	—	—	..	—	....
16	52	**Market Drayton**	arr.	—	—	1 40	—	WO	5 45	6 20	8 12	..	10 18	10 40	12 16	12 55	2 0	2 33	3 28	..	..	4 15	5 45	..	6 18	..
			dep.	—	—		—	—	6 30	6 30	8 17	8 30	10 21	10 50	12 21	1 15	2 30		3 33	4 30	....	4 50	6 35	....	6 24	..
20	11½	Adderley ..	,,	—	—		—	—		—	8 25	CR	10 29	—	12 29	—	2 50	..	3 41	4 38	..	—	—	....	6 32	....
22	7	Audlem	arr.	—	—	Return to 9.35 p.m. ex Stoke.	—	—	For Stoke on Trent Returns at 10.30 a.m.	—	—	CR	10 33	CR	12 33	—	—	....	3 46	4 42	....	—	—	....	6 37	..
			dep.	—	—		—	—		—	8 31	—	10 36	—	12 36	—	3 5	..	3 50	4 46	..	—	—	..	6 41	....
27*	39	Nantwich	,,	—	—		—	5 40		—	8 40	—	10 45	—	12 50	1 55	3K35	....	4 0	4 54	....	5 20	7 20	....	6 53	..
32	—	**Crewe**	arr.	1 35	2 0		2 40	5 55		7 10	8 50	9 30	10 55	11 30	1 0	2 10	3 50	..	4 12	5 5	..	5 35	7 35	..	7 5	..
—	—	**Crewe**	dep.	2 45	2 35		4 0	6 25		....	9 12	....	11 5		1 10	....	3 50	....	4 25	5 20	....	....	9 20	....	7 15	....
		Stockport	arr.	—	—		—	—		..	9 45	..	11 56	..	1 45	..	—	..	5 4	5 58	..	..	—	..	7 48	..
		Edgeley Junction	,,	3 45	—		5 0	7 30		....	—	....	—	....	—	....	6 55	....	—	—	....	....	10 25	....	—	....
		Longsight ..	,,	—	—		5 45	—		..	—	..	—	..	—	..	—	..	—	—	..	..	—	..	—	....
		Manchester (Lon. Rd)	,,	—	—		—	—		....	9 57	....	12 8	....	1 58	....	—	....	5 16	6 10	....	....	—	....	8 0	..
		,, (L'pl. Rd)	,,	—	—		6 20	8 30		..		..		..		..	—	..			..	..	—	..		....
—	—	Huddersfield	,,	5 30	—	....	....	10 40	....	....	....	....	....	....	....	....	9 5	....	....	....	....	....	—	....	....	..
—	—	Halifax	,,	7 30	—	..	..	12 20	..	..	..	..	..	..	..	..	4 50	..	..	..	..	..	—	..	..	..
—	—	Bradford	,,	7 35	—	....	....	12 55	....	....	....	....	....	....	....	....	3 50	....	....	....	....	....	3 50	....	....	....
—	—	Leeds	,,	7 27	—	..	..	1 35	..	..	..	..	..	..	..	..	11 30	..	..	..	..	..	3 5	..	..	..
		Liverpool (Edge Hill)	,,		4 0	....	....	10 20	....	....	....	....	....	....	....	....		....	....	....	....	....	11 40	....	....	....
		Preston	,,	..	5 25	..	..	7 40	..	..	..	..	..	..	..	..	..	..	..	..	..	.	11 0	..	..	..

F These Trains will stop at Wellington for examination purposes only. H To convey mixed Traffic. K Arrives at Nantwich at 3.30 p.m.
L Calls at Crudgington to pick up Passengers for Crewe or beyond. * Distance at Junction Points.

WELLINGTON, MARKET DRAYTON AND CREWE—*Continued.*

DOWN TRAINS. WEEK DAYS.

STATIONS.		24	25	26	27	28	29	30	31	32	33	34	35	36
		U	F		A	F	C	F		F	F			
		Goods. MO	Brocoli Train.		Passenger.	W'ster&Crewe Vegetable Express Train.	Wol'hampton and Crewe Goods.	W'ster &Crewe Veg'ble Train.		Exp. Veg'table Train for Yorkshire.	Exp. Veg.'Trn. W'cester. to Manchester.	Exp. Veg'table Train Worcester to Crewe.		
		P.M.	P.M.		P.M.	P.M.	P.M.	P.M.		P.M.	P.M.	P.M.		
London	dep.	....	....	....	4 45	....	....	....	....	....	....	....	....	....
Basingstoke ..	,,	..	..	..	—	RR	..	RR	..	..	..	..	..	..
Reading	,,	....	....	....	—	....	....	....	....	....	....	....	....	....
Oxford	,,	..	..	..	6 9	..	..	..	..	..	....	..	..	..
Bordesley Junction	,,	....	RR	....	—	....	RR	....	....	....	S	....	....	....
Hockley	,,	..	..	..	—	..	..	..	..	..	..	RR	..	..
Worcester	,,	H	....	....	—	5 J 50	....	7N10	....	7 30	7 50	8 5	....	....
Victoria Basin ..	,,	2 35	4 35	..	—	—	6 30	—	..	—	—	—	..	..
Oxley Siding	arr.	2 45	4 40	....	—	7 32	6 35	8 45	....	9 23	9 35	10 5	....	....
	dep.	3 0	5 30	..	—	8 20	7 20	9 12	..	9 37	9 55	10 25	..	..
Wellington ..	arr.	4 25	6 18	....	—	—	8 35	10 0	....	—	—	—	....	....
Wellington	dep.	6 0	6 30	..	8 55	9 5	9 10	10 10	..	10 28	10 40	11 13	..	..
Crudgington	,,	—	F	....	Sat.	—	—	F	....	—	—	—	....	....
Peplow	,,	—	—	..	Sat.	—	—	—	..	—	—	—	..	..
Hodnet	,,	—	—	....	9 13	—	—	—	....	—	—	—	....	....
Tern Hill ..	,,	—	—	..	—	—	—	—	..	—	—	—	..	..
Market Drayton	arr.	6 40	—	..	9 22	9 40	9 45	—	..	11W3	11W15	—	..	..
	dep.	7 30	7 15	....	9 25	9 45	9 50	—	....	11 0 8	11 0 20	—	....	....
Adderley	,,	—	—	..	Sat.	—	—	—	..	—	—	—	..	..
Audlem	arr.	—	—	....	9 34	—	—	—	....	—	—	—	....	....
..	dep.	—	—	..	9 36	—	—	—	..	—	—	—	..	..
Nantwich	,,	8 15	7 45	....	9 48	—	—	11 10	....	—	11 55	—	....	....
Crewe	arr.	8 30	7 56	..	9 58	10 25	10 45	11 25	..	11 45	12 10	12 35	..	..
Crewe	dep.	9 20	9 20	....	10 18	....	....	....	....	....	12 42	Returns 12.0 noon ex Crewe.	....	....
Stockport ..	arr.	—	—	..	11 15	..	..	Returns at 10.15 a.m. Coupled to No. 33	..	Returns 2.0 a.m. ex Crewe.	—		..	..
Edgeley Junction	,,	10 25	10 25	..	—	..	..		..		1 40		..	..
Longsight ..	,,	—	—	....	—	....	....		....		2 22		....	....
Manchester(Lon. Rd.)	,,	—	—	..	11 28	..	..		..		—		..	..
,, (L'pl. Rd.)	,,	—	—	....	....	....	....		....		2 50		....	....
Huddersfield	,,	—	—	..	..	..	..		..		Returns 10.15 a.m. ex Crewe.		..	..
Halifax	,,	—	—	....	....	....	....		....				....	....
Bradford	,,	3 50	3 50	..	..	..	..		..				..	..
Leeds	,,	3 5	3 5	....	....	....	....		....				....	....
Liverpool (Edge Hill)	,,			..	..	..	..	..	..	..			..	..
Preston	,,	....	..	....	..	..	..	....	....	..		..	....	....

SUNDAYS.

STATIONS.		1	2	3	4	5	6	7	8	9	10	11
		B	F	B	B	B	B	B	A			
		B'dsly, W'hptn & Yorkshire Exp. Goods.	W'cster, L'pool & North Exp. Goods.	N. S. Goods Train.	B'gham, W'ptn & L. & Y. Exp. Goods.	Express Goods Birm'gham&c. to North.	W'hampton & North Fast Goods.	Wolv'hampton and Crewe Goods.	Passenger.			
		P.M.	P.M.	A.M.	P.M.	P.M.	A.M.	P.M.	P.M.			
London	dep.	Starts on Sat'day.	Starts on Sat'day night.	Worked by N. S. Engine over G. W. Line	Starts on Sat'day night.	9 50	....	....	....	....	....	....
Basingstoke ..	,,					9 30	..	..	..	..	..	..
Reading	,,					9 55	....	....	....	....	....	....
Oxford	,,					12 10	..	..	..	..	..	..
Bordesley Junction	,,		....		....	A.M.	....	....	....	....	....	....
Hockley	,,	—	..		..	—	.	..	..	..	..	..
Worcester	,,	—	8 25		....	—	. .	....	....	....	....	....
Victoria Basin ..	,,	—	—		11 20	3 15	..	5 15	..	..	..	..
Oxley Siding	arr.	9 58	11 0		11 25	3 25	....	5 25	....	....	....	....
	dep.	11 5	11 45		12 20	3 55	4 40	5 55	..	..	..	..
Wellington ..	arr.	11 55	12 30		1 10	—	5 30	6 45	....	....	....	....
Wellington	dep.	12 5	12 45	1 0	1 20	4 40	5 40	6 55	7 40	..	..	..
Crudgington	,,	F	—	—	—	—	—	—	7 49	....	....	....
Peplow	,,	—	—	—	—	—	—	—	7 58	..	..	..
Hodnet	,,	—	—	—	—	—	—	—	8 4	....	....	....
Tern Hill ..	,,	—	—	—	—	—	—	—	—	..	..	..
Market Drayton	arr.	—	—	1 40	—	WO	6 20	7 30	8 13	..	..	..
	dep.	—	—	Return to 9.35 p.m. ex Stoke.	—	—	6 30	7 50	8 19	....	....	....
Adderley	,,	—	—		—	—	—	—	8 27	..	..	..
Audlem	arr.	—	—		—	—	—	—	8 32	....	....	....
..	dep.	—	—		—	—	—	—	8 36	..	..	..
Nantwich	,,	—	—		—	5 40	—	8 25	8 50	....	....	....
Crewe	arr.	1 35	2 0		2 40	5 55	7 10	8 40	9 0	..	..	..
Crewe	dep.	2 45	4 0		4 0	3 45	—	12 25	9 6	....	....	....
Stockport ..	arr.	—	RR		RR	—	—	—	9 43	..	..	..
Edgeley Junction	,,	3 45	5 0		5 0	7 46	—	1 25	—	....	....	....
Longsight ..	,,	—	5 48		5 48	8 50	—	2 15	—	..	..	..
Manchester(Lon. Rd.)	,,	—	—		—	9 6	—	2 40	9 55	....	....	....
,, (L'pl. Rd.)	,,	—	6 15		6 15	9 30	—	3 0	..	..	..	..
Huddersfield	,,	5 30	—		....	—	....	....	....	....	....	....
Halifax	,,	—	—		..	—	..	..	..	..	..	..
Bradford	,,	—	—		....	—	....	....	....	....	....	....
Leeds	,,	7 27	—	..	..	—	..	..	..	..	..	..
Liverpool (Edge Hill)	,,		3 55	....	....	2 20	....	....	....	....	....	....
Preston	,,	..	5 40	..	..	9 35	..	..	..	..	..	..

F These Trains will stop at Wellington for examination purposes only, **H** To convey Mixed Traffic. **J** 4.0 p.m ex Littleton and Badsey. **N** 6.15 p.m. ex Evesham.

WELLINGTON, MARKET DRAYTON AND CREWE.—*Continued.*

UP TRAINS—WEEK DAYS.

STATIONS.	1	2	3	4	5	6	7	8	9	10	11	12	13	14	15	16	17	18	
		B	B	B	B	B	B	A	D	C	B	A	C	D	E	C	A	D	
		Goods.	Exp. Goods for Bir. W.M. Dist. and Worcester.	Goods.	Crewe and Oxley Goods.	Fast Goods.	Express Goods.	Passenger.	Goods.	Goods.	Express Goods.	Passenger.	Goods.	Stoke and Salop Goods.	Passenger. O	Goods.	Passsenger.	Local Goods.	
																		arr.	dep.
		A.M.	A.M.	P.M.	A.M.	A.M.	A.M.	A.M.	A.M.	A.M.	A.M.	A.M.	A.M.	P.M.	A.M.	NOON.	A.M.	P.M.	A.M.
Liverpool (Edge Hill) dep.	..	..	12 5	..	..	12 30	..	..	..	..	..	..	..	..	..	..	..	..	..
Preston .... ,,	....	RR	—	....	RR	12 20	....	....	....	....	....	....	....	....		....	....	....	....
Leeds .. .. ,,	..	Return to 6.30 p.m. from Victoria Basin.	—	8 40	Sundays excepted.	—	..	..	..	12 15	..	..	..	..	Will run on alternate Tuesdays. First date May 3rd.	..	..	..	8 35
Bradford .... ,,	....		—	—		—	....	....	....	10 15	....	....	....	....		....	....	—	5 0
Halifax .. .. ,,	..		—	—		—	..	..	..	—	..	..	..	..		..	..	—	..
Huddersfield(H'house) ,,	....		—	—		—	....	....	....	—	....	....	3 24	....		RR	....	—	9 52
Manchester(L'pool Rd.),,	..		—	—		—	..		..	M	..	..	—	..		..	..	—	—
Do. (London Rd.) ,,	....		—	—		—	....	....	....	—	....	8 35	—	....		....	11 50	—	—
Longsight .. .. ,,	..		—	—		—	..	..	..	—	..	—	—	..		..	—	—	—
Heaton Norris .... ,,	....		—	12 40		1 50	....	....	....	5 45	....	—	7 15	....		....	—	—	12 10
Stockport .. .. ,,	..		—	—		—	..	..	..	—	..	8 47	—	..		..	12 4	—	—
Crewe .... arr.	....		1 35	1 55	M	3 15	....	....	....	7 10	....	9 25	8 45	....		....	12 52	1 35	—
Crewe .... dep.	....	12 30	2 0	RR 2 30	3 20	4 30	5 20	6 55	G 7 30	M 7 30	8 30	9 40	M 10 15	....		12 0	1 7	—	2 40
Nantwich .. .. ,,	..	M	M	—	—	M	—	7 5	—	J	—	9 50	—	..		—	1 17	2 50	•3 25
Audlem .... ,,	....	....	—	M	—	—	—	7 18	7 55	7 55	M	10 3	—	....		—	1 30	3 40	4 0
Adderley .. .. ,,	..	..	—	—	—	—	—	7 24	—	—	—	10 9	—	..	..	—	1 36	4 10	4 20
Market Drayton arr.	....	1 15	—	3 20	4 0	5 10	6 0	7 30	8 15	8 15	—	10 14	11 0	12 15	....	12 45	1 42	4 30	—
Market Drayton dep.	..	1 40	—	3 40	4 10	5 20	6 10	7 34	8 45	8 35	9 15	10•18	11 10	2 50	*11 45*	12 55	1W50	—	5 5
Tern Hill .. .. ,,	....	---	—	—	—	—	—	—	CR	—	—	—	—	3 15	—	—	—	—	—
Hodnet .... ,,	..	—	—	—	—	—	—	7 44	9 5	J	—	10 28	—	4 10	*11 54*	—	2 0	C	R
Peplow .. .. ,,	....	—	—	—	—	—	—	7 51	9 20	—	—	10 34	—	4 35		—	2 7	C	R
Crudgington .... arr.	..	—	H	—	—	—	H	7 59	—	—	H	10 42	H	4 45	..	—	2 15	5 45	—
Crudgington .... dep.	....	—	—	—	—	—	—	8 3	9 35	—	—	10 45	—	5 45	....	—	2 18	—	•6 30
Wellington .... arr.	..	2 25	3 20	4 25	4 50	6 10	6 55	8 13	9 55	9 15	9 55	10 55	11 50	6 0	..	1 40	2 28	6 50	—
Wellington .. dep.	..	2 40	3 30	4 40	5 10	6 25	7 5	8 26	10 15	9 35	10 10	11 10	11 55		..	2 5	2 30	—	7 0
Oxley Siding .. arr.	....	3 40	4 25	5 45	6 10	7 20	8 0	—	12 40	11 5	12 15	—	12 50	Return of 3.30 a.m. ex Salop.	....	2 55	—	8 5	8 35
Oxley Siding .. dep.	..	4 20	4 50	6 10		9 5	8 30	—	1 0	11 20		—	2 55		..	4 20	—		
Victoria Basin .... arr.	....	4 30	—	6 20	....	—	8 40	—	1 5	11 25	....	—	—		....	—	—	....	....
Worcester .. .. ,,	..		8 23		..	2 28		—			..	—	6 25		..	7 35	—	..	..
Hockley .... ,,	....	....		....	....		....	—	....	....	....	—	Return of 7.50 p.m. from W'str.		....		—	....	....
Bordesley Junction ,,	..	..	Return of 7.30 p.m. ex W'str.	..	..	..	..	—	..	..	..	—			..	..	—	..	..
Oxford .... ,,	....	....		....	....	....	....	10 50	....	....	....	1 57			....	....	5 40	....	....
Reading .. .. ,,	..	..		..	..	..	..	11§33	..	..	..	2§45			..	..	6 27	..	..
Basingstoke .... ,,	....	....		....	....	....	....	—	....	....	....	—			....	....	—	....	....
London .. .. arr.	..	..		..	..	..	..	12 15	..	..	..	3 30			..	..	7 35	..	..

G This Train to run on Mondays only and work the Cattle from the Local Stations to Wellington.

H These Trains will stop at Wellington for examination purposes only.

J This Train does the Lawton Siding work. When not running Mr. Gibson must advise Mr. Cox and arrange for the following train to do the Lawton work. To stop at Nantwich and Hodnet on alternate Tuesdays—Hodnet Sale days.

K To take forward from Market Drayton and Wellington Potato traffic for South Wales to go forward by the 9.45 p.m. ex Chester. It is important this Train should leave Wellington punctually.

L This Train to be marshalled as follows :—Engine, Trucks for London and intermediate Stations to Wolverhampton—Trucks. for Worcester, Wolverhampton, and W. M. Stations—Trucks for Stations between Worcester and Oxford—Brake Van.

O With Passengers arriving by N. S. Train due at Market Drayton 11.47 a.m., which Train will run through to Hodnet. To be worked by Engine and Men of N. S. Pass. Train from Stoke, to return to Market Drayton at once. Mr. THOMAS, Hodnet, to count the Passengers alighting from the Special, and advise Superintendent's Office of the number.

V Runs on Thursdays and Fridays.

W Can leave Platform 1.47 p.m.

WELLINGTON, MARKET DRAYTON, AND CREWE—*Continued.*

WEEK DAYS—*Continued.*

STATIONS.	19	20	21	22	23	24	25	26	27	28
	A	A	B	A	A	B	B	B	B	B
	Passenger.	Passenger.	**Goods.**	Passenger.	Passenger.	Mrkt. Drayton and Salop **Goods.**	**Goods** N.S. Express.	M'chstr. B'stoke & Southampton Express **Goods.**	Return Brocoli Train.	M'chstr. Yks. Exp. **Goods** for W. M. Disct. & Worcester.
	P.M.	P.M.	P.M.	P.M.	P.M.	P.M.	P.M.	P.M.	P.M.	P.M.
Liverpool (Edge Hill) dep.	..	..	..	..	..	..	..	..	..	9 5
Preston .... ,,	....	....	....	....	....	K	....	1 45	....	—
Leeds .. .. ,,	..	..	..	..	..	..	Worked by N. S. Engine over G. W. Line.	—	..	—
Bradford .... ,,	....	....	....	....	....	....		—	....	—
Halifax .. .. ,,	..	..	..	..	..	..		—	..	—
Huddersfield (H'house) ,,	....	....	....	....	....	....		—	....	—
Manchester (L'pool Rd) ,,	..	..	..	..	..	..		8 25	..	9 40
Do. (London Rd) ,,	2 10	4 15	....	5 17	7 0	....		—	....	—
Longsight .. .. ,,	—	—	..	—	—	....		—	..	10 5
Heaton Norris .... ,,	—	—	....	—	—	....		—	..	—
Stockport .. .. ,,	2 22	4 30	..	5 30	7 12	..		—	..	—
Crewe .... arr.	2 55	5 3	....	6 25	7·45	....		9 52	RR	11 30
Crewe .... dep.	3 10	5 10	5 20	6 50	8 10	....		10 2	10 45	L 11 45
Nantwich .. .. ,,	3 20	5 20	5 35	7 0	8 20	..		—	—	—
Audlem .... ,,	3 31	5 33	—	7 13	8 33	..	..	—	—	—
Adderley .. .. ,,	3 36	5 39	—	7 19	8 39	..	....	—	—	—
Market Drayton arr.	3 42	5 45	6 10	7 25	8 45	....	..	W O	11 25	12 25
Market Drayton dep.	3 45	5 50	6 40	7X30	Works 9.45 p.m. Goods Market Drayton to Shrewsbury.	9 45	10 50		11 35	12 35
Terne Hill .. .. ,,	—	—	—	—		—	—	—	—	—
Hodnet .... ,,	3 54	6 0	—	7 40		—	—	—	—	—
Peplow .. .. ,,	3 59	6 7	—	7 47		—	—	—	—	—
Crudgington .... arr.	4 7	6 15	—	7 55		—	—	—	—	—
Crudgington .... dep.	4P9	6 20	—	8 0		—	—	—	—	—
Wellington .. arr.	4 18	6 32	7 25	8 10		10 30	11 35	—	12 20	—
Wellington .... dep.	4 42	6 50	7 35	..		Worked by Engine of 8.10 p.m. from Crewe. Runs to Salop.	..	11 22	12 30	1 20
Oxley Siding .. arr.	—	—	8 35	....			....	12 22	1 30	2 20
Oxley Siding .. dep.	—	—	8 50	..			..	12 40	1 50	3 0
Victoria Basin .... arr.	—	—	8 55	....			....	—	1 55	—
Worcester .. .. ,,	—	—	..	..			..	—		5 50
Hockley .... ,,	—	—	....	....			....	1 10	....	—
Bordesley Junction ,,	—	—	..	..			..	—	..	—
Oxford .... ,,	7 16	9 16	....	....			....	5 20	....	7 0
Reading .. .. ,,	8§ 0	10§2	..	..			..	—	..	8 55
Basingstoke .... ,,	—	—	....	....			....	5 20	....	10 0
London .... ,,	8 45	10 45	..	..			..	6 50	..	12 5

SUNDAYS.

STATIONS.	1	2	3	4	5	6	7	8	
		B	B	B			A	B	
		Express Goods for Southampton, Birmingham, WM. district, and Worcester.	Goods. RR	Goods.			Passenger.	Goods.	
		A.M.	A.M.	A.M.			A.M.	A.M.	
Liverpool (Edge Hill) dep.	..	..	..	..	..	..	..	..	..
Preston .... ,,	....	....	....	....	....	....	....	....	....
Leeds .. .. ,,	..	..	..	..	..	..	..	..	..
Bradford .... ,,	....	....	....	....	....	....	....	....	....
Halifax .. .. ,,	..	..	..	..	..	..	..	..	..
Huddersfield (H'house) ,,	....	....	....	....	....	....	....	....	....
Manchester (L'pool Rd) ,,	..	..	..	..	..	..	..	..	..
Do. (London Rd) ,,	....	....	....	....	....	....	....	....	....
Longsight .. .. ,,	..	..	..	..	..	..	..	..	..
Heaton Norris .... ,,	....	....	....	....	....	....	....	....	....
Stockport .. .. ,,	..	..	..	..	..	..	..	..	..
Crewe .... arr.	....	....	....	....	....	....	....	....	....
Crewe .... dep.	....	2 0	2 30	4 30	....	..	8 0	8 30	....
Nantwich .. .. ,,	..	—	—	—	..	....	8 10	—	..
Audlem .... ,,	....	—	—	—	..	....	8 23	—	....
Adderley .. .. ,,	..	—	—	—	..	....	8 29	—	..
Market Drayton arr.	....	—	3 20	5 10	....	..	8 35	9 5	....
Market Drayton dep.	..	—	3 40	5 20	..	....	8 37	9 15	..
Terne Hill .. .. ,,	..	—	—	—	..	..	—	—	..
Hodnet .... ,,	....	—	—	—	....	..	8 47	—	....
Peplow .. .. ,,	..	—	—	—	..	..	8 56	—	..
Crudgington .... arr.	....	H	—	—	....	..	9 4	—	....
Crudgington .... dep.	..	—	—	—	..	..	9 6	—	..
Wellington .. arr.	....	3 20	4 25	6 10	....	....	9 15	10 0	....
Wellington .... dep.	..	3 30	4 40	6 25	..	..	..	10 30	..
Oxley Siding .. arr.	....	4 25	5 45	7 20	....	....	....	11 20	....
Oxley Siding .. dep.	..	4 50	6 10	7 40	..	..	..	11 50	..
Victoria Basin .... arr.	....	—	6 20	7 50	....	..	....	11 55	....
Worcester .. .. ,,	..	8 5	..	..	..	..	..	..	..
Hockley .... ,,	....	....	....	....	....	....	....	....	....
Bordesley Junction ,,	..	..	..	..	..	..	..	..	..
Oxford .... ,,	....	....	....	....	....	....	....	....	....
Reading .. .. ,,	..	..	..	..	..	..	..	..	..
Basingstoke .... ,,	....	....	....	....	....	....	....	....	....
London .... ,,	..	..	..	..	..	..	..	..	..

§ Slip Coach.

P Crudgington to wire Wellington when there are Passengers in the 3.10 p.m. ex Crewe for the Bristol Express.

X Can leave Platform 7.28 p.m.

Up Goods running through Market Drayton.

Enginemen of Up Goods Trains fully loaded from Crewe and not requiring to take water at Market Drayton must give a Crow on passing Adderley during the day, and Audlem at night, and the Signalman at Adderley or Audlem, as the case may be, will then advise the Market Drayton Junction Signalman that the approaching Train is prepared to run through Market Drayton without stopping.

Code.—Asia.
Text of Message represented by Code.—
Coming Train does not want to stop at Market Drayton.

NORTH STAFFORDSHIRE TRAINS.

STATIONS.	WEEK DAYS.											SUNDAYS	
	G. W. Goods to Stoke.	Passenger.	Passenger.		Passenger.	Passenger.	Passengers Wednesdays only.		Goods.	Passenger.	Goods	Passenger.	Passenger.
M'Drayton. dep.	A.M. 6 30	A.M. 8 30	A.M. 10 30	....	P.M. 12 30	P.M. 3 35	P.M. 4 45	....	P.M. 5 30	P.M. 6 55	P.M. 8 45	A.M. 9 52	P.M. 7 25
STATION.	Passenger Wednesdays only.	Passenger.	Passenger. MO	Passenger.	G. W. Goods ex Stoke.	Passenger.	Goods.	Passenger.	Passenger Saturdays excepted.	Passenger Saturdays only.	Goods.	Passenger.	Passenger.
M'Drayton arr.	A.M. 9 50	A.M. 10 6	A.M. 11 0	A.M. 11 40	P.M. 12 15	P.M. 1 35	P.M. 5 5	P.M. 5 37	P.M. 8 10	P.M. 9 16	P.M. 10 30	A.M. 9 39	P.M. 9 16

BR (LMR) Working Timetable, 8th June to 20th September, 1953

Down Trains. WELLINGTON, MARKET DRAYTON AND CREWE. Week Days.

Mile Post Mileage from Paddington via Oxford M.	C.	Distance from Wellington M.	C.	STATIONS.	Ruling Gradient 1 in	Allow for Stop. Mins.	Allow for Start. Mins.	Point-to-Point Times "C" Head Code Mins.	Point-to-Point Times "D" Head Code Mins.	Point-to-Point Times "E" Head Code Mins.	Point-to-Point Times "F" Head Code Mins.	Point-to-Point Times "H" "J" "K" Head Codes Mins.
				Oxley Sidings								
—	—	—	—	Oxley Siding North ←■								
—	—	—	—	Hollinswood								
161	28	—	—	**WELLINGTON**	104 F.		1					
164	8	2	61	Longdon Halt	104 F.							
166	3	4	55	Crudgington	186 R.	1	1					12
167	18¼	5	71¼	Rowton Halt	150 R.	—	—		—	—	—	—
168	34¼	7	11	Ellerdine Siding	264 F.	—	—		—	—	—	—
168	39¾	7	12	Ellerdine Halt	264 F.	—	—		—	—	—	—
170	16	8	69	Peplow	594 R.	1	1					10
172	29	11	2	Hodnet	343 R.	1	1					5
173	32¾	12	6	Wollerton Halt	220 F.	—	—		—	—	—	—
175	7	13	60	Tern Hill	220 R.	1	1					6
177	79	16	52	**MARKET DRAYTON**	165 R.	1	1	23	25	30	34	7
181	39	20	12	Adderley	220 R.	2	1					9
182	54	21	27	Coxbank Halt	131 F.	—	—		—	—	—	—
183	34	22	7	Audlem	131 F.	2	1					5
185	47¼	24	20¼	Coole Pilate Halt	150 R.	—	—		—	—	—	—
188	66¼	27§	39	Nantwich Junction	150 R.	1	1	15	18	21	24	13
—	—	—	—	Nantwich	330 F.	1	1		2	2	2	4
—	—	32	27	**CREWE**	160 R.	1		7	8	9	11	12
—	—	§ Dist. at Jct. Points.		Stockport								
—	—			Manchester { London Road								
—	—			Manchester { Liverpool Rd.								

STATIONS.			F Freight. MX arr.	F Freight. MX dep.		F 10.50 p.m. Stourbridge Junction (via Wombourn) Freight. arr.	dep.	F Freight RR arr.	dep.	F 9.45 p.m. Worcester Freight. arr.	dep.		
			a.m.	a.m.		a.m. M	a.m. X	a.m. M	a.m. O	a.m. M	a.m. X		
Oxley Sidings			—	12 1					1 30	12 23	1 40		
Oxley Siding North			12	4		1	1	1	33	1	43		
Hollinswood			12	39		1	36	[illegible]	[illegible]	2	18		
WELLINGTON			12	48		1	45	2	17	2	27		
Longdon Halt			—	—		—	—	Light Engine to run if no traffic.		—	—		
Crudgington			—	—		—	—			—	—		
Rowton Halt			—	—		—	—			—	—		
Ellerdine Siding			—	—		—	—			—	—		
Ellerdine Halt			—	—		—	—			—	—		
Peplow			—	—		—	—			—	—		
Hodnet			—	—		—	—			—	—		
Wollerton Halt			—	—		—	—			—	—		
Tern Hill			—	—		—	—			—	—		
MARKET DRAYTON			1 230	W1 33		2 200	W2 30	2	51	3 2	L3 12		
Adderley			—	—		—	—	—	—	—	—		
Coxbank Halt			—	—		—	—	—	—	—	—		
Audlem			—	—		—	—	— •	—	—	• —		
Coole Pilate Halt			—	—		—	—	—	—	—	—		
Nantwich Junction			1	58		2	55	3	20	3	41		
Nantwich			—	—		—	—	—	—	—	—		
CREWE			2 12	Z		3 9	—	3 34	—	3 55	—		
Stockport													
Manchester { London Road													
Manchester { Liverpool Rd.													

Down trains must not be delayed at Audlem for tickets when running late.

L.M.R. (NORTH STAFFORD SECTION) TRAINS.

Head Code	K		B	K		B		B	K	WEEKDAYS.				B					SUNDAYS.				
STATION.	N'c'tle Jct. Frght		Pass.	N'c'tle Jct. Frght		Pass.		Pass. SO	Stoke Frght					Pass.									
	a.m.		a.m.	a.m.		p.m.		p.m.	p.m.					p.m.									
Market Drayton dep	6 33		8 42	10 9		12 18		7 45	3 45					7 0									
Silverdale Junction pass.	C6 348		C8 428	C10108		C12 198		C7 448	C3 468					C7 18									

Z—After arrival at Crewe, engine and trainmen to be utilised to transfer W.R. Goods brake vans from Gresty Lane Down Sidings to Gresty Lane Up Sidings, as required.

WELLINGTON, MARKET DRAYTON AND CREWE—continued.

Down Trains. **Week Days.**

Head Code	F			D		E		H		H				C		D		B		H			
STATIONS.	1.55 a.m. Kingswinford Junction Freight. Via Wombourn			Leeds (Neville Hill) MSX Crewe SO Freight		Crewe Freight.		3.45 a.m. Freight ex Coton Hill.		Freight				9.45 p.m. G.S. ex Eastleigh		12.55 a.m. Didcot Freight.		Passenger.		4.40 a.m Oldbury and Langley Gr'n to Haverton Hill Freight.			
	MX			Y		MO								MX		MSX				MSX RR			
	arr.	dep.		arr.	dep.	arr.	dep.	arr.	dep.	arr.	dep.			arr.	dep.	arr.	dep.	arr.	dep.	arr.	dep.		
	a.m.	a.m.		a.m.	a.m.	a.m.	a.m.	a.m.	a.m.	a.m.	a.m.			a.m.	a.m.	a.m.	a.m.	a.m.	a.m.	a.m.	a.m.		
Oxley Sidings	..	....	....	—	4 0	—V	4 0	....	....	....	4 55	....	....	....	....	....	..	....	....	....	....	....	....
Oxley Siding North ←■	2	40	..	4	3	4	3	..	..	4	58	..	..	5	45	6	5	..	..	7	33	..	..
Hollinswood'	3 16	* 3 30	....	—	—	4	33	....	....	5	40	....	....	—	—	6 42	7•5	....	....	8	11	....	....
WELLINGTON	3	40	..	4	38	4	42	4 17	5 10	5 49	6 0	..	..	6 20	6 50	7	14	—	7 30	8	22	..	..
Longdon Halt	—	—	....	—	—	—	—	—	—	—	—	....	....	—	—	—	—	—	—	—	—	....	....
Crudgington	—	—	..	—	—	—	—	—	—	—	—	..	..	—	—	—	—	—	7 38	—	—	..	..
Rowton Halt	—	—	....	—	—	—	—	—	—	—	—	....	....	—	—	—	—	—	—	—	—	....	....
Ellerdine Siding	—	—	..	—	—	—	—	—	—	—	—	..	..	—	—	—	—	—	—	—	—	..	..
Ellerdine Halt	—	—	....	—	—	—	—	—	—	—	—	....	....	—	—	—	—	—	7 44	—	—	....	....
Peplow	—	—	..	—	—	—	—	—	—	—	—	..	..	—	—	—	—	7 47	7 49	—	—	..	..
Hodnet	—	—	....	—	—	—	—	—	—	—	—	....	....	—	—	—	—	7 53	7 55	—	—	....	....
Wollerton Halt	—	—	..	—	—	—	—	—	—	—	—	..	..	—	—	—	—	7 57	7 58	—	—	..	..
Tern Hill	—	—	....	—	—	—	—	—	—	—	—	....	....	—	—	—	—	8 1	8 4	—	—	....	....
MARKET DRAYTON	4 140	W4 24	..	5	3	5	12	5 52	—	6 42	6 53	..	..	7	20	7	39	8 9	8 15	9 30	W9 8	..	..
Adderley	—	—	....	—	—	—	—			—	—	....	....	—	—	—	—	8 20	8 21	—	—	....	....
Coxbank Halt	—	\ —	..	—	—	—	—	..	..	—	—	..	..	—	—	—	—	8 23	8 24	—	• —	..	..
Audlem	—	—	....	—	—	—	—	....	....	—	—	....	....	—	—	—	—	8 26	8 28	—	—	....	....
Coole Pilate Halt	—	—	..	—	—	—	—	..	..	—	—	..	..	—	—	—	—	—	8 33	—	—	..	..
Nantwich Junction	4	49	....	5	21	5	33	....	....	7	21	....	....	7	37	7 58	• 8 5	—	—	9	40	....	....
Nantwich	—	—	..	—	—	—	—	..	..	—	—	..	..	—	—	—	—	—	8 39	—	—	..	..
CREWE	5 3	—	....	5 32E	O6¶5	5 45	—	....	....	7 38	—	....	....	7 45	—	8 17	—	8§47	—	957CE	CT109	....	..
Stockport	..	..	..		..	..	..	..	..	..	..	..	..	..	..	..	..	..	..	Arr. Neville Hill 3.3 p.m. N.E.R. work forward as convenient.		..	..
Manchester { London Road	....	....	....	....		....	....	....	....	....	....	....	....	....	....	....	....	....	....			....	....
Manchester { Liverpool Rd	..	..	..	¶—	MSX	..	..	..	..	..	..	..	..	..	..	..	..	..	..			..	..

V—An engine is authorized to work coupled to this train from Oxley Sidings to Crewe with Vacuum Brake connected to train.

Y—Worked by L.M.R. engine off 8.50 p.m. Manchester to Oxley Sidings.

§—Advertised Crewe arrive 8.49 a.m.

WELLINGTON, MARKET DRAYTON AND CREWE—continued.

Down Trains. **Week Days.**

Head Code	B		F		K		D		B		B		F		F		B	B					
STATIONS.	Passenger.		Freight.		Freight.		4.30 a.m. MSX Basingstoke Freight.		9.32 a.m. Worcester Passenger.		Passenger.		10.20 a.m. Empties ex Worcester via Wombourn.		Freight. SX		Pass. WSX	Passenger. WSO					
	arr.	dep.	arr.	dep.	arr.	dep.	arr.	dep.	arr.	dep.	arr.	dep.	arr.	dep.	arr.	dep.	dep.	arr.	dep.				
	a.m.	a.m.	a.m.	a.m	a.m.	a.m.	a.m.	a.m.	a.m.	a.m.	p.m.	p.m.	p.m.	p.m.	p.m.	p.m.	p.m.	p.m.	p.m.				
Oxley Sidings	....	....	—	9 40	....	....	....	....	....	....	....	....	....	....	—	1 30	....	....	....	....	....	....	....
Oxley Siding North ←	..	..	9	43	..	..	10	44	11	28	..	..	12	49	1	33	..	..	..	..	..	..	..
Hollinswood	....	....	10	18	....	....	—	—	—	—	....	....	1	24	2	8	....	....	....	....	....	....	....
WELLINGTON	—	10 0	10	27	—	11 20	11	40	12 7	12 15	—	1 0	1	33	2	17	2‡49	—	2‡49	..	..	..	..
Longdon Halt	—	10 5	—	—	—	—	—	—	—	12 20	—	1 5	—	—	—	—	2 54	—	2 54	....	....	....	....
Crudgington	—	10 10	—	—	11 33	11 58	—	—	12 24	12 26	—	1 10	—	—	—	—	2 59	—	2 59	..	..	..	..
Rowton Halt	—	10 14	—	—	—	—	—	—	12 29	12 30	1 13½	1 14	—	—	—	—	3 3	—	3 3	....	....	....	....
Ellerdine Siding	—	—	—	—	12 5	12 12	—	—	—	—	—	—	—	—	—	—	—	—	—	..	..	..	..
Ellerdine Halt	—	10 18	—	—	—	—	—	—	—	12 34	1 17½	1 18	—	—	—	—	3 7	—	3 7	....	....	....	....
Peplow	1021½	10 23	—	—	12 17	12 26	—	—	1237½	12 39	—	1 22	—	—	—	—	3 12	—	3 12	..	..	..	..
Hodnet	—	10 28	—	—	12 33	1 6	—	—	—	12 44	—	1 27	—	—	—	—	3 17	—	3 17	....	....	....	....
Wollerton Halt	1030½	10 31	—	—	—	—	—	—	1246½	12 47	1 29½	1 30	—	—	—	—	3 20	—	3 20	..	..	..	..
Tern Hill	—	10 36	—	—	1 14	1 21	p	m.	—	12 52	1 34	1 36	—	—	—	—	3 25	—	3 25	....	....	....	....
MARKET DRAYTON	1041½	10 45	11 20	W1112	1 33	1 55	12	5	1257½	1 0	1 42	—	2 8	—	2520W	CR3 2	3 30	—	3 31	..	..	..	..
Adderley	1050½	10 51	—	—	2 7	2 15	—	—	1 5½	1 6	Engine returns working 3.20 p.m. Freight ex Market Drayton.		Engine and Van to Coleham 2†35 p.m.	..	—	—	....	—	3 36	....	....	....	....
Coxbank Halt	1053½	10 54	—	—	—	—	—	—	1 8½	1 9				..	—	—	..	—	3 39	..	..	..	..
Audlem	10 56	10 58	—	—	2 23	2 31	—	—		1 12				....	—	—	....	—	3 42	....	....	....	....
Coole Pilate Halt	—	11 3	—	—	—	—	—	—	—	1 17				..	—	—	..	—	3 46	..	..	..	..
Nantwich Junction	—	—	11	37	2	48V	12 24*	12 50	—	—				....	3	27	....	—	—	....	....	....	....
Nantwich	—	11 10	—	—	C	R	—	—	—	1 24				..	—	—	..	—	3 52	..	..	..	..
CREWE	11¶18	—	11 51	—	3 7	—	1 2	—	1§32	—				..	3 41	—	..	4‡‡0	—	....	....	....	....
Stockport	....	....	....	....	....	....	....	....	....	....				....	....	....	....	....	....	....	....	....	....
Manchester { London Road	..	..	..	..	..	..	..	..	..	..				..	..	..	..	..	..	..	..	..	..
Manchester { Liverpool Rd.	....	....	....	....	....	....	....	....	....	....				....	....	....	....	....	....	....	....	....	....

§—Advertised Crewe arrive 1.36 p.m.

‡—Advertised Wellington depart 2.45 p.m.

‡‡—P.B. arrive 4.1 p.m.

¶—Advertised Crewe arrive 11.21 a.m.

V—On Saturdays, Nantwich Junction 2.46 * 2.50, arrive Crewe 3.8 p.m.

WELLINGTON, MARKET DRAYTON AND CREWE—continued.

Down Trains. **Week Days.**

Head Code	D		D		B		H			B		H		D		E	
STATIONS.	Freight.		1.20 a.m. Tavistock Junction Freight. SX		Passenger.		Freight			Passenger.		Freight.		Freight. 8.35 p.m. Worcester. SX		Freight. 8.35 p.m. Worcester. SO	
	arr.	dep.	arr.	dep.	arr.	dep.	arr.	dep.		arr.	dep.	arr.	dep.	arr.	dep.	arr.	dep.
	p.m.	p.m.	p.m.	p.m.	p.m.	p.m.	p.m.	p.m.		p.m	p.m.	p.m.	p.m.	p.m. V	p.m. ia	p.m. V	p.m. ia
Oxley Sidings	—	4 0	....	....	..	..	—	5 40	..	..	..	—	8 0	Wom	bourn	Wom	bourn
Oxley Siding North ←	4	3	4	24	....	....	5	43	....	....	....	8	3	10	41	10	41
Hollinswood	—	—	—	—	..	..	6	21	..	..	..	8	41	—	—	11	11
WELLINGTON	4	39	5	0	—	5 55	6	32	....	—	9 25	8 54	9 37	11	17	11	20
Longdon Halt	—	—	—	—	—	6 0	—	—	..	—N	9 30	—	—	—	—	—	—
Crudgington	—	—	—	—	6 4	6 6	—	—	....	9 34	9 36	—	—	—	—	—	—
Rowton Halt	—	—	—	—	—	6 10	—	—	..	—	9R40	—	—	—	—	—	—
Ellerdine Halt	—	—	—	—	6 12	6 14	—	—	....	—	9 44	—	—	—	—	—	—
Peplow	—	—	—	—	6 17½	6 18	—	—	..	9 47½	9 49	—	—	—	—	—	—
Hodnet	—	—	—	—	—	6 23	—	—	....	—	9 54	—	—	—	—	—	—
Wollerton Halt	—	—	—	—	—	6 26	—	—	..	—	—	—	—	—	—	—	—
Tern Hill	—	—	—	—	6 30	6 32	—	—	....	—	9 59	—	—	—	—	—	—
MARKET DRAYTON	5	4	5 26	5 46	6 37½	6 42	7	12	..	10 5	10 10	1026OW	10*45	11	42	11	50
Adderley	—	—	—	—	6 47½	6 48	—	—	....	1015½	10 17	—	—	—	—	—	—
Coxbank Halt	—	—	—	—	—	6 52	—	—	..	1019½	10 21	—	—	—	* —	—	—
Audlem	—	—	—	—	6 54	6 56	—	—	....	—	10 24	—	—	—	—	—	—
Coole Pilate Halt	—	—	—	—	—	7 2	—	—	..	—	—	—	—	a.m.	a.m.	—	—
Nantwich Junction	5 22*	5 51	6 6	* 6 12	—	—	7 39	*8 5Y	....	—	—	11 13	*11 25	12	1Z	12	11
Nantwich	—	—	—	—	—	7 9	—	—	..	10 32	10 34	—	—	—	—	—	—
CREWE	6 3	—	6 24	—	7 18	—	8 23Y	—	....	10 42	—	11 43	—	12 12	—	12 23	—
Stockport	....	....	..	..	..	..	..	..	..	..	..	..	..	..	..	..	..
Manchester { London Road.	..	..	....	....	....	....	....	..	....	....	....	....	....	....	....	....	....
Manchester { Liverpool Rd.	....	....	..	..	..	..	..	..	..	..	..	..	..	..	..	..	..

N—Calls to set down passengers. **R**—Thursdays and Saturdays only. **Y**—On Tuesdays and Saturdays, Nantwich Junction dep. 8.40, Crewe arr. 8.58 p.m.

Z—On Saturdays, 13th June to 29th August, inclusive, pass Nantwich Junction 12/6 a.m., arrive Crewe 12.17 a.m.

WELLINGTON, MARKET DRAYTON AND CREWE—continued.

Down Trains. **Sundays.**

Head Code	F		F		F		F		E		F		B		D	D		E	B	
STATIONS.	Freight		10.50 p.m. (Saturdays) Stourbridge Junction (Via Wombourn) **Freight.**		9.45 p.m. (Saturdays) Worcester **Freight.**		1.45 a.m. Kingswinford Junction **Freight.**		**Freight.** V		**Freight.**		Passenger.		4.30 a.m. Basing stoke **Frght**	12.10 a.m. Tavistock **Freight.**		**Frght**	Passenger. Z	
	arr.	dep.	arr.	dep.	arr.	dep.	arr.	dep.	arr.	dep.	arr.	dep.	arr.	dep.	dep.	arr.	dep.	dep.	arr.	dep.
	a.m.	a.m.	a.m.	a.m.	a.m.	a.m.	a.m.	a.m.	a.m.	a.m.	a.m.	a.m.	a.m.	a.m.	a.m.	a.m.	a.m.	p.m.	p.m.	p.m.
Oxley Sidings	....	**12 1**	....	....	**12 23**	**1 40**	—	—	—	**4 0**	—	**7 30**	....	....	**10§ 6**	**11 6C**	**T1111**	**1 30**	....	....
Oxley Siding North ←■	12	4	1	1	1	43	2	40	4	3	7	33	..	..	10 9	11	14	1 33	..	..
Hollinswood	12	39	1	36	2	18	3	15	4	33	8	8	....	....	—	—	—	2 3	....	....
WELLINGTON	12	49	1	46	2	27	3	24	4	49	8	17	—	**9 15**	10 46	11	50	2 12	—	**10 55**
Longdon Halt	—	—	—	—	—	—	—	—	—	—	—	—	—	9 20	—	—	—	—	**N**	11 2
Crudgington	—	—	—	—	—	—	—	—	—	—	—	—	—	9 25	—	—	—	—	11 6	11 8
Rowton Halt	—	—	—	—	—	—	—	—	—	—	—	—	—	9 29	—	—	—	—	—	—
Ellerdine Halt	—	—	—	—	—	—	—	—	—	—	—	—	—	9 33	—	—	—	—	—	—
Peplow	—	—	—	—	—	—	—	—	—	—	—	—	9 36½	9 37	—	—	—	—	11 16	11 18
Hodnet	—	—	—	—	—	—	—	—	—	—	—	—	—	9 42	—	—	—	—	11 23	11 25
Wollerton Halt	—	—	—	—	—	—	—	—	—	—	—	—	—	9 45	—	p.m.	p.m.	—	—	—
Tern Hill	—	—	—	—	—	—	—	—	—	—	—	—	—	9 50	—	—	—	—	11 30	11 34
MARKET DRAYTON	**1 23 0**	**W1 33**	**2 20 0**	**W2 30**	**3 2**	**L3 12**	**3 58 0**	**W4 8**	5	19	**8 52 0**	**W9 2**	**9 55½**	**10 0**	11 10	**12 16**	**12 36**	2CR 42	**11 40**	**11 45**
Adderley	—	—	—	—	—	—	—	—	—	—	—	—	—	10 6	—	—	—	—	11 51	11 53
Coxbank Halt	—	—	—	—	—	•	—	—	—	—	—	—	10 8½	10 9	—	—	—	—	—	—
Audlem	—	—	—	—	—	—	—	—	—	—	—	—	10 11	1011½	—	—	—	—	11 57	12 0
Coole Pilate Halt	—	—	—	—	—	—	—	—	—	—	—	—	1015½	10 16	—	—	—	—	—	—
Nantwich Junction	1	58	2	55	3	45	4	32	5	33	9	37	—	—	11 28	12	55	3 3	—	—
Nantwich	—	—	—	—	—	—	—	—	—	—	—	—	—	10 23	—	—	—	—	12 8	12 10
CREWE	**2 12**	—	**3 9**	....	**3 59**	—	**4 46**	—	**5 45**	—	**9 41**	—	**10 33**	—	**11 39**	**1 6**	—	**3 15**	**12‡18**	—
Stockport	..	..	..	..	..	..	..	..	..	..	..	..	..	..	§ arr. Oxley Sdgs. 10.1 a.m.	..	..	..	..	..
Manchester { **London Road**	....	....	....	....	....	....	....	....	....	....	....	....	....	....		....	....	....	....	....
Manchester { **Liverpool Rd.**	..	..	..	..	..	..	..	..	..	..	..	..	..	..		..	..	..	..	..

N—Calls to set down passengers.

V—See note, page 130

Z—Recovery time allowed at stations. Every effort must be made to recover lost time if train running late.

‡—P.B. 12.26 a.m.

Up Trains. CREWE, MARKET DRAYTON AND WELLINGTON Week Days.

Time Allowance for Freight Trains. See page 2

STATIONS.	Ruling Gradient 1 in	Allow for Stop. Mins.	Allow for Start. Mins.	Point-to-Point Times "C" Head Code Mins.	Point-to-Point Times "D" Head Code Mins.	Point-to-Point Times "E" Head Code Mins.	Point-to-Point Times "F" Head Code Mins.	Point-to-Point Times "H" "J" "K" Head Codes Mins.
Manchester { Liverpool Rd.	....	....	....	....	....	....	....	....
Manchester { London Road	..	..	..	..	..	..	..	..
Stockport	....	....	....	....	....	....	....	....
CREWE	..	..	1	..	..	..	..	..
Nantwich	330 R.	....	....	....	....	....	....	....
Nantwich Junction	100 R.	1	1	6	7	9	10	12
Coole Pilate Halt	210 R.	....	....	....	....	....	....	....
Audlem	131 R.	1	2	..	..	..	..	13
Coxbank Halt	131 R.	—	—	....	....	....	....	—
Adderley	131 R.	1	2	..	..	..	..	6
MARKET DRAYTON	190 R.	1	1	17	20	23	27	9
Tern Hill	165 F.	1	1	..	..	..	..	7
Wollerton Halt	220 F.	—	—	....	....	....	....	—
Hodnet	220 R.	1	1	..	..	..	..	6
Peplow	297 R.	1	1	....	....	....	....	5
Ellerdine Halt	264 R.	..	..	..	..	..	..	..
Rowton Halt	264 R.	....	....	....	....	....	....	....
Crudgington	150 F.	1	1	..	..	..	..	10
Longdon Halt	104 R.	....	....	....	....	....	....	....
WELLINGTON	104 R.	1	..	25	28	33	38	14
Hollinswood	....	....	....	....	....	....	....	....
Oxley Sidings North ←■	..	..	..	..	..	..	..	..
Oxley Sidings	....	....	....	....	....	....	....	....
Stourbridge Junction	..	..	..	..	..	..	..	..
Worcester (Shrub Hill)	....	....	....	....	....	....	....	....

Head Code	E	E	F		F		E		A		F		H		F
STATIONS.	Stoke Gifford Frght via Wombourn MSX	Stoke Giffo'd Frght MO V	Hockley Freight. Y MX		Hockley Freight. U SO		Moreton Cutting Freight. MX		Passenger to Donnington (Not Advertised) MO		Oxley Freight. MX		Worcester (via Wombourn) Freight.		Oxley Frght MO
	dep.	dep.	arr.	dep.	arr.	dep.	arr.	dep.	arr.	dep.	arr.	dep	arr.	dep.	dep.
	a.m.	a.m.	a.m.	a.m.	a.m.	a.m.	a.m.	a.m.	a.m.	a.m.	a.m.	a.m.	a.m.	a.m.	a.m.
Manchester { Liverpool Rd.	....	....	....	....	....	....	....	....	....	....	....	....	....	....	Starts from Gresty Green
Manchester { London Road	‡	..	Starts from	Gresty Green	Starts from	Gresty Green	Starts from	Gresty Green	..	..	Starts from	Gresty Green	Starts from Gresty	Lane	
Stockport	....	....							....	....					
CREWE	12 5	*12 55*	—	1 4	—	*1 10*	--	1 30	—	*1§35*	—	3 35	—	4 50	*5 30*
Nantwich	—	—	—	—	—	—	—	—	—	—	—	—	—	—	—
Nantwich Junction	12 15	*1 5*	1	15	*1*	*21*	1	40.	*1*	*43*	3	46	5	3	*5 41*
Coole Pilate Halt	—	—	—	—	—	—	—	—	—	—	—	—	—	—	—
Audlem	—	—	—	—	—	—	—	—	—	—	—	—	—	—	—
Coxbank Halt	—	—	—	—	—	—	—	—	—	—	—	—	—	—	—
Adderley	—	—	—	—	—	—	—	—	—	—	—	—	—	—	—
MARKET DRAYTON	12 38	*1 28*	1	42	*1*	*48*	2 40	W2 9	*2§ 0*	*2 5*	4 14 0	W4 19	5 32 0	W5 39	*6* 0W*14*
Tern Hill	—	—	—	—	—	—	—	—	*2§10*	*2 18*	—	—	—	—	
Wollerton Halt	—	—	—	—	—	—	—	—	—	—	—	—	—	—	Arr. Market Drayton 6.9 a.m.
Hodnet	—	—	—	—	—	—	—	—	—	—	—	—	—	—	
Peplow	—	—	—	—	—	—	—	—	—	—	—	—	—	—	
Ellerdine Halt	—	—	—	—	—	—	—	—	—	—	—	—	—	—	
Rowton Halt	—	—	—	—	—	—	—	—	—	—	—	—	—	—	
Crudgington	—	—	—	—	—	—	—	—	—	—	—	—	—	—	
Longdon Halt	—	—	—	—	—	—	—	—	—	—	—	—	—	—	
WELLINGTON	1 11	*2*	2	20	*2*	*26*	2	43	*2§35*	*2 45*	4 59	5 27	6	22	*6 53*
Hollinswood	1 28	*2 13*	2	38	*2*	*39*	3	2			5	42	6 39	7 22	*7 6*
Oxley Sidings North ←■	1 55	*2 40*	3	8	*3*	*9*	3	32	..	..	6	12	8	1	*7 36*
Oxley Sidings		*2 43*	3 11CT	CR3 25	*3 12*	—			....	....	6 15	—	—	—	*7 39*
Stourbridge Junction	..						Via Wombourn		..	..			9 25	9 55	
Worcester (Shrub Hill)	....	....	....	....	....	....			....	....	....	....	12Z15	—	....

L.M.R. (NORTH STAFFORD SECTION) TRAINS.

Head Code		K	B		B	K	K		B			K	B	WEEK DAYS.							SUNDAYS.			
STATION.		4.55 a.m. Stoke Frgt.	Pass.		Pass.	9.25 a.m. Stoke Frght SX	9.25 a.m. Stoke Frgt. SO		Pass. SO			12.25 p.m. Stoke Frgt.	Pass.											
		a.m.	a.m.		a.m.	a.m.	a.m.		p.m.			p.m.	p.m.											
Silverdale Junction	pass	C5 56§	C8 21§	..	C9 45§	C11 25§	*C11 40§*	..	*C1 18§*	..	..	C2 54§	C5 36§	..	..	..	..	..	..	..	..	..	..	..
Market Drayton	arr.	5 57	8 22	..	9 46	11 26	*11 41*	..	*1 19*	..	..	2 55	5 37	..	..	..	..	..	..	..	..	..	..	..

U—Applies on Saturdays, 13th June to 29th August, inclusive. **V**—Starts from Gresty Green. Runs via Wolverhampton, Dudley and Worcester. **Y**—On Saturdays, 13th June to 29th August, inclusive, **starts at** 1.10 a.m. and runs as shewn in next column. **Z**—Worcester Yard. §—Market Drayton and Tern Hill tickets collected at Crewe, and Trench Crossing and Donnington tickets at Wellington. ‡—Startsfrom Gresty Green.

CREWE, MARKET DRAYTON AND WELLINGTON—continued.

Up Trains. Week Days.

Head Code	B		H		B		K		F	
STATIONS.	Passenger.		Oxley Freight. SX		Passenger and Milk Train.		Wellington Freight.		Oxley Freight.	
	arr.	dep.	arr.	dep.	arr.	dep.	arr.	dep.	arr.	dep.
	a.m.	a.m.	a.m.	a.m.	a.m.	a.m.	a.m.	a.m.	a.m.	a.m.
Manchester Liverp'l Rd	....	....	Starts from	Gresty Green	....	....	Starts from	Gresty Lane	Starts from	Gresty Lane
Manchester London Rd	..	..			..	..				
Stockport	....	....			....	....				
CREWE	—	6 5	—	6 50	..	..	—	7 5	—	8 45
Nantwich	6 13	6 1	—	—	....	....	—	—	—	—
Nantwich Junction	—	—	7	8	..	..	7	18	8	56
Coole Pilate Halt	—	—	—	—	....	....	—	—	—	—
Audlem	6 22	6 24	—	—	..	..	7 32	7 52	—	—
Coxbank Halt	6 26	6 27	—	—	....	....	—	—	—	—
Adderley	6 30	6 31	—	—	..	..	C	R	—	—
MARKET DRAYTON	6 37	6 42	7 320	W7 37	—	8 0	8 10	8 40	9 24 OW	9 25
Tern Hill	6 47	6 51	—	—	—	8 6	8 49	9 5	—	—
Wollerton Halt	—	—	—	—	8 9¼	8 10	—	—	—	—
Hodnet	6 56	6 58	—	—	8 12¼	8 14	9 13	9 28	—	—
Peplow	7 2	7 4	—	—	8 18	8 20	9 35	9 59	—	—
Ellerdine Halt	7‡7½	7‡ 8	—	—	8 23¼	8 24	—	—	—	—
Rowton Halt	CR¶	7 12	—	—	—	8 28	—	—	—	—
Crudgington	7 15	7 17	—	—	8 31	8 33	10 11	10 44	—	—
Longdon Halt	—	7 22	—	—	—	8 39	—	—	—	—
WELLINGTON	7 28	—	8 21	* 8 35	8 45	—	11 0	—	10	8
Hollinswood	....	....	8 53	*10 20	....	....	....	....	10 22	*11 15
Oxley Sidings North ←■	..	..	10	59	..	..	..	..	10	46
Oxley Sidings	....	....	11 2	—	....	....	....	....	11 49	⊥

Head Code	B		F		F		E		B		F	G		
STATIONS.	Passenger V		Oxley Freight.		Stourbridge Junction Freight. SX		Moreton Cutting Freight. SX		Passenger.		Oxley Fr'ght SX	Engine and Van to Coleham.		
	arr.	dep.	arr	dep.	arr.	dep.	arr.	dep.	arr.	dep.	dep.	arr.	dep.	
	a.m.	a.m.	a.m.	a.m.	a.m.	a.m.	p.m.	noon	p.m.	p.m.	p.m.	p.m.	p.m.	
Manchester Liverp'l Rd	....	....	Starts from	Gresty Green	Starts from	Gresty Green	Starts from	Gresty Green	....	....	Starts from Gresty Green	After working 10.20 a.m. Worcester.		....
Manchester London Rd	..	..							..	..				..
Stockport	....	....							....	....				....
CREWE	—	9 30	—	9 50	—	11 0	—	12 0	—	12§56	1 30	....	....	..
Nantwich	—	9 39	—	—	—	—	—	—	—	1 5	—	..	..	....
Nantwich Junction	—	—	10	1	11	11	12	10	—	—	1 41	....	....	..
Coole Pilate Halt	9 45	9 45½	—	—	—	—	—	—	—	1 12	—	..	..	....
Audlem	9 48½	9 49	—	—	—	—	—	—	—	1 16	—	....	....	..
Coxbank Halt	—	9 52	—	—	—	—	—	—	—	1 20	—	..	..	....
Adderley	—	9 55	—	—	—	—	—	—	—	1 23	—	....	....	..
MARKET DRAYTON	10 1	10 4	10 29	10 54	11 390	W1144	12 340	W1239	1 29	1 32	2N19	—	2†35	....
Tern Hill	—	10 10	—	—	—	—	—	—	—	1 38	—	—	—	..
Wollerton Halt	—	10 14	—	—	—	—	—	—	—	1 42	—	—	—	....
Hodnet	1016½	10 17	—	—	—	—	—	—	—	1 46	—	—	—	..
Peplow	—	10 22	—	—	—	—	—	—	—	1 51	—	—	—	....
Ellerdine Halt	—	10 26	—	—	—	—	—	—	—	1 55	—	—	—	..
Rowton Halt	—	10 29	—	—	—	—	—	—	—	1 58	—	— •	—	....
Crudgington	—	10 33	—	—	—	—	—	—	2 1	2 4	—	—	—	..
Longdon Halt	—	10 38	—	—	—	—	—	—	—	2 9	—	—	—	....
WELLINGTON	10 43	—	11 34*	1153Y	12	23	1	13	2 15	—	2 58	3†15	3†25	..
Hollinswood	....	....	12 9	*12 30	12 37	* 1 10	1	26	....	....	3 17	....	....	....
Oxley Sidings North ←■	..	..	1	1	1	46	1	52	..	..	3 47	..	..	..
Oxley Sidings	..	..	1 4	—			Via Wombourn		....	....	3 50	....	....	....

N—Arrives 2.9 p.m. OW

V—H. and C. traffic not conveyed by this train except from Crewe (off L.M.R.) and from Market Drayton, unless specially authorized.

¶—To call at Rowton Halt, if required, to pick up passengers. Enginemen to keep sharp look-out for passengers wishing to join train.

‡—Stop not advertised.

Y—On Saturdays dep. Wellington 12.0 noon, Hollinswood 12.16/12.40, Oxley North 1/11, Oxley 1.14 p.m.

§—P.B. Crewe depart 12.53 p.m.

CREWE, MARKET DRAYTON AND WELLINGTON—continued.

Up Trains. **Week Days**

Head Code	H	B		B		F		B		H		H		B		D		F		F		F	
STATIONS	Shrewsbury Frght	Passenger. WSX		Passenger. WSO		Oxley Freight.		Passenger D		Oxley Freight.		Oxley Freight.		Passenger.		Y Oxley Freight. SX		Y Oxley Freight. SO		Worcester (via Wombourn) Freight. SX		Worcester (via Wombourn) Freight SO	
	dep.	arr.	dep.	arr.	dep.	arr.	dep.	arr.	dep.	arr.	dep.	arr.	dep.	arr.	dep.	arr.	dep.	arr.	dep.	arr.	dep.	arr.	dep.
	p.m.	p.m.	p.m.	p.m.	p.m.	p.m. Starts Gresty	p.m. from Green	p.m.	p.m.	p.m. Starts Gresty	p.m. from Green	p.m. Starts Gresty	p.m. from Green	p.m.	p.m.	p.m.	p.m.	p.m.	p.m.	p.m. Starts Gresty	p.m. from Lane	p.m. Starts Gresty	p.m. from Lane
Manchester { Liverpool Rd.	....	....	....	....	....			....	....					....	....	....	....	....	....				
Manchester { London Road	..	..	..	..	..			..	..					..	..	—	8 50	—	7 15				
Stockport	....	....	....	....	.....			....	....	....	....	....	....	....	....	—	—	....	....	....	....	....	....
CREWE	..	..	..	—	3 15	—	3 55	—	5D10	—	5 35	..	8 5	—	8 52	9V55 CO	T10 24 W	9 V5 CO	T9 55 W	—	11 30	—	11 30
Nantwich	....	....	....	—	3 24	—	—	—	5 21	—	—	—	—	—	9 1					—	—	—	—
Nantwich Junction	..	..	..	—	—	4	6	—	—	5	48	8	18	—	—	10	32	10	6	11	41	11	41
Coole Pilate Halt	....	....	....	3 30	3 30½	—	—	—	5 28	—	—	—	—	—	9 8	—	—	—	—	—	—	—	—
Audlem	..	..	..	3 33½	3 34	—	—	—	5 32	—	—	— •	—	—	9 12	—	—	—	—	—	—	—	—
Coxbank Halt	....	....	....	—	3 37	—	—	5 34½	5 35	—	—	—	—	—	9 15	—	—	—	—	—	—	—	—
Adderley	..	..	..	—	3 40	—	—	—	5 38	—	—	—	—	—	9 19	—	—	—	—	—	—	—	—
MARKET DRAYTON	3 20	—	3 50	3 46	3 50	4 340	W4 39	5 45	5 50	6 17	6 40	8 47	8 53	—	9 27	10	52	10 340	W1040	12 90	W*1218	12 90	W12*18
Tern Hill	—	—	3 56	—	3 56	—	—	—	5 56	—	—	—	—	—	9 33	—	—	—	—	—	—	—	—
Wollerton Halt	—	—	4 0	—	4 0	—	—	5 59½	6 0	—	—	—	—	—	—	—	—	—	—	—	—	—	—
Hodnet	—	4 2½	4 3	4 2½	4 3	—	—	6 2½	6 3	—	—	—	—	—	9 40	—	—	—	—	—	—	—	—
Peplow	—	—	4 8	—	4 8	—	—	—	6 8	—	—	—	—	—	9 45	—	—	—	—	—	—	—	—
Ellerdine Halt	—	—	4 12	—	4 12	—	—	6 11½	6 12	—	—	—	—	—	—	—	—	—	—	—	—	—	—
Rowton Halt	—	—	4 15	—	4 15	—	—	6 15R	6 16	—	—	—	—	—	—	—	—	—	—	—	—	—	—
Crudgington	—	—	4 19	—	4 19	—	—	—	6 20	—	—	—	—	9 52	9 54	—	—	—	—	—	—	—	—
Longdon Halt	—	—	4 24	—	4 24	—	—	SO	6 25	—	—	—	—	—	—	—	—	—	—	—	—	—	—
WELLINGTON	4 4	4F35	—	4F35	—	5 19	5 23	6 31	—	7	23	9	36	10 4	—	11	20	11	19	12	57	1	2
Hollinswood	Wellington dep. 4.35 p.m.	....	....	....	....	5 38	* 6 10	....	....	7 39	8 25	9	51	....	....	11	31	11	32	1	10	1	15
Oxley Sidings North ←—		..	..	..	..	6	41	..	..	9	4	10	29	..	..	11	54	12	2	1	40	1	45
Oxley Sidings		....	....	....	....	6 44	—	....	....	9 7	—	10 32	—	....	....	11 57	—	12 5	—	—	—	1 48	3 15
Stourbridge Junction		..	..	..	..			..	..					..	..					2 48	3 15	—	—
Worcester (Shrub Hill)		....	....	....	....	....	....	....	....	....	....	....	....	....	....	....	....	....	....	4H52	—	4 40	—

D—Calls daily at Willaston 5.15/5.16 p.m.
R—Calls Thursdays and Saturdays only.
F—Five minutes recovery time Longdon Halt to Wellington.
V—Gresty Lane.
H—On Sundays arrives Worcester 4.40 a.m.
Y—Worked by L.M.R. Engine (7.15 p.m. SO ex Manchester runs under "E" Head Code to Crewe).

CREWE, MARKET DRAYTON AND WELLINGTON—continued.

Up Trains. Sundays.

Head Code	F			H		H		F		B		F		F		F		F		F		B	
STATIONS.	Hockley Freight.			Oxley Freight.		Oxley Freight.		Oxley Freight.		Passenger.		Oxley Freight.		Oxley Freight.		Oxley Freight		Oxley Freight.		Oxley Freight.		Passenger.	
	arr.	dep.		arr.	dep.	arr.	dep.	arr.	dep.	arr.	dep.	arr.	dep.	arr.	dep.	arr.	dep.	arr.	dep.	arr.	dep.	arr.	dep.
	a.m.	a.m.		a.m.	a.m.	a.m.	a.m.	a.m.	a.m.	a.m.	a.m.	a.m.	a.m.	a.m.	a.m.	a.m.	a.m.	a.m.	a.m.	p.m.	a.m.	p.m.	p.m.
Manchester Liverpool Rd.	....	....	....	....	....	....	....	....	....	....	....	....	....	....	....	....	....	....	....	....	....	....	....
Manchester London Road	..	..	..	..	..	..	..	..	..	..	..	..	..	..	..	..	..	..	..	..	..	..	..
Stockport	....	....	....	....	....	....	....	....	....	....	....	....	....	....	....	....	....	....	....	....	....	....	....
CREWE	—	1Z4	..	—	3Z35	—	4Z50	—	6Z0	—	6 40	—	6Z55	—	8Z30	—	9Z30	—	11Z30	—	11Z50	—	8 35
Nantwich	—	—	....	—	—	—	—	—	—	—	6 49	—	—	—	—	—	—	—	—	—	—	—	8 44
Nantwich Junction	1	15	..	3	48	5	3	6	11	—	—	7	6	8	41	9	41	11	41	12	1	—	—
Coole Pilate Halt	—	—	....	—	—	—	—	—	—	—	6 56	—	—	—	—	—	—	—	—	—	—	—	—
Audlem	—	—	..	—	—	—	—	—	—	—	7 2	—	—	—	—	—	—	—	—	—	—	—	8 52
Coxbank Halt	—	—	....	—	—	—	—	—	—	7 4½	7 5	—	—	—	—	—	—	—	—	—	—	C‡R	8 55
Adderley	—	—	..	—	—	—	—	—	—	—	7 8	—	—	—	—	—	—	p.m.	p.m.	—	—	—	8 58
MARKET DRAYTON	1	42	....	4 17O	W4 27	5 32 O	W5 42	6 39O	W6 44	7 14	7 20	7 34O	W7 44	9 9O	W9 14	10 9O	W1014	12 9O	W1214	12 29O	W1234	9 4	9 6
Tern Hill	—	—	..	—	—	—	—	—	—	—	7 26	—	—	—	—	—	—	—	—	—	—	—	9 12
Wollerton Halt	—	—	....	—	—	—	—	—	—	7 29½	7 30	—	—	—	—	—	—	—	—	—	—	—	—
Hodnet	—	—	..	—	—	—	—	—	—	7 32½	7 33	—	—	—	—	—	—	—	—	—	—	—	9 18
Peplow	—	—	....	— *	—	—	—	—	—	—	7 38	— *	—	—	—	—	—	—	—	—	—	—	9 23
Ellerdine Halt	—	—	..	—	—	—	—	—	—	7 41½	7 42	—	—	—	—	—	—	—	—	—	—	—	—
Rowton Halt	—	—	....	—	—	—	—	—	—	—	7 46	—	—	—	—	—	—	—	—	—	—	—	—
Crudgington	—	—	..	—	—	—	—	—	—	—	7 50	—	—	—	—	—	—	—	—	—	—	—	9 31
Longdon Halt	—	—	....	—	—	—	—	—	—	—	7 55	—	—	—	—	—	—	—	—	—	—	—	—
WELLINGTON	2	20	..	5	12	6 25	6 55	7	23	8 1	—	8	30	9	53	10	53	12	53	1	13	9 40	—
Hollinswood	2	33	....	5	27	7	12	7	36	....	....	8	43	10	6	11	6	1	6	1	26	....	....
Oxley Sidings North ←	3	8	..	6	1	7	50	8	6	..	..	9	13	10	36	11	36	1	36	1	56	..	..
Oxley Sidings	3 6C	T3 11	....	6 4	—	7 53	—	8 9	—	....	....	9 16	—	10 39	—	11 39	—	1 39	—	1 59	—	....	....

Z—Gresty Green

‡—Calls at Coxbank Halt to set down on notice to Guard at Audlem.

Appendix Eight

Locomotive Allocations - Wellington and Crewe

Wellington

At 1st January, 1921

Dean '645' class 0-6-0PT	759
Armstrong '517' class 0-4-2T	842, 1424, 1485
Dean '1501' class 0-6-0ST	1510
Dean '1501' class 0-6-0PT	1554
Dean '655' class 0-6-0ST	1748, 1778
Dean '655' class 0-6-0PT	1787, 2710
Dean '1901' class 0-6-0PT	1914
Dean '3206' class 'Barnum' double-framed 2-4-0	3220
Dean '3232' class single-framed 2-4-0	3234, 3240
	Total: 14

At 1st January, 1934

Dean '645' class 0-6-0PT	768
Dean '1501' class 0-6-0PT	1514, 1524
Dean '655' class 0-6-0PT	1787, 2706, 2716, 2717, 2720
Dean '3206' class 'Barnum' double-framed 2-4-0	3210, 3216, 3222
Dean '3300' class 'Bulldog' double-framed 4-4-0	3309 *Maristow*
Collett '5101' class 2-6-2T	5129
Collett '58XX' class 0-4-2T	5810
	Total: 14

At 31st December, 1947

Dean '2021' class 0-6-0PT	2030
Dean '3300' class 'Bulldog' double-framed 4-4-0	3417 *Lord Mildmay of Flete*
Collett '57XX' class 0-6-0PT	3732, 3775, 5758, 9624, 9630, 9639
Churchward '43XX' class 2-6-0	5309, 5332
Churchward '44XX' class 2-6-2T	4400, 4403, 4406
Collett '5101' class 2-6-2T	5127, 5135, 5137, 5178
	Total: 17

At July 1951

Hawksworth '16XX' class 0-6-0PT	1619
Dean '2021' class 0-6-0PT	2030
Collett '57XX' class 0-6-0PT	3613, 3687, 3732, 3749, 3760, 5758, 7754, 9624, 9630, 9639, 9742
Churchward '44XX' class 2-6-2T	4401, 4405, 4406
Collett '5101' class 2-6-2T	4154, 5109, 5125, 5138, 5139, 5178
	Total: 22

At May 1958

Hawksworth '16XX' class 0-6-0PT	1663
Collett '57XX' class 0-6-0PT	3732, 3744, 3760, 4605, 5758, 7754, 9630, 9639, 9741, 9774
Collett '5101' class 2-6-2T	4110, 4120, 4158, 5167
BR Standard class '3' 2-6-2T	82004, 82006, 82009
	Total: 18

At 1st January, 1962

Collett '57XX' class 0-6-0PT	3626, 3732, 3744, 4605, 9630, 9636, 9639, 9741, 9774
Collett '64XX' class 0-6-0PT	6421, 6429
Ivatt class '2' 2-6-2T	41201, 41204, 41232, 41241
Stanier '3P' class 0-4-4T	41900
	Total: 16

At Closure, 10th August, 1964

Collett '57XX' class 0-6-0PT	3776, 9639, 9774
	Total: 3

Crewe, Gresty Lane

At 1st January, 1921

Gooch '131' class double-framed 0-6-0	312
Armstrong '360' class 0-6-0	363
Dean '3252' or 'Duke of Cornwall' class curved double-framed 4-4-0	3267 *Cornishman*
Dean '3300' or 'Bulldog' class double-framed 4-4-0	3314 *Mersey*, 3362 *Albert Brassey*, 3400 *Winnipeg*
	Total: 6

At 1st January, 1934

Dean '3300' or 'Bulldog' class double-framed 4-4-0	3405 *Empire of India*
	Total: 1

NB: The situation at this date would appear to be transitional in that at least one other locomotive would have been due to be allocated here within the next month.

At 31st December, 1947

Collett '57XX' class 0-6-0PT	3749
Collett '5101' class 2-6-2T	4154, 5139
	Total: 3

Appendix Nine

Ruling Gradients

Wellington to Wellington (Drayton Junction)	1 in 104	Falling
Wellington (Drayton Junction) to Longdon Halt	1 in 104	Falling
Longdon Halt to Crudgington	1 in 186	Rising
Crudgington to Rowton Halt	1 in 150	Rising
Rowton Halt to Ellerdine Halt	1 in 264	Falling
Ellerdine Halt to Peplow	1 in 594	Rising
Peplow to Hodnet	1 in 343	Rising
Hodnet to Wollerton Halt	1 in 220	Falling
Wollerton Halt to Tern Hill	1 in 220	Rising
Tern Hill to Market Drayton	1 in 165	Rising
Market Drayton to Adderley	1 in 220	Rising
Adderley to Coxbank Halt	1 in 131	Falling
Coxbank Halt to Audlem	1 in 131	Falling
Audlem to Coole Pilate Halt	1 in 150	Rising
Coole Pilate Halt to Nantwich (Market Drayton Junction)	1 in 150	Rising
Nantwich (Market Drayton Junction) to Nantwich	1 in 330	Falling
Nantwich to Crewe	1 in 160	Rising

'Hall' class 4-6-0 No. 5919 *Worsley Hall* on a down part-fitted freight approaching Adderley station on 12th August, 1961. *Michael Mensing*

Appendix Ten

Chronological list of important events

1849	SBR/SUR Joint Line from Shrewsbury through Wellington opened (1st June)
1854	SBR absorbed by GWR (1st September)
1858	LNWR Shrewsbury to Crewe line opened (1st September)
1860	NMDR first meeting of provisional company (23rd August)
	NMDR plans deposited (28th November)
1861	NMDR incorporated (7th June)
	First official meeting of NMDR company (21st June)
1862	LNWR Shrewsbury to Crewe line doubled
	Contract issued to Brassey & Field to construct NMDR (10th March)
	WDR incorporated (7th August)
	GWR agreed to work NMDR (19th October)
	First official meeting of WDR company (4th November)
	WDR plans deposited (29th November)
1863	NMDR line inspected by Board of Trade official (16th October)
	NMDR line opened to passengers and goods (19th October)
1864	Working agreement of WDR by GWR approved (30th January)
	Contract issued to Brassey & Field to construct WDR (1st June)
	Act authorising transfer of WDR upon completion to GWR (14th July)
1866	Contract for doubling NMDR issued to Brassey & Field (5th March)
	Expected completion date of WDR (May)
1867	NMDR doubling completed (July)
	WDR and NMDR double line first inspected by Board of Trade official (23rd July)
	WDR and NMDR double line finally inspected by Board of Trade official (8th October)
	WDR and NMDR double track opened (16th October)
	GWR services through to Manchester inaugurated (1st November)
	Formal agreement for amalgamation of WDR with GWR (16th December)
	Wellington locomotive shed completed (April)
1868	Act passed authorising amalgamation of WDR with GWR (12th July)
*c.*1870	Crewe, Gresty Lane shed opened
1870	NSR line from Newcastle to Market Drayton opened (1st February)
	Peplow station opened (14th November)
1873	GWR authorised to make arrangements for amalgamation of NMDR (21st July)
1877	WDR Board sealed agreement for amalgamation with GWR (30th August)
1897	GWR absorbed NMDR (1st July)
1899	Tern Hill station opened (3rd April)
1928	Ellerdine Siding opened (28th February)
1930	Ellerdine Halt opened (7th July)
1931	Wollerton Halt opened (2nd November)
1934	Coxbank Halt opened (23rd June)
	Longdon Halt opened (20th October)
	Market Drayton shed closed (8th December)
1935	Tern Hill site purchased for development as RAF station
	Rowton Halt opened (29th June)
	Coole Pilate Halt opened (17th August)
	Little Drayton Halt opened (14th September)
1941	Little Drayton Halt closed (6th October)
1950	Line from Nantwich to Crudgington transferred to LMR

1950 Wellington shed transferred to WR, Wolverhampton District (February)
1951 Crewe, Gresty Lane shed transferred to LMR (July)
1954 Willaston station closed (6th December)
1956 Stoke to Market Drayton passenger service withdrawn (5th May)
1957 Hack Green Box opened (23rd June)
1962 'Pines Express' route commenced over line (10th September)
1963 Crewe, Gresty Lane shed closed (17th June)
Wellington to Nantwich passenger service withdrawn (9th September)
'Pines Express' route discontinued over line (9th September)
Wellington shed transferred to LMR (9th September)
1964 Wellington shed closed (10th August)
1966 Madeley Chord to Market Drayton line closed completely (August)
1967 Madeley Chord to Market Drayton line closed officially (9th January)
Wellington to Nantwich closed completely (8th May)

Ivatt class '2' 2-6-2T No. 41232 arrives at Adderley with the 5.18 pm Crewe-Wellington service on 12th August, 1961. *Michael Mensing*

Bibliography and Acknowledgements

Primary documentation has been accessed at the following locations:

Public Record Office (now National Archives), Kew - Minutes and records of the Nantwich & Market Drayton Railway Company, and the Wellington & Drayton Railway Company. Selected records of the Great Western Railway, and the London & North Western Railway.

National Railway Museum, York - Working timetables of the Great Western Railway, and the Western Region, and London Midland Region of British Railways.

Telford Library - *Wellington Journal*, and *Wellington Journal & Shrewsbury News*.

Nantwich Library - *Nantwich Guardian*.

Market Drayton Library - *Newport & Market Drayton Advertiser*.

Shropshire Archives - *Shrewsbury Chronicle*, Deposited Plans for the NMDR and the WDR, Ordnance survey maps.

Cheshire Records Office - Ordnance survey maps.

Author's collection - Working Timetables and Sectional Appendices, 1881 Census.

The following secondary sources of information have been consulted:

The Story of Market Drayton to the Early 20th Century by N. Rowley (Redverse Ltd, 1987)

Audlem - The History of a Cheshire Parish and its Five Townships by F.A. Latham *et al.* (Audlem Local History Group, 1997)

Rowton Recorded by Elizabeth Jordan (AJF Publications, 2000)

A Brief History of RAF Tern Hill by Group Captain D.A. Toon (published privately, *c.*1978)

The Oxford Companion to British Railway History by J. Simmons and G. Biddle (Oxford University Press, 1997)

The Midland Railway North of Leeds by P.E. Baughan (Guild Publishing, 1987)

The North Staffordshire Railway by Rex Christiansen (David & Charles, 1971)

Locomotive and Train Working in the Latter Part of the Nineteenth Century, Volume Two by E.L. Ahrons (W. Heffer & Sons, 1952)

The Great Western North of Wolverhampton by Keith M. Beck (Ian Allan, 1986)

Rail Centres: Shrewsbury by Richard K. Morriss (Ian Allan, 1986)

Transport in the Whitchurch Area, Part II, Canals and Railways by D.P. Barnard

Thomas Brassey: Railway Builder by Charles Walker (Frederick Muller, 1969)

Encyclopaedia of British Railway Companies by C. Awdry (Guild Publishing, 1990)

'Madeley and Leycett Collieries' by Allan C. Baker, *Industrial Railway Record* No. 161

A Regional History of the Railways of Great Britain Volume 7, The West Midlands by Rex Christiansen (David & Charles, 1973)

By Rail to Wombourn by Ned Williams (Uralia Press, 1977)

The Wenlock Branch by Ken Jones (Oakwood Press, 1998)

The Shropshire Union Railway by Bob Yate (Oakwood Press, 2003)

Crewe Station, Traffic & Footplate Working in the 1950s by Bill Rear (Ian Allan, 1999)

Tales of the Great Western Railway by O.S. Nock (David & Charles, 1984)

'Samuel Morton Peto' by Adrian Gray, *Backtrack*, Vol. 16, No. 4 (April 2002)

History of the Great Western Railway by Peter Semmens (Guild Publishing, 1985)

Branch Line Memories by Lewis Reade (Atlantic, 1983)

'Intruders at Crewe' by Allan C. Baker, *British Railway Illustrated*, Vol. 10. (December, 2000)

Crewe Locomotive Works and Its Men by Brian Reed (David & Charles, 1982)

The Stoke to Market Drayton Line by C.R. Lester (Oakwood Press, 1983)

Directory of Railway Stations by R.V.J. Butt (Patrick Stephens, 1995)

A Register of Halts and Platforms 1907-79 by C.R. Clinker (Avon Anglia, 1979)

Great Western Railway Halts, Volumes One and Two by Kevin Robertson (Irwell Press, 1990 and the author 2000)
Track Layout Diagrams of the GWR and BR Western Region, Section 32, East Shropshire (Second Edition) by R. A. Cooke (1994)
Steaming Through Shropshire, Part One by Michael Clemens (Video by B & R Video Productions, 1999)
Shropshire Railways Remembered by Leslie Oppitz (Countryside Books, 1993)
Crewe and Nantwich, A Pictorial History by Richard Simpson (Phillimore, 1991)
Locomotives of the Great Western Railway, Parts 1 to 10, RCTS, 1951 to 1966.
Locomotives at the Grouping No. 3 - London Midland & Scottish by H.C. Casserley and S.W. Johnston (Ian Allan, 1974)
Locomotives at the Grouping No. 4 - Great Western Railway by H.C. Casserley and S.W. Johnston (Ian Allan, 1974)
GWR Locomotive Allocations, First and Last Shed, 1922 to 1967 by J.W.P. Rowledge (David & Charles, 1986)
Great Western Railway Locomotive Allocations for 1921 by I. Harrison (Wild Swan Publications, 1984)
Great Western Railway Locomotive Allocations for 1934 by N. Pocock and I. Harrison (Wild Swan Publications, 1987)
An Historical Survey of Great Western Engine Sheds, 1837-1947 by E. Lyons and E. Mountford (Oxford Publishing Co. 1979)
An Historical Survey of Great Western Engine Sheds, 1947 by E. Lyons (Oxford Publishing Co. 1974)
The Handbook of Steam Motive Power Depots, Volume 2, Central England, East Anglia and Wales by Paul Smith (Platform 5 Publishing, 1989)
LMS Engine Sheds, Volume Four, The Smaller English Constituents, by C. Hawkins and G. Reeve (Wild Swan, 1984)
'Proposed Marshalling Yards at Shrewsbury and Gloucester', *Railway Magazine*, February 1961.
'The Beyer '99' and '140' Class Saddle Tanks' by Bob Miller. *The Industrial Locomotive* No. 111, 2004.
Contemporary traffic reports from various issues of *Railway Magazine, Trains Illustrated, Modern Railways* and *Railway Observer*.

I should also like to record the help and advice received from many individuals. In particular, former railwaymen Peter Bushell, Cliff Carr, George Finney, Don Houlston, Albert Simester and Mark Temple, along with Allan Baker, Keith Beddoes, Malcolm Fletcher, Jon Maden, Don Rowland and Ted Talbot. Thanks must also go to the staff of the libraries at Crewe, Nantwich, Newport, Market Drayton, and Telford, and at the county records offices at Chester, Shrewsbury and Stafford, as well as the National Railway Museum, York and The National Archives, Kew for their assistance. Finally, but not least, to my wife Sandra, for her forbearance and encouragement during the lengthy time it took to research and write this book.

Index